Prai

"The Rowley/Haltem   shows how they have been able to win jaw-dropping over again. This is a particularly useful guide for lawyers like myself, who tend to stay too much in our heads and need help becoming 'human' in the courtroom. A must-read for 2013."

—Rick Friedman, author of *Rules of the Road, Polarizing the Case,* and *Becoming a Trial Lawyer;* member of the Inner Circle of Advocates and the International Academy of Trial Lawyers; recipient of the 2004 Steven J. Sharp Award

"In this treasure of a book, the authors offer the real secret for being a great trial lawyer with a trial track record to back it up. Out of all the books about trials, this one is revolutionary because it offers the real secrets of success with examples from actual trials. This is a book with a message every trial lawyer should read and apply."

—Paul Luvera, member and past president of the Inner Circle of Advocates, member of the American College of Trial Lawyers and the International Academy of Trial Lawyers

"Nick Rowley proves that some young men have old souls, and wisdom to boot!"

—Geoffrey Fieger, winner of more multimillion-dollar awards than any attorney in the country, Democratic Party nominee for governor of Michigan in 1998

"Brutally honest. A must-read for any trial lawyer."

—Honorable Peter J. Polos (retired)

"I salute Nick Rowley and Steve Halteman for their professional dedication and personal courage in the defense of their clients' rights and to their conviction to their clients. I have had the privilege to work with both authors and can substantiate that the substance of this book is not fictional, but is, unarguably, fact."

—Marc R. Lebed, MD, MDR; OB-GYN; visiting lecturer at Pepperdine University School of Law, UC Davis Medical School, UC San Diego Medical Center; cofounder and codirector of Medical Dispute Professionals

Trial by Human

Nicholas Rowley and Steven Halteman

Trial Guides, LLC

Trial Guides, LLC, Portland, Oregon 97210

Copyright © 2013 by Trial Guides, LLC. All rights reserved.

TRIAL GUIDES and logo are registered trademarks of Trial Guides, LLC.

ISBN: 978-1-934833-81-0

Library of Congress Control Number: 2013937010

These materials, or any parts or portions thereof, may not be reproduced in any form, written or mechanical, or be programmed into any electronic storage or retrieval system, without the express written permission of Trial Guides, LLC, unless such copying is expressly permitted by federal copyright law. Please direct inquiries to:

Trial Guides, LLC
Attn: Permissions
2350 NW York Street
Portland, OR 97210
(800) 309-6845
www.trialguides.com

Interior design by Laura Lind Design

Jacket design by Theodore Marshall

Printed and bound in the United States of America.

This book is printed on acid-free paper.

To those who have the courage to stand up for their fellow humans against the big bullies. Without you, our "justice" system would be without justice, lost forever. With you, we can change the world.

—Nick Rowley

To my little girl, Fumiko, aka Superfly, my favorite little girl in the whole wide world, and to my father, George Benton Halteman, who lives on through me.

—Steve Halteman

All proceeds received by the authors from the sale of this book will be donated to Trial Lawyers' Charities of Los Angeles.

Table of Contents

Publisher's Note ix
Acknowledgments. xi
Downloadable Transcripts xv
Introduction. 1

1. Trial by Human Starts with You 7
2. Pick a Case, Find a Human, Learn a Story 29
3. Chapters of the Human Story 39
4. Discovering Your Clients' Human Stories 61
5. Trial and Dealing with the Worst. 75
6. Focus Groups 85
7. Mini–Opening Statement. 89
8. Nick's View of Voir Dire. .93
9. Steve's View of Voir Dire 127
10. Opening Statement. 145
11. Bring Life to the Courtroom 165
12. Witness Examinations. .175
13. Direct Examination 211
14. Cross-Examination 219
15. Keeping Connected with the Jury during Trial. . .231
16. Closing Argument 237
17. Talking about Money. .257
18. Life Lessons. 271

19. Closing Thoughts	279
Appendix: The *Blunt* Trial in Six Acts	285
Index	299
About the Authors	307

Publisher's Note

This book is intended for practicing attorneys. This book does not offer legal advice and does not take the place of consultation with an attorney or other professional with appropriate expertise and experience.

Attorneys are strongly cautioned to evaluate the information, ideas, and opinions set forth in this book in light of their own research, experience, and judgment; to consult applicable rules, regulations, procedures, cases, and statutes (including those issued after the publication date of this book); and to make independent decisions about whether and how to apply such information, ideas, and opinions to a particular case.

Quotations from cases, pleadings, discovery, and other sources are for illustrative purposes only and may not be suitable for use in litigation in any particular case.

The cases described in this book are actual cases, and the names and other identifying details of participants, litigants, witnesses, and counsel have not been fictionalized except where otherwise expressly stated.

All references to the trademarks of third parties are strictly informational and for purposes of commentary. No sponsorship or endorsement by, or affiliation with, the trademark owners is claimed or implied by the author or publisher of this book.

The author and publisher disclaim any liability or responsibility for loss or damage resulting from the use of this book or the information, ideas, or opinions contained in this book.

Acknowledgments

Nick Rowley

To my beloved friends, family, and mentors. Deryl Edwards, Mark Helm, and Courtney Yoder are three young trial lawyers like me who started this journey with me, and with whom I have tried cases over the years. I met each of them at Gerry Spence's Trial Lawyers College in Dubois, Wyoming, and they have become my best friends in this world.

Mark and Deryl died since I started this book; they died way too young. They were the most loyal of humans.

Courtney, thank all the stars in the sky, is still here, trying cases, inspiring me, with so many years to come. She is my best friend in this world and the one who inspires me most. She is the most amazing trial lawyer I have ever seen in a courtroom and the most amazing human being I know. Courtney is our future, trying case after case and paying forward what she has been taught at the Trial Lawyers College. She has been a mentee and a mentor of mine for many years. Thanks, Courtney, for always believing in me even when nobody else did.

Gerry Spence has seen and experienced a lot through his eighty-four years of life. He is our teacher, and he brought us all together. Thank you, Gerry, for your love and relentless belief in me as a person and as a trial lawyer. Gerry is a living prophet of feeling, truth, and justice. If you want to be a trial lawyer, to be a human who stands for justice, and if you had only one hour to absorb the energy and spirit of the guru, the most real and precious Trial by Human lawyer, the one person you want to spend that hour with is Gerry Spence. Drive as far as it takes, walk as far as you must, pay whatever it takes to get the ticket, and spend time with Gerry Spence. If you say you can't afford it, I say you can't afford not to.

If there is one person who has had the most influence on me, whose soul lives within mine when I stand before a jury, it is old man Spence. He is the prophet of justice of our time, the Trial by Human lawyer of all time. There is no human like this old man in our universe. The journey I, or we, are embarking upon started with Spence. The old man started a college in the middle-of-nowhere cowboy country, Dubois, Wyoming. This is where I was first taught. The college puts on four-day and multiweek programs throughout the year; check out the schedule at triallawyerscollege.com. You must attend if you want to travel this journey and be the best you can be.

Gary Dordick has become the big brother that I never had. Gary is not only one of the most successful trial lawyers in history, but he has also been a personal mentor to me since more than ten years ago when I was a law clerk. Gary and his wife, Nava, have always been there for me through thick and thin, and what I have to give and pay forward is very much because of them. Anytime you can, go see Gary in a courtroom, meet with him, hear him speak, and learn from him. You are cheating yourself if you miss it. He is always willing to take the time to help young trial lawyers and even old ones.

William "Wild Bill" Ritner is a man from Nebraska whom I first worked for as a medical malpractice defense lawyer in Southern California. He let me take as many non–med mal plaintiffs' cases as I could sign up, and helped me build my practice and go out on my own. He showed me that it is OK to be myself and wear cowboy boots to court, and that the way to win a case is to get your jury to care.

Rick Friedman is one of my inspirations. Anything Rick has written is a must-read. I have read and studied all of his books. If you want to be a trial lawyer, follow and learn from Rick.

Thanks to my partners John Carpenter, Paul Zuckerman, and Steven Glass. They give me unconditional support and are the forces behind and beside me when I am in trial. I am part of what I believe to be the greatest law firm ever. I would not be where I am without Paul, John, and Steve and the rest of our team at Carpenter, Zuckerman & Rowley.

And thanks go to my children. I have eight of them. I work hard and stand up for people to make this world better, and no matter where I am in the world, whatever I am doing, you are with me and my beating heart, and on the forefront of my mind, Tristan Charles Rowley, Corban Anthony Rowley, Nicholas Charles Rowley Jr., Evan Justice Rowley, Elan Lethaniel Rowley, Finlay Justice Rowley, Coralin Joy Rowley, and Emma Belle Rowley. I love you all so very much. I always wanted to be a dad and have a lot of kids. You give me endless love and all make me so very proud.

Steve Halteman

I raise my glass to the following:

To the Halteman clan: George, Myrna, Jen, Jill, and Beth. We are never alone.

To Naomi and Fumiko and all the good years.

To Nick Rowley for opening the door.

To Jim O'Donnell, who introduced me to the unusual.

To my brother, Brian Krupinsky.

To the friendship of Walter Menck, Dave Hirsh, Rob Begley, and Jeff Carter. Wherever, whenever, it's always a laugh.

To the Mississippi River crew: Tony Rowley and Joe Krueger. This is the next generation of hard-core adventurers.

To my favorite left-brained lawyers, Robert Ounjian and Rod Ritner, who are fortunately unable to dance with "R" and shoot pool at the same time.

To Tina Ricks, Bekah Krueger, Tiffany Chung, Steve Glass, Regan Fisher, and Brian Simmons. Thanks for the charitable hand-holding during the writing process.

To the clients who trusted our approach.

And finally, to all the travelers whom I have crossed paths and swapped stories with.

My thanks to you all for the shine you have brought to my life.

Downloadable Transcripts

The authors have provided a number of transcripts from some of their actual trials to accompany this book. These transcripts offer concrete examples of the Trial by Human method and the specific strategies the authors describe within these pages.

To download these files to your computer, smartphone, or tablet, use the following link:

http://www.trialguides.com/resources/downloads/trial-by-human

Introduction

Nick Rowley

Too often, we have heard lawyers complain that successfully trying cases requires too much money and experience, and that the odds are stacked against them. We are here to tell you that to try cases, you do not always need a bunch of money to pay experts or lots of experience. First, you need courage. Second, you need to love your client and the jury. We want you to commit yourself to a new method of practicing law—a method we call Trial by Human.

This method includes acknowledging that law school, for the most part, fails to teach much of anything about being a real trial lawyer. The place to go to learn about the case is not an office or a conference room, where you will sit reading records and depositions. Instead, leave your suit and tie at the office, and drive to your client's home. Sit down and have dinner with your client and his family in their home, wear regular everyday clothes, and establish a real human connection. You cannot expect a jury to care and to be human if you have not done so yourself.

Few lawyers are real trial lawyers. To be a real trial lawyer, you have to try cases regularly. You have to be willing to take on the risk of rejection, failure, and immense pain. Real trial lawyers will suffer no matter how good they become. But, as any real trial lawyer knows, when you win a trial, there is no feeling like it in the world. The feeling of success, purpose, and overwhelming emotion is a life high that only those of us who have tried cases and won can understand.

We are the turning points of every case. If we could find a way to unify better and stop the constant greedy competition for the "big" and "good" cases, and instead pay forward what we learn to the less advantaged, less lucky lawyers, we can become much more powerful than our common enemies. I am starting out by saying this because I have seen too much greed and ego in our profession, and it is something I have been guilty of and struggle to change. What we do needs to be about more than money and ego. Those things do not win over juries and don't help us connect with clients. We need to be better. We can be better.

I often think of the younger, less experienced versions of me, the help I needed, the help that I was given, and the times when the luckier and more successful lawyers refused to give because they preferred to hoard it all for themselves. I am where I am very much because of the help and guidance I received from others. By writing this book for you, I am paying forward what I have learned so far, and I ask that you do the same.

We always want to hear how great we are, to have people tell us about our good parts and the impressive things we do. We love being adored. However, that is not what helps us become the best, not at all. To improve our trial skills, our practice, and our lives, we must commit to constructively criticizing ourselves. If we are committed, we can always get better. Gerry Spence, who is still trying cases, will tell you that he is still working to be a better trial lawyer, and more importantly, a better human. I am trying to do the same.

In this book, we are going to tell you about our journey, which includes winning and also losing. None of us want to talk about our losses. It is painful, embarrassing, and something that we want to erase from the record books. But in order to improve ourselves, and to help others, we need to embrace and to relive our losses. We need to share our losses with those we seek to help. The best and bravest trial lawyers I know lose cases. They would tell you that they often learn more from losing than from winning. I will tell you that.

My friend and coauthor on this book is Steve Halteman, a jury consultant and trial strategist who has worked on many of my cases. Steve will explain his human perspectives and how we have evolved together and developed our method, Trial by Human. Together, we will discuss our preparation for cases and trials, what has worked, and what has not.

We must bring humanity and dignity back to the courtroom and be able to deal with the struggles of talking to jurors about difficult things, such as money. We can become close to being invincible, but it is only through the power of the heart, soul, and brutal honesty in the courtroom that we can do this.

If You Are an Enemy

If you are an enemy reading this book—say, an insurance defense lawyer, or a government attorney using the power of the state to put people in cages for as long as possible rather than rehabilitate them—then your soul may burn by reading any part of this book. Magic makers have sealed this book to curse anybody who reads it with an evil purpose, such as trying to bully ordinary people who are standing up for themselves against the elite power structure in the United States. Reconsider the harm you are doing to people and society. Soften your heart and help the people who are in need, rather than making their lives worse and helping the insurance defense industry.

What Is a Trial by Human Lawyer?

Real trial lawyers, Trial by Human lawyers, are a unique breed of warrior. We must develop more of these lawyers to create the change our justice system needs. This book is written for those who have the courage to stand up for their fellow humans against the big bullies.

Courage is the basic ingredient necessary for battles. We cannot go out and buy courage. We cannot mimic it from watching somebody else. So where do we get it? Courage is something we must find within ourselves.

Fighting courageously does not mean we stop being smart, that we lose our tempers, or recklessly run the gauntlet. Courage is the basic ingredient: the gunpowder. We still need the gun, the bullet, the sight, the barrel, and the trigger. But without the gunpowder, you cannot shoot. The good thing about having this ingredient within us is that once we tap in and find it, there is an unlimited supply.

Many of us have lost our courage. We don't know when we lost it, or where it went, but it appears to be gone. For some, courage is something we don't believe we have enough of. And, for others, the courage is fake. We will talk more about courage later. For now, just think of the times you have had courage, the times you lacked courage, and the times when you wish you had more.

True warriors are not defined by their wins, but by their ability to stand up and find courage again and again, regardless of the number of times they've been beaten and even knocked out cold.

THE DISEASE AFFECTING OUR JUSTICE SYSTEM

Insurance companies have injected antilawsuit propaganda into the minds of our jurors. Many people think of lawsuits for money as dirty and greedy. Many people are turned off by our system of justice. Because of this, our system is dying. Most Americans don't know about the crisis, or don't believe it exists. Ordinary people, the people we represent, have been convinced that there is nothing wrong with our system. Worse, the American public has been brainwashed to believe that trial lawyers—the ones who are there for them at their most desperate moment—are the bad guys. Many of our jurors and our judges have been brainwashed.

It is our duty to fix the brainwashing. We must inoculate. And to do this, we have to start in our schools (high schools, colleges, and most definitely law schools), because the propaganda is being injected into the students and implanted into our youth. Far too often, young jurors, college students, have a bad view of money lawsuits and the core belief that they are wrong and frivolous.

Everywhere we turn, we are told not to go to trial. Courts order people into mediation, and accused people are forced into plea bargains for crimes they did not commit. Judges warn us not to go to trial and successfully pressure lawyers into giving up and settling cases for far less than true justice.

Effectively, the power structure is steadily killing the jury trial method. Less and less money is paid to settle legitimate cases. Laws like the "three strikes" mandate life imprisonment for twenty-year-olds for minor crimes. Judges warn those who are mustering the courage to go to trial about the dangers. Statutes punish those who will not be beaten into a cheap settlement. Jurors are poisoned with propaganda before they ever show up for jury duty. Our media praise juries for convictions, and insult and punish juries when they bravely find the unpopular truth. The Nancy Graces of the world rally the public to convict without a trial, and the politicians who instill fear into their constituents about trial lawyers damaging our country make it easy for people to just give up. Many times, lawyers themselves succumb and force clients to settle cases rather than go to trial.

Not enough people address this problem. When we pick up a book on becoming more effective at trying cases, we don't hear enough about the virus infecting our justice system. We don't hear the brutal truth that real trial lawyers are a dying breed. I know this because I have seen the numbers dwindling. Our leaders among trial lawyers smile and talk about justice, but I question whether they truly do care or whether they are mostly in it to get rich or stay rich.

I would rather hear about how much better the world would be if we helped develop more Trial by Human lawyers, teaching them how to find their courage and win the cases that deserve to be won.

1

TRIAL BY HUMAN STARTS WITH YOU

Nick Rowley

In order for this book to have its full effect, we are going to ask that you do something. This is something you may not have done before. There's a good chance that if you think you have, you really have not. Trust us with this. Do this exercise.

Get out a note pad. There are some questions and answers we ask that you write out. They are not questions for us. They are questions for you! You, the human! The human who loves, feels, hurts, cares, hates, betrays, fears, loses his or her cool, offends, regrets, and who has that so very important ego to protect. Do not use a computer to do this. Use a blank piece of real paper and a pen or pencil. Stay away from the computer when you read this book. Even if the very notion of having to get out a paper and pencil and write at the beginning of reading a book is annoying to you, give it a shot. Try something different.

You need to be brutally honest in going through this exercise and answering the questions. "Brutal honesty" is a phrase you will see a lot of in my writings and when I am in trial. I start every trial with this phrase, and it's one of the methods we are going to learn about and practice. The end result is you being more effective at every part of being you.

I write to you and pour out my heart and soul with the hope that if you have been beaten down, you can find the courage to pull yourself back up, keep fighting the enemy, and never give up. This is for you if you have suffered the deep, sharp, and chronic pain of rejection, so piercing that you can still place your hand on your chest and take a deep breath and feel it. Feel that pain, such that the depth of it brings tears to your eyes. This feeling is not one that can be contrived; rather, it overwhelms, takes control, and creates a glow of truth around your body, one that brings out the humanity in other humans. By feeling these emotions, you will allow other people to relate to you more closely.

Those who can feel, who still have their humanity and are not afraid to share it and show it, are the most powerful lawyers to try cases. What do we mean by having "humanity"? We're referring to people who are able to truly feel their own emotions and empathize with others. They acknowledge their flaws and are motivated to fix them. They are authentic, honest, and able to communicate truth in a sincere way. Those are the ones who can be the most successful. Those are the warriors who can keep the fire alive and provide hope for the future of justice.

We are going to learn to identify and embrace the parts of us that are good, bad, and even ugly. When we learn to do this with ourselves and to accept ourselves, we will be able to better understand and communicate with those humans we need in our lives and those humans who are involved with our cases.

The human, the whole you, the "brutally honest" you, the one who wants to be a more successful trial lawyer and better human being and is willing to continuously struggle to get there—that is where we must start. My mentor, the best trial lawyer in history, Gerry Spence, taught me that "it all begins with you."

The answers to the questions we are going to go over are not something you need to share, not with anybody. However, we suggest that you write them down. Go to a quiet, peaceful place. No cell phone. No text messaging or emails. No iPod. No sounds of the hustle and bustle of modern life. Spend some time pondering and feeling the questions. Ask them out loud to yourself. Hear the words you say; feel them. Don't jump to answer each question. Take your time. Answer them. Listen to whether the answers are true. Are you being brutally honest? The answers might bring tears. Tears are good. They are produced by raw, brutally honest human emotion, our feelings. True tears do not lie.

When we do this exercise, we might find that the answers are not brutally honest. If we cannot be brutally honest with ourselves, then how can we begin to connect with our clients and our jury? The answer is that we can't. If we sugarcoat, if we hold back the brutal honesty and are unwilling to share our true feelings and beliefs, then we have no right to ask our clients or jurors to do what we need them to do. So, it might be tough to do this exercise. And, that's OK. It may take a lot of work; it sure did for me! I remain a work in progress.

So, commit to yourself. Commit to working on being brutally honest, and promise yourself that you will do whatever it takes to get there. In the end you will have evolved to a better version of the human being that exists within your body.

Here are the questions. Write each question out one by one. Do not start answering them until you write them all out. Some of these questions I learned from others; some of them Steve and I wrote.

1. Who am I?
2. What am I?
3. What are the things I am most afraid of? Why?
4. What do I really care about? Money? Fame? Myself? Other people?
5. How selfish am I? Why? Is it OK to be as selfish as I am? Why?
6. Why am I really reading this book?
7. Do I like my current professional life, or do I want to change it? Why?

8. What are the things I dislike most about myself? Why?

9. What are the things I like about myself? Why?

10. What is the best thing about me?

11. What is the worst/ugliest thing about me as a person (not physical appearance, but rather what is beneath the surface)?

12. How do other people see me?

13. Do I show others, including jurors, my true self?

14. Do I even know my true self?

15. What are the monumental experiences in life that brought me to where I am and made me the way I am?

16. What are the things I want to change about myself? Why?

17. Apart from money, success, and changing my physical appearance, what do I want most in my life? If I could push a button and make my life different tomorrow, how would it be? Why?

18. Am I mostly happy or sad? What makes me this way?

While you are doing this, don't ask for solutions. Don't judge your answers. Just focus on writing brutally honest answers. Accept that the answers are what they are and don't necessarily need fixing. There doesn't need to be a solution to everything. But knowing who we are is important to the process we are going to teach you.

We make it a point to get you away from your appearance. It is rare to find a person who doesn't want a different nose, face, breasts, penis, feet, belly, and so on. Those are the surface things, the things that take us away from the human being that we are, and the things that we all (certainly including me) get too tied up with.

So, before you read any further, take some time and answer these questions. Think about these questions again after you are done with the book, and think about them the next time you are about to step in front of a jury. Our answers often change. For me, they have certainly changed over the years. Write out the answers and put them somewhere safe.

To help you with this step, we are going to tell you a bit about us. We are digging deep and sharing things with you in the hope that you will do the same for yourself. Why reveal all of this personal information? Well, I have been taught that if you want a person to open up, you need to show them how, by first doing it yourself. I will answer the questions I am asking you to write out and answer. Steve will answer these questions too. We are not asking you to do something that we ourselves are not willing to do first. You need to be in touch with, and connected with, yourself and know your good, bad, and ugly in order to be brutally honest and connect with your client and the jury. So we are going to tell you our stories and who we are, including the good, the bad, and the ugly.

Nick Rowley

I was born in Stormlake, Iowa. My earliest memories are running around our little white farmhouse, patrolling through our garden to scare away the rabbits, going to my grandparents' farm in Jefferson, Iowa, and seeing all my cousins, aunts, and uncles. My grandparents had a red farmhouse with a big red barn and raised cattle, hogs, and chickens, and tended to endless fields of corn and soybeans.

Life was perfect during my first years, as I remember them. My dad, aside from being a hardworking man from sunrise to sundown, was also a stoner, a hippie, and had hair down to his waist. After a drastic change in the livestock industry in Iowa, my dad decided to leave the small farming town we lived in and pursue his dream of being an artist. So, off we went to the University of Iowa, Iowa City, where we lived in family student housing for the next four years. I was exposed to many different cultures, and I loved it. Many of the kids in student housing were from other countries and were of different color and spirit than what I was used to. At this point in my life, I did not know or understand prejudice. My parents were liberals and I was a carefree kid. My mother was my everything, and she was a sweet, loving mom.

Things changed a few years later. When I was seven years old, my dad's first teaching job took us to Nogales, Arizona, a town on the border with Mexico. During this time, I learned Spanish fluently. I also learned what racism and prejudice were firsthand, and I was on the receiving end. I was the only blond-haired white kid in my class, one of a few in the entire school. Those Mexican kids were mean, and in turn, I learned how to be mean. Starting at age seven, I learned to fight and cuss with the best of them.

In Nogales, I wasn't just bullied. I was brutalized. Classmates and neighbor kids beat, tormented, and humiliated me, multiple times a week, for five straight years of my childhood (before I moved back to Iowa at age twelve). I did not have a big brother to stand up for me. I didn't have any friends. I was the oldest of my brothers and sisters. I was the one who had to become tough to protect them against very horrible bullies, kids whom I still believe were evil.

We were very poor. Often, we had no hot water and no running vehicle, and we rarely had a phone line. Adding to this, my parents had their own major issues from their childhoods, and they were still children having children.

It was during this time in my life when my parents split up. My mother had an affair and left my father for a Vietnam veteran, a Navy SEAL: the complete opposite of my father. Mom moved back to Iowa with my six younger brothers and sisters when I was in fifth grade. The same issues that plagued my parents when they were married to each other continued when they eventually remarried. My parents and stepparents all fought horribly, and they were always splitting up and getting back together.

When my parents divorced, I refused to abandon my father. My mother had been the most important person in my life, the only person I really loved. When I realized what was going on, and why my mother left my father, I stayed with my father because I was afraid he would kill himself. I was angry, and I lost my connection with my mom. My dad went into a deep depression. At times, I moved back and forth between Iowa and Arizona, and then to California, where my dad eventually moved. Things did not go well. I got in a lot of trouble, challenged all authority, and moved out at age fifteen after a fistfight with my dad. I became emancipated at age sixteen and joined the military on my seventeenth birthday.

Growing up, I had a choice to either be broken or strong. I chose strong. There was no room for me to complain or ask for help. It didn't do any good anyway. I learned very young that I was the only one who could protect me. I was not a whiner. I learned that whining made me weak. I had to stand on my own.

Moving out at age fifteen was the beginning of my life. I graduated from high school at age sixteen. From age twelve, I worked as much as I could, often full time. I worked as a paper delivery boy, as a farmhand, as a small engine mechanic, and on a cement crew building pig confinements in Iowa. I did roofing jobs and worked fourteen-hour days on different construction crews. Even on the days I was "on vacation," I worked. I would work or go to the office or study on every holiday. I served on active duty from 1994 to 1998 and was in the army reserves for three years after that. I worked without a day off up until age twenty-eight.

The G.I. Bill got me through college and law school. I moved to California for law school at the University of La Verne, not even knowing the difference between an ABA school and a Cal Bar–approved school. I finished law school in 2001, studied like a crazy person, and passed the bar exam on my first attempt.

Brutal honesty: I have often been my own worst enemy. I am in a constant struggle to be a better human, to lessen my ego-driven desires, and to focus more on the people I love. I work to identify my faults, and I strive to improve upon them. I have made progress, but I have so much further to go. I am better than I used to be as a human. I have discovered those people I enjoy being around—those who are honest with me, steadfast, and true—and spend more and more time with them. I have become a more dedicated father. However, I often feel I have progressed forward only to realize I am worse off than when I began my journey. I have an ego that has often controlled my insecurities and that has needed constant love, attention, and validation. My insecurities have also been my drive. Sometimes I have not wanted to change anything about me, as selfish as that is.

Anger and rage. I am still an angry person—I have been since I was young. I control it now and use it as a source of power rather than something that is destructive. The personal work I have done over the years has helped me realize that the anger comes from scars within me, deep wounds, experiences I had growing up, starting in Nogales, Arizona, through my time in the service, and betrayals I have been victim of as an adult.

Impulsive is a word that most people who know me well would say describes me. *Spontaneous* is the word I prefer, because it sounds better. I am a flawed person who acts on impulse, overwhelms myself, and spreads myself way too thin. I live with fear and anxiety, and often with the overwhelming feeling of the whole world on my shoulders. I have a constant fear of death and loss. I was still a teenager, a combat medic, when I was trained to deal with death by being detached. I was trained to become numb, and I did. Life and death became no big deal for me. I saw it. I felt it. I was trained to help deliver it.

For many years, what I experienced as a soldier did not affect me on the surface. Then suddenly, it changed. Visions and sounds started coming into my head, and I was unable to stop or control them. Work shut them out when it first began, after I lost a few loved ones. It began during law school, and I worked full-time, usually more than fifty hours per week, so I could shut it out.

Until recently, I have been a very lonely person. I don't like to be alone. Even when I am with somebody, I am alone. Because of this, I have made decisions that were wrong and that have hurt people I love. Until now, it has been impossible for me to trust women. I felt the betrayal and loss of my mother as a fresh wound. I have not spent enough time with my children.

Getting to where I am now has been a lot of work. I still have a life of work ahead. I went through many years anxious and depressed. An example of the anxiety I will share happened a year ago: I was on a plane to Los Angeles, looking at snowcapped mountains; it was a beautiful view. Without any notice, I had a ten-minute panic or anxiety attack: heart racing, respiratory rate up, heart thumping in my chest. This is something I have experienced many times since serving in the military. It's fear of death.

It's the only thing I fear. I am not afraid of flying, just of dying. I have had no problem jumping out of a plane, driving fast, driving motorcycles, doing dangerous and adrenaline-rushing activities, and living on the edge. But death is something I fear immensely, and this has disabled me regularly. The lack of control and the unknown is what I fear.

There was no rhyme or reason for when my anxiety would come and go. It came from a culmination of experiences. There have been times in my life and in the military where I have been trapped, stuck alone, and I believed I would never see another human being again, sure to die. People close to me have died. People I cared about died right in front of me. Patients and soldiers whose lives were in my hands died even though I tried my best to save them. I sometimes wake drenched in sweat just hours after falling asleep, unable to catch my breath, everything vivid as if I am still in those places. So I am, I have been, disabled at times by my brain—fortunately, not permanently or continuously, just sometimes, and it is better now. This is who I am, a man who is afraid. Yet many people, those who don't know what is inside me, describe me as fearless.

About five years ago, my wife and I lost a child. The grief brought all those other losses to the surface. It was raw. The hurt, the fear, and reliving many experiences I had when I was a medic became unbearable. The frequency and intensity got worse and worse, and out of control. The more I tried to ignore it, the worse it became. I worked harder and longer to fill my mind with other things, and distanced myself from my family.

It got to the point where I would find myself crying while alone, driving in the car, up in the middle of the night, unable to sleep. So I filled my life with more and more work, trial after trial, always keeping myself surrounded by people. For a long time, I never talked to anybody about it. Finally, I went to some therapy and support groups. It turned out that I had never grieved for many of the deaths of people who were important to me.

I found ways to temporarily avoid dealing with the problems. Being in love helps; being loved helps. Staying busy and ignoring what I need as a human does not help. For a while, I was running all over trying cases. I did everything I could to try case after case. One day I'd be in Iowa. Two days before that, Chicago. The next day, Los Angeles, then to New York or Florida. My life and schedule were in constant flux. Going to battle for clients, one after the next, meant I didn't have to focus on myself. And, if I died along the way, then I would never have had to face my demons. I thought that working constantly and having no time alone was good, and eventually the struggle with myself would pass or I'd grow up; keeping crazy busy with trials, I would never have time to be lonely. Focusing on work and others can be much easier than focusing on myself. And maybe I thought that by fixing other people's problems, I might fix myself. So when I wasn't helping others and I had space to think and reflect, I would get depressed and my anxiety worsened. So my method, in the long run, didn't work.

I still try lots of cases, but I have started to slow down. I saw a therapist and got some good direction. I am a quick study, I got the help I needed, and I even started taking antianxiety medication. I started reading books, working on myself, and most importantly, being brutally honest about my relationships, happiness, unhappiness, and loneliness.

I have started facing the experiences that haunt me. It is with the realization that I am flawed, but that I am in fact in control of the rest of my life, that I have decided to make life different from this point forward. I continue to work very hard to make changes. I am learning how to live happily and to enjoy life more. I am getting there, but sometimes it is still a day-to-day struggle.

As a father, I have always cuddled my children. I love to sing, and I know without doubt that I fill my children with love and attention that is unique and special. I tell them stories, ones that are old and many that I create. My stories for them are fun, and each child plays a part and has special names as characters in the stories. When I am present, I am a fun-loving father. I hope that makes up a bit for not being a come-home-every-day father.

My children know I am out in battle, slaying dragons and standing up for people against bullies. Physically and emotionally, I am in the heat of a battle. I talk to my children almost every day, but I have not spent enough time with them and have not been an everyday dad. My place over the years has been standing in front of juries, fighting bullies and protecting people who would otherwise have no chance in the world but for me. But, even with that, I know that children and mothers need a father at home, and there is no substitute for my absence. I can only strive to be present more, physically and emotionally. The one thing I tell my children every time I can is: "No matter where I am in the world, I miss you and I love you more than anything."

Up until now, my favorite times and places in this world have not been on vacations and home with my family. This is my brutal honesty. I feel very bad about this truth, but it is who I am. I heard a great man, my mentor Gerry Spence, once say that regrettably, he thought he was not a good father because he focused on being a great trial lawyer instead of being the father that he now wishes he had been. I have followed a similar path, but am struggling, trying to get better at balancing this.

What I wanted to be most in the world was a good provider for my family. I am a great provider, but I am not the best father. So what I wanted to be the most in the world, because it is what I grew up without (a good financial provider), is insufficient. I have worked so hard on being a good provider that I have missed my kids' concerts, parent-teacher conferences, and dinners around the family table. The times I was there for my children's concerts and games, I could see the happiness in their eyes. Therefore, I know the disappointment they must have felt the many other times when I was not there. For the next thirty-five years of my life, I am set on changing this!

Even though I appreciate what I went through and who I am, I have flaws that I must deal with every day. My chronic wounded ego and anger can be brutal enemies, which I have to fight. But I need them both. They are often my source of power and motivation. The key is controlling them and finding balance with the love I have within me.

What I like most about myself is my ability to love other humans. I am a lover and protector. I have always wanted storybook love and companionship. I've been this way since I was a kid.

I have always been one to come to the aid of others without thinking twice. It has always been instinct for me, and it has been that way since I was a child. I didn't stand up for others because it felt good. I just did it because it was the right thing to do.

Making people feel good about themselves, seeing the beauty and goodness of who they are, is also something I am very good at and love to do. I am able to be brutally honest with people who need to hear the good things about themselves. Again, that is something I starved for as a child. When I am with my children, I am connected tight with them. I do my best to make up for my absence. I embrace them, fill them with attention, turn off my phone, and give them love.

I have always extended my hand to help almost anybody in need. I rarely say no to a request for help from another, even if I hardly know the person, and even if we are strangers.

I feel much older than I am. I have always felt that I have an old soul. I love old people. Where I come from, there are no face-lifts or cosmetic surgery. Old people are beautiful. I hope I get to be old someday, see my children have children, and be there for their games and activities.

I love the people who are less fortunate in our world. I enjoy being around the poor more than I do being around the rich. But I question whether that is because I have that luxury, or maybe it is because I used to be very poor.

When it comes to those in the higher echelons, the people we are supposed to bow down to and defer to, even the great ones whom I actually respect, my mentors, I butt heads. Part of it is that I want to prove I am just as good as they are. Part of it is that I want them to know my value, because I doubt it myself when I look in the mirror. The other reason is that those on thrones, sitting up high, need to be reminded that they are just humans, just a few cars and bank accounts away from being in a very different set of shoes. The rich are not better than the poor; often, it is the opposite. Those with fancy homes are no better than the men and women walking into homeless shelters, living in the slums, or pushing grocery carts. We are just a few strokes of bad luck away from where they are. We are all humans with similar stories, just a few shades of gray apart.

I am not one to complain or seek attention because of what I went through. I wouldn't trade any of what I went through for anything; it all made me strong and became the foundation of who I am, the good, the bad, and the ugly. Experiences turned out to be both curses and blessings. Good, bad, and ugly—they forged me into who I am.

You want to be the best you can be. I want to be the best ever! That is, the best version of me ever. There are many "bests." This is not a world where there is only one best. Once, my goal was to be better than everybody else as a trial lawyer. Now I just want to be among the best when it comes to our side of this war. I want there to be many bests. The more bests who exist thirty years from now, when it comes to Trial by Human lawyers, the better our country and justice system will be. Gerry Spence is the best of his time. His goal, as I have heard and believe it, is to make many more bests. That is my goal too. We need to dedicate ourselves to making each other better.

In order to be great trial lawyers, the best trial lawyers, we must first become better people by better knowing ourselves and how we can improve ourselves. I look forward to a life of passion, love, commitment, and living life to its fullest. I am not naïve, however, to think that I can have that without a lifetime of personal work.

If we can learn to love ourselves and our clients unconditionally, and be brutally honest about who we are as humans—good, bad, and ugly—then we will become more powerful than our opponents. Our opponents will be weak because they are fake, false, and without love.

STEVE HALTEMAN

When I am not consulting on a trial somewhere in the United States or mediating a dispute somewhere else, I am home in Costa Rica with my wife and nine-year-old daughter. In my spare time, I run long distances, bodysurf, and design and build both houses and unusual furniture. I also try to help out at the nonprofit school my wife and her business partner founded here in Costa

Rica. I'm constantly in search of building projects so that I can keep my special crew of Costa Rican men employed and content.

Most recently, I have been working on finishing the restoration of a long project, mating a 1951 GMC truck body with a 1995 Chevy Tahoe frame and motor. The goal is the ultimate Costa Rican off-roader. I am doing the work in Costa Rica between trials in the United States. My thought processes are similar, while my clothes and vocabulary are not.

The rest of the story, or how I stumbled into becoming a trial consultant, is as follows. One day, one of my wife's oldest friends, John, visited Costa Rica. John Carpenter is a trial lawyer in L.A. He brought along some friends, one of whom was from Iowa, but seemed more like from another planet. Enter Nick Rowley. At some point, it came out that I have a law degree, taught law in Japan, and served as a night court commissioner. As aligned or misaligned as the stars are, Nick and I shared our life stories up on the side of a mountain and became fast friends of the same cloth. We believe our world only has hope if people are willing to become humans again. As Nick always insists on personal histories, here is mine.

My father was a preacher with four churches in western Pennsylvania. My mother stayed at home until she returned to teaching some years later. I was born in 1963, just a few miles from where an airplane would one day crash into a field on September 11th.

My earliest memory was of seeing semifrozen people huddled in our living room as I came down the stairs in the morning. Our house lay on the alternate to the turnpike. When snow shut the turnpike down, people would try to make it home using the alternate. The police brought the lucky ones to the preacher's house. They took the unlucky ones elsewhere.

One day, when I was three, not long after my sister was born, my father came home and announced that things were warming up between Russia and the USA, so we should go over and have a look around.

I spent my fourth birthday in Leningrad. Somehow, my parents shipped our Dodge van to Poland and procured a six-month camping visa to the Soviet Union, and we roamed, overstaying our visa by many months. My fate was sealed by events I had no say in.

We returned to the States with eight dollars. Dad took on three churches, my parents had two more daughters in Maryland, and we settled down for seven years. Then my father stumbled upon the Mojave Desert. He made another announcement, and our family moved across the country to a part of the California Mojave Desert called California City. My father took on two churches. There, I learned how to run far and catch snakes, and I also learned about the injustice of being the shortest kid in high school. To pass the time, I bought an old MG convertible and tried to restore it. At that point, I was still small enough to fit in the car. Yet, my father made another announcement. No more churches; we were moving to Nevada.

Nevada was where I learned about perception and understanding themes. Between my sophomore and junior years, I grew eight inches. At the end of that growth spurt, I arrived at my new high school. In California, no girl ever looked sideways at the desert midget I was, a kid who spent his hours looking for snakes. In Nevada, the perception and themes were different. Now, I was the tall, filled out, blond surfer boy from California. Growing eight inches, driving my convertible, and coming from California labeled me a cool surfer kid who was the one to hang out with, though the waves of Southern California remained far out of reach for us desert kids. Almost overnight, I had become socially desirable. The world saw a different person. I didn't. The human me, my feelings, beliefs, insecurities, and attitudes, had not changed, not one iota. I remained the kid who was happiest driving through the cold back roads of the USSR with my parents and sisters, trying to learn a new language, and meeting people.

Off to college, education secondary to fun, my first serious girlfriend, and the inevitable, suicide-worthy broken heart. I was so depressed after that breakup that I could not continue with my education. I returned home with an announcement of my own for Mom and Dad. I had decided to take the year off to relax on the couch and take stock of my life. My parents said, "No you're not." A conversation followed that has since thrown my life sideways.

My dad asked me how much money I had in the bank.

"Fifteen hundred dollars."

"So you'll need to get a job."

That didn't excite me.

"Well, then why don't you hit the road?"

"Hit the road?"

"Tell you what, Son," he said. "I'll match your $1,500. Travel the world and go for as long as the money lasts you."

It was George Orwell's year, 1984. The wall still stood. I was twenty years old. My father's parting wisdom was, "Hitchhike. It's cheaper."

So I took my father's advice and always hitched, always alone—through Europe to Turkey, then through the Middle East, into Africa, finally arriving in Egypt. I traveled through Eastern Europe behind the Iron Curtain. I learned parts of different languages, customs, religions, cultures, and learned much about the commonness of humanity.

Surprisingly, there were so many similarities between different cultures and religions. I learned that Muslims, Christians, Jews, Hindus, Buddhists, and so on, are born, develop, reproduce, eat, breathe, live, die, mourn, and love very similarly.

What lessons did I learn? One, that collecting experiences rather than money would be my goal in life. Two, always go with my gut. Without exception. When I was about to climb into a car with people I didn't know, whom I didn't share a language or culture with, whose motivations were unclear, I had one best friend: my gut. Three, if I wanted to learn about people, I needed to *listen to them*. Shut up and listen. Listen with my heart and ears. That is how I learned to hear things worth hearing. Four, that in 1984, $3,000 bought you about nine months of very frugal travel.

I came back to finish college, and with no other prospects, ended up going to law school. San Diego is a great place to live, but a poor choice to endure the drudgery of law school. Distractions abounded. After two years of hovering at the bottom of my class, I lost interest in the program altogether. From my perspective, law school was a fraud. At a minimum, it lacked a hook for my attention and it revealed the shallowness of my intellect. Regardless, I was done. After repeated inquires, the admissions office confessed that a two-year leave of absence was possible. So I packed again and headed to Turkey. I took a few classes, and then flew to Egypt, where my plan was to follow the Nile to its headwaters.

This is when I met a woman from California named Naomi. She was hanging out in Cairo. We teamed up and headed south. In southern Sudan, we ran into the civil war. What to do? We turned west and dropped into the Central African Republic, crossed Zaire, went through Uganda, and eventually arrived in Kenya. This trip from Egypt ended up taking over ten months. We starved, were in gun battles, ate anything, were arrested, were jailed, and saw unexplainable things. We also survived, grew close, and opened our eyes wide. This new collection of life and cultural experiences provided more education than what I had been getting in law school. And the tuition was cheaper.

After wandering around Eastern Africa, Naomi and I took a break. She stayed in Africa and I left for India and Nepal. This was before the Internet and cell phones, so we stayed in touch by telegram, paying by the word. In Africa, I had studied the act of being patient. In India, I perfected the act by wandering around for six months. Nothing moves in India at the pace you prefer.

Eventually, Naomi and I reunited in Thailand. We rounded out the last of my two-year escape from law school by seeing Asia. Naomi went to Japan to teach, and I returned to San Diego to get a piece of paper. What did I learn? One, that perhaps I'd be happier living overseas. Two, that people watching is great entertainment, but to do it without judgment is extremely challenging. And three, it was time to settle down and start a legal career.

I returned to law school. All I remember about finishing law school was the monotony of trying to stay awake in class, and my guess that most of what I was learning had nothing to do with being a practicing lawyer. Following a squeeze-by graduation, I was hired by a big-name firm in Las Vegas, I got a nice plush office, and I bought some suits. Soon thereafter, my dad showed up and took a look around.

I puffed out my chest and said, "Well, Pop, what do you think? Your son has arrived, eh?"

Very calmly, he said, "I don't know, Son. This doesn't seem like you."

He was right; it didn't. My experiences growing up, coupled with world travel and the love I had for different cultures, made the idea of spending my life as an attorney-at-law less than desirable. I left for Japan.

Naomi and I married. We lived and taught in Japan for ten years. I taught English and U.S. law. In Japan, I learned that everybody has a public face and a private face. The two are not necessarily similar.

Our time in Japan had a great fringe benefit: six months of vacation per year. To Naomi and me, that meant six months of travel per year. For ten years, we traveled the world six months out of each year. The way we traveled was on the cheap: we would stay in hostels, eat what the locals eat, do what the locals do. Learning and becoming part of the different cultures was our preference.

At the end of the nineties, Naomi was hit by a drunk driver in Japan while riding her bike. It was a good way for any husband to learn hate. The surgeries she needed required us to return to the States. We settled in Maryland.

I tried work as a cabinetmaker, handyman, and wilderness skills instructor for Outward Bound, but I finally had to make some decent money, so I got involved with the U.S. legal system. I applied and was hired as a district court commissioner, serving as a night court judge. Most of what I did was set bail and decide whether to release criminal defendants who were arrested at night. I usually went with my gut, but I was proven a few times to be wrong. Specifically, I recall a few parking lot video surveillance tapes that police officers forced me to watch. Some of the accused I had released took my goodwill only to go out into the court parking lot and break into police cars. Some people just don't want to go home. I could relate to that.

In 2004, with my wife put back together and a new baby daughter named Fumiko in our arms, we headed south to Costa Rica, where we had purchased some land in the early 1990s. That is where we have been ever since.

Enter Nick Rowley. The above conversation concluded, though with a few more stories added trying to make me seem more like Indiana Jones.

Maybe after a few beers, Nick leaned forward and said, "How would you like to come help me on my next trial?"

I said, "What's that got to do with my life story?"

Nick said, "Never mind that; it's a simple question."

"What would I do exactly?"

"Help pick the jury, watch the trial, tell me what you think in the role as a juror."

"Hell, I don't know. I've never even seen a jury picked. I have no idea how it is done."

Nick smiled and said, "Exactly. This is why I need you."

That is how it began, how I became a jury consultant and trial strategist many years and trials ago.

I do not maintain any license to practice law in any state as a matter of personal choice. I probably couldn't pass a bar exam anyway. I do not do legal research or write briefs. What I do is to stay in touch with the humanity in the courtroom. My job is to stay in tune with the human story: to keep the case grounded at the basic levels of humanity and feeling that drive the decisions jurors make.

Focusing on the "human" aspect of a case is a nebulous concept if ever there was one. I'll try to clarify. Human beings' right brains dominate. I believe that most jurors will take a creatively told story to prove a point any day over a detailed, long, verbal, left-brained explanation delivered from a lectern. I count myself in that group.

What Nick and I do is always different. However, we approach every case beginning with the client, and we discover the human stories. My approach to trial has and continues to evolve. Still, common threads exist and continue to exist. I'll speak of these common threads throughout the book, but first some unfinished business.

If you've made it this far, you're aware of the chronology of my life. I haven't answered the hard questions Nick suggested earlier. There's a reason for that. Publicly analyzing one's personal issues is something I don't like, and I don't want people to do it to me. That's not to say I don't privately wrestle with my issues and demons. It's just that I am not open to discussion, unlike Nick, who puts it all out there. After looking for ways to avoid answering, I have recognized the fairness of answering, and that we should never ask others to do what we are unwilling to do ourselves. I'm not afraid of the answers, just about publicly revealing them. So I guess I will just have to jump. Or walk away from the book.

I've decided to jump.

1. Who am I?

    I am a forty-nine-year-old male in the midst of a midlife crisis, wondering which way to turn.

2. What am I?

    A human being who is finally learning that life is harder than I always thought. A human being who is good at many things, but a master of none.

3. What are the things I am most afraid of? Why?

    Rejection, because I like being liked more than I should. I am afraid of the second half of my life being a letdown. I am also afraid of turning out to be a coward in the toughest situations ahead of me.

4. What do I really care about? Money? Fame? Myself? Other people?

    My daughter most of all. Second, what other people think of me. Third, the unknown and what's around the corner.

5. How selfish am I? Why? Is it OK to be as selfish as I am? Why?

    I am very selfish. I put my happiness first. Even before that of my family. I can even be selfish in the face of generosity. I am ashamed of that and hope to be better.

6. Why am I really reading this book?

    Let's try: why am I writing this book? First, Nick asked. Second, I've always wanted to tackle writing a book. (Next, for something completely unheard of, I'm going to try my hand at a novel.) And third, my ego loves to hear me say, "I have a book coming out."

7. Do I like my current professional life, or do I want to change it? Why?

    Not right now, but I get bored easily and am not one to stay in one place for too long. Right now, I have a good balance, but I have no idea how long it will last.

8. What are the things I dislike most about myself? Why?

    That I never properly grieved for my father. I wasn't there the day he died, and I feel horrible about that. I want, but am struggling hard, to be a better father. My daughter is growing up, and I don't believe I am good enough to be the father she needs in the years to come. I am unable to forgive when I should. I hold grudges. While I put out a front of being very confident, I am in fact often insecure, which makes me feel like a fake. I can be arrogant given the right set of circumstances. Sometimes I should shut up.

9. What are the things I like about myself? Why?

    I'm self-entertained. I enjoy being with people or alone equally. I generally try to do the right thing. I side with the underdog. I am a calm person and think before I act. I'm allergic to panic. I would rather build something with my own hands that is worth less than take from somebody else and have better.

10. What is the best thing about me?

    That I make my own way in the world, and always will.

11. What is the worst/ugliest thing about me as a person (not physical appearance, but rather what is beneath the surface)?

    I'll keep that one private, as you can do with yours, but trust me: I know what it is. This is an important thing for us to know about ourselves, to know what is ugly and how to beat it back.

12. How do other people see me?

    Ah, the great unanswerable question. Not a clue. I know it depends on the context of our interaction, but why some look at me favorably and others do not is quite mysterious.

People are just too complex to give a general answer to this one. Sorry, I get a failing grade on number twelve.

13. Do I show others, including jurors, my true self?

    Only after evaluating the other person for trustworthiness. Or after a number of beers.

14. Do I even know my true self?

    I thought I did, but with so many major shifts going on, I'm beginning to doubt it. I have a plan, though, to get reacquainted.

15. What are the monumental experiences in life that brought me to where I am and made me the way I am?

    The big six would be getting molested at four years of age; rolling my convertible MG at age seventeen; hitchhiking alone from London to Cairo at a young age; meeting Naomi, my wife-to-be, in Cairo in 1989; the birth of my daughter; and the death of my father.

16. What are the things I want to change about myself? Why?

    I'd like to become deeper in thought as well as calmer. I'd like to simplify myself a great deal. I'd like to believe in a God.

17. Apart from money, success, and changing my physical appearance, what do I want most in my life? If I could push a button and make my life different tomorrow, how would it be? Why?

    I'd move the clock back two years and make the changes that I should have made, and be there when my father died, holding his hand.

18. Am I mostly happy or sad? What makes me this way?

    I'm happy 80 percent of the time, and sad 20 percent of the time. I have always been lucky that way. Although a big shock has been that as I age, the times of sadness are in the ascendency.

I need a beer. And I suspect you are wondering how any of the above is going to help you in the courtroom. This is a fair question, and one that we will try to answer starting with chapter 2.

Pick a Case, Find a Human, Learn a Story

Nick Rowley

Find a case or two in your office that is most important to you, and also find at least one case that you don't like, that you wish would disappear, and you wish you no longer had any responsibility for. Then ask yourself these questions:

- Why are you on these cases?
- Is the most important thing about these cases how much money you are going to put in your own pocket at the end of the day?
- What do you know about your clients?
- Do you even like your clients? If so, why? If not, why?
- Do you really care about your client, or do you care more about the money?
- Where are you in your own life emotionally and psychologically that influences the answers to these questions?

You need to answer and deal with these harsh questions, and be brutally honest with yourself. The business of the law practice can consume your humanity, and so can life's other stressors. Not being brutally honest about why you have a case in your hands can have devastating consequences.

Have you sat down and spent any real time with these clients, face-to-face, breaking bread, sharing a meal, in regular, everyday human clothing? If not, you need to. You may have the index information on the case—some photographs, a police report, some medical records, date of birth, contact information—but what do you really know about these human beings and their lives? What makes them tick, and what do they love? Who do they love? What are their fears? What medicine is in their cabinets? What does it smell like to be in their home and car or truck? What things do you have in common? We want to challenge you to find out these answers and experience these feelings.

Spend quality time with your clients and witnesses in their worlds. Cook for them. Have them cook for you. Cook together. Food is something that brings people together. Look at photo albums. Share life stories. Connect. Try talking about everything other than the case.

You might find yourself falling in love with another human being, and if so, that is a very good thing. It is good because you have the obligation, the duty, to bring a group (a jury) of other humans into your client's world. These other humans probably live in similar worlds. They need you to be the medium. You, the attorney-at-law, truly are an outsider in this case. You will remain that way until you change.

This is such an important thing to understand in order for you to be the best and apply the Trial by Human method. You first must become human again. If you are as human with your client and the jurors in the courtroom as you are with your best friend, then you don't need to read this book. You've got it down. But if you feel a void between yourself and your client or between yourself and the jurors, then read on. When you figure this out, when you are done with your test cases, if you feel a difference, win or lose, you must do it again and again and again.

You have to be willing to do what you ask the jurors to do, which is to care and connect with your client and your cause. If you don't care about your client enough to do these things, why should the jury care about your client?

For now, either carry on reading but put a bookmark in this chapter to remind yourself to come back to this section later, or stop reading this book and go meet with some of your clients. At least pick up the phone and have a regular human conversation. Shake it up a bit. Call and say, "I just want to learn about you and I want to tell you about myself," or "We have a big fight ahead of us and it would mean a lot to me if we could spend some time together as regular people."

If you don't have time to do any of this, then you won't fully succeed and accomplish what this book can provide for you. In that case, you can continue to read and find some things that might work in your bag of tricks. We all have our bags, but they are what we use to get a hung jury on a case that should result in acquittal, or what we use to get a million-dollar verdict on a five-million-dollar case. And, sometimes, when we reach into our bags of tricks, we pull out what ends up being a piece of shit. We didn't expect it, and we are stuck standing there with shit in our hands, there in the courtroom, for all to see. Our client is at the table, afraid and helpless, and we are exposed as the tricksters that we are.

We want you to try something different, and to put the bag of tricks aside. We want you to stand in court as the voice of a fellow human whom you love and care about. Someone you see as family, a human you would truly break down and cry for, whom you are honored to spend time with, and whom you care about.

Tom Valens

I have something to share with you. There is an experience that helped me a lot as a trial lawyer. It is a case I had many years ago, and that ended up being one of my first "big wins." It didn't start out as a win. It started out as a shitty case that I did not want anything to do with. My client, Tom Valens,[1] was a man I did not like. Actually, that is putting it mildly. I hated the man and described him with a multitude of choice words. I could not stand his voice. The sight of him shook me, and I dreaded having to deal with him.

It was 2005, and I was twenty-seven years old. We were in a conservative place. I had never tried a case in this county before. Other attorneys told me it was a bad place to be a plaintiff in a medical malpractice case. Tom was a jerk. He was cocky, demanding, a know-it-all, and in my opinion, not credible. He complained way too much, and about everything. His entire case sucked. He seemed to me to be an exaggerator. To top it off, Tom did not like me.

There I was, standing in front of the courthouse on the first day of trial, and I didn't want to be there. This was going to suck. I was going to lose, and I was going to get sued. I was there because a lawyer I had previously employed had signed up the case, but failed to work it up. It was too late to get out of it—the lawyer in my firm who had been responsible for this file had since left—and I was standing there in front of the courthouse because I didn't want an ugly situation to get worse. I was going to spend the next couple weeks with a crazy, angry, untrustworthy man who exaggerated everything. I hated life. My law practice was not something I enjoyed. I was sick of trying cases and dealing with clients who complained and expected miracles. I was becoming bitter. Tom's case was one that motivated me to think of quitting the practice of law, or even switching to doing med mal defense work, where I knew I could make steady money and feed my ego with win after win in the courtroom.

There was no expert on liability, causation, or damages. Each expert I talked to didn't like the case. The one treating physician who did have a supportive opinion, and who had agreed to testify against the defendant physician, had died.

The more I looked into the case—reviewing all the medical records, Tom's underlying workers' compensation file, and the

---

1. This name has been fictionalized for confidentiality.

defense expert reports—the worse it got. I had even called opposing counsel and tried to get the case settled for $30,000, which was the reporting limit in California. I offered to eat all costs and waive attorney's fees. I told Tom his case sucked, and he said he would sue me if I withdrew from the case. Out of my own stupidity, my malpractice insurance policy had lapsed at the time.

Tom was claiming big economic damages from a misdiagnosis of a blood disorder called hemochromatosis (too much iron in the blood, resulting in oxidative damage to the tissues). The problem was that Tom had claimed in his workers' comp case that a back injury rendered him unable to work. He also claimed psychiatric injury and permanent disability in the workers' comp case.

It was as ugly as ugly could be. The insurance defense lawyers not only refused to settle for the $30,000, but they also refused to settle for $0 and a waiver of costs. Defense counsel insisted they would win a defense judgment and put a lien on Tom's house. I could not stand Tom, so my motivation for pushing forward was that I promised the defense that if they did not pay the $30,000, I would make it my priority in life to win this case. I gave them my word. Tom had in fact been misdiagnosed, and at this point, the defense refused to allow an honorable retreat and decided to be bullies. I hate bullies, and I hated the defense more than I hated my client.

It was time for expert designation. To oppose a summary judgment motion, I only had a few days. The treating doctor, who was going to give us a declaration to beat the summary judgment motion, had died. Late at night, digging through the file and preparing a letter to Tom explaining that we were going to lose the case and asking for his permission to try to negotiate a waiver of costs and dismiss the case, I looked at the retainer agreement.

The retainer agreement provided that the client was responsible for all costs. This was the ace in the hole. I thought I found a way to escape. I called Tom and asked him for $30,000 to try the case. I knew he couldn't pay, and I thought I had my way out. I told him that under the contract, he was obligated. He took out a line of credit on his house that day and gave me a check. Shit!

I then went through a service to find an expert to get a declaration to defeat the summary judgment motion. I did that, and the expert said he would testify at trial. I started to see that I could win the case on the medicine. I took the depositions of the defense experts, Harvard-trained doctors, who called Tom's case as ugly and frivolous as ugly and frivolous could be.

Time for trial. No continuance. The court was ready for us, and the defense was ready to go. I had an opening prepared. I had some good facts on the misdiagnosis, but causation and damages were tough, and the prior workers' comp case claimed that everything Tom was blaming the medical defendant for was a work-related injury.

I took a long time picking a jury. We got a good jury. I ended my opening statement by telling the jury how the defendant physician would be proven untrustworthy: he was a man who falsified medical records and was disciplined by the medical board for doing so. The judge granted a mistrial motion. The defense had no motion *in limine* on file on this issue, so I thought it was fair game. The judge was not upset with me, and he scolded defense counsel for not making a motion *in limine*. The court would bring in a new jury the next morning.

Tom was not bothered. He gave me a pat on the back and a half hug, told me that it would be OK, that I did a good job. This man believed in his case, and for the first time, I saw that he, undeservingly, believed in me. Deep in his core, Tom knew that he could win his case as long as he had a capable trial lawyer who would care about him. He never imagined winning it as big as we did, and neither did I.

At this point, the evening after the mistrial, Tom and I went out and had a beer together. We sat down together outside the courtroom for the first time. We agreed that we did not like each other, but we had a job to do. After a few beers, a good steak dinner, and story after story about how we grew up tough and worked hard as soon as we were old enough to pick up a shovel, Tom and I fell in love with each other. Tom was just like me as a kid. He moved out when he was fifteen years old. He worked hard, and his record was impeccable. He was a smart guy. He loved being on a boat in the ocean. He had worked on fishing boats, but now because of his injuries, he could not be on the water anymore. He loved to work with his hands, but now his hands did not work. He loved to barbecue. That was one of the few things he was still able to do.

He told me about his workers' comp case, and I truly listened to him for the first time. This was the ugly part of the case I had to deal with. But for the first time, I truly listened to this broken man and his explanation. For the first time, I was not thinking of him as a fraud. I felt humbled and ashamed of myself inside. Tom explained how the work injury existed, and was real, and how it happened, but that the reason he hadn't healed was this nasty disease, hemochromatosis. (A two-year buildup of iron in his blood from the time that the defendant physician should have picked up on it resulted in oxidative damage to the soft tissues and the joints in Tom's body.)

It was at this point that I really paid attention to Tom's hand. It wasn't a hand anymore. It was like a claw. I asked him to take off his shoes, and I saw that his feet were also deranged. I always saw Tom clenching a fist and waving his fist, which led me to believe he was angry and intimidating. The truth was that he didn't want to look that way. His hand was stuck in that position, in a contracture, and expressing anger was how he coped with his pain. This was not mentioned in any medical records or depositions. The defense experts mentioned that he always spoke and shook his fist at them. Little did they know. I had spent my preparation of this case focusing on incomplete medical records, not spending time with my client listening to his story. Joint pain was mentioned, but not these derangements/contractures of his hand and both feet, which were clearly visible once I took the time to look.

I didn't sleep that night. I stayed up writing frantically. The story was entirely different now. I understood, and felt in my soul, what happened to Tom. I saw how the medical doctors betrayed and ignored him. I knew it, and the reason why I knew it was because I was guilty of doing the same thing to him, not listening or caring.

The next day, I picked the jury much more efficiently, in less time. I was confident in the case, and I didn't need to precondition the jury. I did the opening statement as Tom's brother: I told his life story, and I showed the jury how I cared about him. I took them inside Tom's life, body, and brain. I took them inside his home. We went to the doctor's office together and talked about what happened there. We went inside the laboratory where Tom's blood was tested, and we read the reports, which ignored the lab test results that showed the abnormal iron levels in his blood.

Tom and I were connected. All we needed was that one evening together: sharing stories, being real, listening to and caring about each other. I learned more about him in that evening than I could have by reading every page in the five boxes of records that were "the case."

I learned that a case is not a box of depositions and records. A case is not what other attorneys-at-law say it is. A case is often much more. If we find the human story and bring that into the courtroom, all things are possible. Even real justice.

After the opening statement in Tom's case, the defense offered the $30,000. We countered at $450,000. The defense lawyer rolled his eyes and told us, "This case is not worth $450,000."

During the rest of the case, the experts did not matter. I kept telling Tom's human story through every witness who got up on the stand. In the end, twelve human beings cared about Tom. That caring started in voir dire and opening. They cared because I cared, because I was now standing up for my friend, not a "client" or "case" that I only knew from boxes of records and depositions, or sitting in my conference room for meetings in uniform. I was the voice and protector of a human I cared about.

The defense lawyer was right that our case wasn't worth $450,000. A week later, the jury gave us $3.7 million, which was a million more than we had asked for. The jury had loved Tom by the end of the opening statement. They connected with him as human beings and cared for him. They hugged him after the verdict.

Since my experience on Tom's case, before I take a case to trial, I spend time breaking bread with my clients and their families, going through photo albums, staying with them at their homes, becoming family with them, and connecting with them as I would do with a human being who is worth caring about.

Your New Insight May Not Always Be Positive

There are some cases where the insight you gain by spending time with a client will reveal weaknesses in your case that you didn't expect. That is also a benefit to you before trial.

You might think you have a perfect case because of clear liability, great property damage, significant lost income, and because the client is an upstanding member of the community. You may think the case is a slam dunk. Spending time with your clients, whom you don't think you need to spend time with because the case is an easy bell ringer, might reveal that the case is not so perfect. And if your gut tells you there is something wrong and that a client is not being 100 percent truthful, do your own investigation and find out the truth before the defense rubs your nose in it in front of a jury.

Most of the time, the information you learn will substantially help your client. In other cases, it helps you to better advise the client. Most importantly, the time you spend with your client will help you to show that you care enough about your client to learn about her, and it will allow you to be credible in front of the jury by telling them the truth.

What about Your Cases?

Learn the lesson I learned with Tom. Spend time with your clients. Get to know them on a first-name basis. Become friends. Don't prejudge your clients as being great cases or bad cases. Just meet them and spend time with them.

Remember, we are not better than our clients, and we are not superior. We have been bestowed the honor of being their voice. In order to do that job, we need to know what makes them tick. We should sit down at the same dinner table. Know them in our gut, not just on paper or by labels. Don't believe that one case is worth more than another because one client was a good income earner and another was not.

Even if you are of a different religion or no religion, go to church with your client. Spend time and get to know the people closest to him. Find out what is beautiful about the human being you are there to stand up for against the bullies. Find out what is ugly. Embrace it all.

Knowing your clients' labels is not enough to truly understand them and be their voice. What I mean by *labels* is that it is not enough to know that, for example, he is a police officer, she is a young nurse and great income earner, he is a factory worker, he is the father of three children, she is just a stay-at-home wife and her kids are out of the home, they were just retired grandparents and there are no real economic damages, and so on.

We need to know: What is our client's favorite thing to do and why? What is his favorite food? What is her favorite place in the world and why? Whom does he love most and why? What is the love? Feel it, make it part of you, make it something you can feel in your gut, understand it, and share it with a group of people that you want to love your client—your jury.

If you are willing to do this and feel it deep within yourself, then you will start to see that so much more is possible in the courtroom. Once the human stories are alive within you, you have authority, credibility, and something nobody else in the case has: compassion. When you have this compassion alive within you, you won't need notes to tell the story. People ask me how I do what I do without notes. This is how.

Chapters of the Human Story

Nick Rowley

We are not yet ready for trial. Hopefully, trial is at least months away. You have your case to work on. In fact, you have chosen two: one you love and one you don't. You have spent time with these two humans, your clients, and shown them the human inside of you. A different relationship hopefully exists than the one that was there before. Your clients trust you more, both of them. The connection has begun. You have a human story growing alive within you, and you are truly starting to care. They are thinking about you as a person, and you are thinking about them as people.

So what do we do with this?

We have some work to do. It is not the work most lawyers do. This is a different type of work. We have to further develop and set up the chapters of the human story.

I am not going to say much about written discovery. You can figure that out on your own or in a practice guide.

Depositions are important, but that does not mean we need to depose everybody. Informal meetings as human beings with the people who are important to the story are the most important things for us to do. We need to realize that people are afraid of us. They fear being used and manipulated. Our profession is not one that people trust. Many people think that when an attorney calls you, the smart thing to do is hang up the phone and get your own attorney.

So how do we prepare the chapters of our story and learn what it is to be inside the skin of your witnesses, the humans who know and have lived the story? The best way I have found is to call them and ask them for help. We tell them that we need to talk to them. We tell them we want to avoid a case having to go to court, or to avoid sending them a subpoena to be a witness in a trial. I am brutally honest with the witnesses and tell them that my goal is to discover the human story. I tell them what part of it they can help me understand. If the defense is being a bully, I tell them. If my client is hurt, I tell them. If I am afraid of them, I tell them. If I feel they are afraid of me, I ask them and we talk about it. Most of the time, I can get witnesses to talk to me. And for those of you who are afraid of making yourselves witnesses in a case by being a lawyer who has interviewed witnesses, just be up-front with the jurors and tell them whom you have met with and how you went about it. Most jurors would expect lawyers to meet with and interview witnesses.

We need to find a way to bring to life every part of the story we are going to tell the jury. As we transition into ways of accomplishing this in the next chapters, I want you to think of your cases and how you can do the same. Hopefully, you can find creative ways to do it even better.

If you have pictures, we want you to put a voice to those pictures. Even sometimes better than pictures, or along with the pictures, you and the humans in the courtroom can bring to life what the pictures or scenes were like by physically reenacting the scenes of the story.

STORIES ARE NOT LIMITED BY WHAT IS ON PAPER

When we prepare the story, we do not start with the medical records. Those are not necessarily the truth of the case. I don't trust medical records. They are touted and fed to courts, experts, and jurors as "official, reliable records," yet medical providers create them after the fact and craft them with carefully chosen words that check boxes so as to not create any trace of negligence. The records are what risk managers, medical peers, the medical board, and lawyers review. So leave room for the possibility that the records might not tell us the truth, the whole truth, and nothing but the truth. Leave room for the possibility that these "bona fide records" are filled with embellishments, stretches, and manipulations of truth, important mistakes, and sometimes even blatant lies. The records often tell us the stories in the scared voices of employees and professionals who care very much about themselves, each other, and their employer, and who are motivated by self-preservation.

We are going to start with the humans who are most accessible to us, the scenes of where things happened, and, most importantly, those who are most important to the case. These people are the injured person and his or her family.

Starting the Story: Sofia Blunt's Case[1]

To give you an example of how we do this, let's start with the case of Sofia Blunt. (The appendix contains detailed information about the facts of this case.) Steve and I were asked to jump into trial on this severe-brain-damage birth injury case in mid-February 2012. The lawyers already on the case told us that winning anything would be very tough because of the venue and the forces we were up against. Friends said not to jump into the case because it was too much work with high risk of a goose egg at the end.

---

1. *Blunt v. Sierra Vista Medical Center,* case number CV 100071, Superior Court of San Luis Obispo County, San Luis Obispo, CA.

Taking the case meant spending two months away from our families in a conservative jurisdiction where it is next to impossible to win a personal-injury case, let alone a malpractice case against a popular doctor and highly regarded local hospital.

We could have listened to that and let fear start building up. Instead, we looked for some strength and motivation. We went to meet little Sofia. Because the case was about her, that is where we decided to begin. What kind of humans would we be if we made our decision about whether to even meet Sofia based on medical records and the statistics that defense lawyers, insurance companies, judges, and even our fellow trial lawyers wave before us to scare us? What kind of humans would we be if we focused on how slim the chances were of winning a medical malpractice case in San Luis Obispo, California? What kind of humans would we be if that were the truth and we did nothing to change it? What type of warriors would we be if we made our decision based on propaganda and fear, and then by looking at and trusting what turned out to be false, misleading medical records?

We chose to believe there were good, caring people in San Luis Obispo who would want to do justice for a deserving case and a deserving plaintiff.

Our First Meeting with Sofia's Family

The meeting was set, unfortunately, in a conference room. I was in jeans and a T-shirt. Sofia was three years old and had a bow in her hair. She was so very beautiful. I sat down on the floor with her and we talked. At times, I didn't even realize she had a disability because her beauty captured me. She had a smile that brightened the room. Even though she could not respond with words, she communicated with me through her eyes, smiles, and body movements.

I fell in love with this little girl. It didn't take long. I had been called upon to protect her, and I would stop at nothing to stand up and battle for her against the enemies. She chose me and I chose her. My partner Robert Ounjian and I would figure out the medical records and experts later. Right then, we began to develop a chapter of the human story that would live and grow within us and that we would later share and pass over as a gift to our jury.

I asked Sofia's mother, Jennifer, to tell me as much about Sofia as she could. Who was Sofia at that time, what did she like and dislike, and what made her happy? That is what I wanted to know. I wanted to see what made her smile. I did this by asking her mom to speak to me as Sofia.

"If Sofia had a voice and I were able to talk to her, what would she say to me?"

I asked Sofia questions, and I learned so much. I learned that Sofia was trapped inside her body, and that she wanted to play with her sister but couldn't. She wanted to try the food that Mom and Dad and her little sister Charlotte ate, but she didn't have the muscle control to swallow, so she couldn't. She loved Barney. I learned that Sofia was very loved and happy, and she was not afraid of anything. She loved to be social. She loved boys and was a flirt. She loved singing and being outside.

In our meeting, I asked Sofia's parents, Jennifer and Andrew, to talk to me as a new neighbor in the community, sitting at a barbecue, instead of as a lawyer. That put them at ease. I was in regular clothes to begin with. We talked. I'm a nice guy, and I have kids, and we connected as parents. I started by telling them about my family, my children, where I am from. I told them about my children and my struggles as a parent. That opened the door and made them comfortable to talk to me.

They told me about Sofia's difficulties and the restrictions on their ability to travel and to go out as a couple. They had to take time off from their careers because taking care of Sofia was a full-time job. But, with all of that, the most important thing I learned was that they were very happy. A happy family. And they wanted me to know that if the lawsuit did not work out for them, they would still be happy, and they would figure out how to get by. Many people would be severely depressed, crying, complaining, and at their wits' end, hanging their life on the lawsuit. Not these parents. Sofia, despite having severe cerebral palsy and being fed through a tube in her stomach, was a blessing to the family. She brought everybody joy and happiness.

Learning this was empowering to me. I realized how much I have to be happy and thankful for. How in the world do I have anything to complain about when this family found happiness and vowed to stay happy and together no matter what? My getting involved with Sofia's care later on helped me understand how happy they were. Caring for Sofia was a joy. She smiled; she was happy and appreciative. She was sweet and cuddly. She was a sponge for love and affection.

Jennifer and Andrew really didn't have any complaints. They were of course afraid for Sofia's future and what would happen if they were not around. That was their reason for the lawsuit. That, and making sure that what happened to Sofia didn't happen again and get swept under the rug. Jennifer and Andrew not only wanted to make sure there was security for Sofia, but they also wanted to make sure their community was safer. They didn't want Sofia to ever be warehoused in some coed group home where she could end up being the victim of abuse and neglect. Jennifer and Andrew pursued the case because nobody had given them answers. Nobody apologized. They felt betrayed and lied to. They forgave the medical providers for that, but they wanted to make sure to protect other patients.

I learned about their backgrounds and where they came from. Jennifer loved to read. She enjoyed surfing and running. Andrew liked to work out; he had a pull-up bar in the doorway to one of the bedrooms. They loved to travel and go to the beach. Their lives were centered around their two little princesses. They were churchgoers. They were healthy eaters. They had a very close-knit family; there were three grandmothers (two biological grandmothers and one step-grandmother) in the room when Sofia was born. They were very trusting people.

I didn't delve deep into what happened with the medicine during this first meeting. This meeting was about learning about them as people. I left this meeting with the themes of the importance of keeping a family together, protecting a child's future, and finding joy in the worst of circumstances as long as there is life and a family gets to stay together.

We made plans for a second meeting in their home. My goal was to experience Sofia's life for myself. I wanted to see and feel what it was like to live in Sofia's home, care for her, and live with her as part of her family. Everything I learned and experienced became a chapter of the story that I had within me to share with the jury.

Waking Up with Sofia

At our next meeting, we made breakfast together in their home, a two-bedroom apartment. I got to see Sofia wake up in the morning and go through everything that her mom and dad had to do to get her up and moving for the day.

My goal with Sofia was to experience her experiences for myself. If she had gastric feedings that needed to be done, I wanted to participate and be involved. I wanted to be there at her home when she woke up in the morning and see what it was like to take care of her. I needed to experience it for myself. I didn't need a "day-in-the-life" video. It would be much more effective and real for me to go myself, experience it, and tell the story to the jurors. Then, I could set a scene, show them the layout of Sofia's home, and show them where the family sits down for breakfast.

I needed to know Sofia's mom and dad as friends, and we needed to trust each other—even love each other. I needed to understand what life was like for them as parents of a child with special needs. The only way to truly understand and be able to share that with a jury was to get involved, hands on, with Sofia's care.

We looked through photo albums. We talked through Sofia's birth and watched the video together. We talked about the entire labor and delivery so I could reverse roles with both Jennifer and Andrew and feel what it was like to be them during the pregnancy and during the delivery.

My goal here was not to do most of the talking; my goal was to be a good listener. During our time together, I learned more and more about them as humans, and more about myself. I left this time together wanting to know, as a parent, what happened to Sofia: wanting an explanation of why my beautiful little girl had cerebral palsy.

We went over the pregnancy month by month and then the admission to the hospital, and then we slowly went over the labor and delivery as though we were there experiencing it there together.

We do this not by asking and answering questions across a desk from each other in a fancy, impressive office. We sit down, somewhere comfortable for the clients, and we talk in the present tense. We go back in time together, hear the sounds, and reenact what the nurses and doctors said to each other.

Medical Records and Depositions

We learn the story firsthand. The story is not dictated by the discovery, depositions, or medical records. We don't need (or maybe don't even have) such things at this point. Another thing to consider is that if you know the client's story within you and that story is much different than what the medical records and depositions of medical witnesses say, then we identify a conflict of truth that can be the turning point or winning point of your case. If the human story within you is the one that is believable, then you can show the defendant's story to be a lie and betrayal.

After going through what we had so far with Sofia's parents, spending time getting to know the family, and igniting a flame of love for them in our hearts, we then looked at the medical records and depositions. We looked for those conflicts.

Oftentimes, those conflicts exist in the medical records. We then have two choices. One is to be afraid and concerned that the medical records are gospel and our clients are made to be liars. The way I prefer to look at it is the way my friend Rolando Hidalgo says it: "How would we like it if the person and his allies who negligently hit and injured us in a car accident were the ones who got to write up the police report?"

You see, I don't trust medical records. They are written after the fact, and medical professionals are taught the CYA method of documenting medical facts. How many times have we ever seen the following in a medical record: "We made a mistake and hurt/killed the patient"? Never! That is the answer to that question.

WHERE ARE YOUR CASES?

I have purposely digressed from talking about developing the story of Sofia and that is because we have to go back and forth. Our first step is to ignite the human story and the connection between us and our clients. That way, we don't see Sofia as a case number. When we think of her, we see a face, we hear sounds, and we taste the food we ate with her family. She is alive within us, part of who we are in this world.

So, readers! Where are you with your cases at this point? I am asking because I want you to work on your own cases as you read this book. At the very least, make a note of what you are going to do. Mark this part of the book for future reference, because *Trial by Human* is a "how to do it the way we do it" guide. This means that we want you working and developing your cases as you read.

Have you gone and spent time with your clients? Please give it a try. Come back and write down what you have learned from meeting with the human beings involved. What do you feel inside? Do you care more deeply than you did before? What are the themes that you have developed? Write them down. Are your clients more than a case name or file number in the office? Are your clients more than an add-up of medical specials? Are you looking at your clients differently than through the insurance company's Colossus system? I hope so!

Keep talking about these humans whom you are honored to represent. Talk about them with people you know, not with other attorneys who don't practice this way, but with your wife or husband, parents, friends, and people in the line at the grocery store. Of course, don't mention names or confidential information, but tell their story. Keep them alive within you. Go to bed and wake up each morning thinking and caring about them as human beings, not legal subjects and case numbers.

Sofia's Case

Official Records Don't Always Tell the Story

This is where we got the medical records. In Sofia's case, those were labor and delivery records. We needed to see where the conflicts were. What parts of the medical records fit with the story and what parts didn't?

In Sofia's case, we found medical records that said that Sofia came out of her mother crying. This clearly conflicted with her father and mother's story that she came out pale, not moving, and looked dead. A nurse wrote down, hours after Sofia was born, that Sofia was crying when she was born. Why would the medical providers who were taking care of Sofia while she was inside of her mother say that she came out full of life? Why would a nurse write down that she was crying? What human reasons would justify writing down lies in medical records? The truth is that these medical providers, like all humans, have a high-stake interest in self-preservation. To say Sofia came out lifeless and looking dead would mean that she was badly hurt before she was ever handed over to the hospital team of pediatric/neonatal specialists.

Test the Discovery of Truth with Focus Groups

In developing the human story, we need to have themes. This is the point where we can do a focus group and compare the different versions of the truth in front of strangers and develop themes. Doing focus groups is simple. David Ball has a video on how to do your own focus groups, and I would suggest getting it to learn how to do them in detail.[2] What I will say is that it is not very complicated and it is not expensive. What you need is six to ten people. You get them together, show them the evidence in a way that does not favor one side of the case or the other, and ask them what their thoughts and beliefs are. Have them meet your clients. See what questions they have for your clients. See what themes

---

2. David Ball, Debra Miller, and Artemis Malekpour, *Focus Groups: How to Do Your Own Jury Research* (Portland, OR: Trial Guides, 2008).

the group develops. Listen. Don't try to sell your case. Learn by listening and connecting. Imagine them as your jury, and you get to talk to them in regular clothes, learn what is important to them in the case, and see what moves them as human beings.

Be Involved with the Story as It Develops

When there are doctors' appointments, go with your client, and go in regular clothes. Figure out what is going on. Feel what it is to be a patient or parent of a patient, sitting there and waiting for the doctor, standing in line for the prescriptions, being examined or seeing your child get poked and prodded. It is your job, and don't think that you have to hide this from the jury. Embrace it. Tell the jury that your job is to make sure that your Sofia gets the best medical care, and to understand what that care is, so that you can be her voice and in turn tell the court and jury. Tell them the brutally honest truth that you have been involved with; tell them about Sofia's parents' decisions for testing and treatment. Ask the jurors how they feel about that in voir dire. It is the truth, we all know it is the truth, so why bullshit about it? You are your client's protector and voice, and you should be involved in and understand what it is like to go through what she must go through.

Go to your client's home early and see how hard it is for her to get out of bed in the morning. You don't need a day-in-the-life video. You need to go there yourself and have the experience. A chapter of your story is much more powerful than a day-in-the-life video would be. In a video, a family member shows the jury how your client is helped out of bed each morning, or helped in the shower, or helped with cooking. Instead, you can show the jury that, because you did it too.

Continue to Be Involved and Develop Story Chapters

Who are the potential witnesses that you will introduce to a jury? We have found that ordinary people, lay witnesses, can be the most important witnesses in a trial. Meeting other family members and having them relive what they saw (for example, what Sofia's grandmas saw) in that labor and delivery room can be the way you discredit all of the medical records, defendant medical providers, and defense experts.

In Sofia's case, one of the grandmothers reenacted and relived Sofia's delivery, saw her head coming out, and described the first minutes of her life. You could hear a pin drop in the courtroom when I asked Sofia's grandmother, "Tell us about baby Sofia crying when she was born, that cry that we all listen for," and the grandmother's response was: "There was no cry. The baby had no life. It looked dead. We were in shock."

And then I turned to the defendant physician while holding up a medical record and said, "But he says and wrote down in the record that Sofia was crying. Is that the truth that you saw with your eyes and heard with your ears?" Again, silence. Disappointment. Betrayal. That is what I felt and that is what the jury felt. Even the defense lawyers kept their heads down in shame. Had I not spent time with Sofia's grandmother, I would have never known her feelings and been able to tap into and share that emotion, sad truth, and betrayal with the jury.

Take every potential witness and meet with them in regular clothes. Get to know their story and what chapter of the story of the case they can help the jury learn and understand.

Being Involved Shapes Which Experts We Truly Need

Too often, lawyers overkill their cases with experts. Spending personal time with Sofia and her family helped us determine which medical experts we really needed at trial. In our cases, we save ourselves and our clients a lot of money being selective about the medical care and experts. We do not want to overkill the case with professionals and paid experts. It can detract from the human story, which we need to portray in order to win the case.

Lay witnesses are just as important—and sometimes even more important—than your expert witnesses. A case with great experts is weak if you don't have the human beings telling the human story as the foundation. A good lay witness whom the jury connects with can beat a strong defense expert.

Here is a general example showing how you would argue this at a mediation, through a deposition, or in a trial:

According to the defense expert, what Andrew Blunt said cannot be true. Andrew Blunt has spent more time with Sofia than all of the experts in this courtroom combined. He knows his little girl and what she needs. He knows she needs twenty-four-hour, around-the-clock care, seven days a week, to protect her. You heard from him. Did you believe him? If you did, and I think you should because . . . If you believe Sofia's father and you know what he told you is the truth, then you can reject what the defense's paid expert witnesses, whom they have given money to for their opinions, had to say.

You could make all of these statements to an expert in a deposition and see what she has to say. Let the defense object; defense lawyers often object to the truth!

I believe that the best way to beat the defense experts is with good lay witnesses whom the jury will connect with. Meet them in regular clothes. Get to know them. Discover the stories of the laypeople involved. Spend time with them during the discovery phase of the case. Tell the defense about them when you respond to discovery.

Lay Witnesses

A lay witness is an "everyday person" witness who doesn't have a dog in the fight in terms of making money off of the case. A lay witness can come into court in regular clothes as a member of the community and help us tell part of the chapters of our story. This can be a neighbor, a coworker, a teacher, a coach, a close family friend.

If you have a client who has trouble walking, then have a lay witness come give some real-life examples of how she has witnessed the walking problems. Don't rely on an expert witness who spent time with your client in an examination room. If the issue is depression, bring in a lay witness to talk about how your client has changed, how your client appears withdrawn, sad, not the same person anymore.

If the issue is brain injury, you need as many lay witnesses as you can to come in and talk about the human being before and how the human being that exists now is different. Then you ask the defense experts, "Did you talk to the people who knew my client before his brain injury, who have seen the change in him as a human being?"

The answer will be no.

Q: Did you read any of their depositions?

A: No.

Q: The reason is that the defense never bothered to take any of those depositions, did they, because they were not helpful to the defense's case, isn't that true?

DEFENSE LAWYER: Objection.

THE COURT: Sustained.

Q: Human beings who don't have a dog in this fight, who are not getting paid tens of thousands of dollars for their opinions, can be valuable sources of information about how a brain injury has affected somebody's life, isn't that true?

A: Yes.

Q: And you don't know what any of them have to say or what they said to this jury, do you?

A: No.[3]

EXPERT WITNESSES

Videotaped Expert Depositions

Other chapters to create in your story are videotaped depositions. You should videotape treating physician and expert depositions if you believe they will be helpful, and then you can use them at

---

3. *Von Normann v. Newport Channel Inn,* case number 30-2010-00423312, Superior Court of California, Orange County, CA.

trial. Jurors love to watch videos. You also deprive the opposition of the ability to effectively cross-examine the treating doctor. Many times, the lower-level insurance defense lawyer is doing the deposition, not the trial lawyer. So take advantage of it. It will save you money and often prove to be a more effective way of presenting the medical aspects of your case.

My practice is, if people are adverse to us, I take video depositions to tell the various chapters of the story, and then tell the jury the story.

For each witness, reverse roles with him or her before the deposition. Get into the skin of that human being. What is really going on inside? What are your motivations? In her skin, do you truly believe that what you are going to say is the truth? Are you spinning the truth? Are you biased, and if so, why? What are you afraid of? What do you care about? Do you believe you are doing the right thing?

Defense Expert Witnesses

As a defense expert, do you believe you are a soldier in this battle? Are you truly independent and don't care about getting another case from the insurance company that hired you? Do you lean in favor of the side that paid you? If you were sitting down having a beer with your best, most trusted friend, what would you admit to him or her? Or is there no way you would admit to the bias and prejudice that exists within you?

Do you have a deposition of the defense expert coming up? If so, find a quiet place, sit down in a chair, and become that expert witness. Crawl into that human being's skin. Who are you? What motivates you? What do you care about? When this forensic evaluation comes into your office, what do you truly believe in your gut? What do you need to make yourself believe in order to be able to live in your skin and sleep soundly at night? What is your goal? Would you be happy to write your five hundredth forensic report to your employer (the insurance company law firm that hired you and sends you business)? Do you really believe what you are writing, that is, that every problem this plaintiff is claiming is untrue? Do you really believe what you are saying, or are you just saying it, cutting and pasting it from the other report you just wrote? If this were somebody important to you, would you believe that the injuries and pains truly exist and are just as bad as she claims?

In Sofia's case, the defense called a pediatric neonatologist from Stanford to testify that Sofia's brain injury was not preventable and that the damage had already been done and would have been done even if she had been timely delivered. This was a subsequent treating physician whom Sofia was transferred to at Stanford Medical Center, and he had not been hired by either side as a retained expert. In preparing for his cross-examination, I thought about who he was and what he believed in. This neonatologist believed he was doing good for the medical profession by coming down to San Luis Obispo to help fight a frivolous lawsuit.

Getting into his skin, I discovered that this expert did not like medical malpractice litigation. He had refused to allow us to interview him and would not speak to us before he testified. We knew his lawyers had talked to the defense lawyers and that they had a plan to sandbag us. This man was coming down from Stanford to San Luis Obispo to kill Sofia's case. He was an assassin. I wanted him to be killed on cross-examination. But I knew that this was not the way to feel about him in order for me to do the best cross I was capable of.

I stepped into his shoes and skin. Here was my train of thought as I "became" him:

> I care about the medical profession, and I hate frivolous lawsuits that drive up my malpractice rates. I don't like greedy money lawyers who sue doctors (my friends and colleagues). With all that, though, I care about my patients. I love these babies that come to me, and I love when I can make them better. Sofia was not a patient I could make better. We cooled her brain on machines, but she was permanently damaged by the time she came to us. That makes me sad. I wish this had never happened to her. But based on what I have been told, what was given to me in the

transfer summaries and what the transferring hospital and doctors (the defendants) told me, there was nothing that could be done for Sofia to being with—this was just a case of bad luck. Integrity is important to me; I love my profession and the truth is important. I would never be a part of a cover-up. And if the truth was that I was lied to or misled, and my patient Sofia was hurt and there was a cover-up, that would really upset me.

On this doctor's cross-examination, I started soft and kind even though he was trying to kill Sofia's case. I asked him about the importance of integrity and truth in medicine. I went through records and showed him how they were untrue and how he had been misled and lied to. I showed him how the defendants had destroyed Sofia's cord blood gas, which would have been smoking gun evidence of the malpractice. By the time I was done, this man was visibly upset, and it wasn't with me or our side of the case. I asked him if he wished he had been told the truth, and he said yes. I thanked him for trying to do all he could for Sofia.

Now think of your own cases. In the skin of the "forensic expert," go back in time to evaluate this human. Why in the world are you even doing this job of completing forensic evaluations for the defense and testifying? Has it become fun for you? Is it more fun than treating HMO patients who annoy you? Have you become numb? Is this job challenging? When you tell the jury that you would rather be back at your office seeing patients, are you really telling the truth, or is that just what you want the world and maybe even yourself to believe? Do you want to make more money doing the job of a defense medical examiner? Do you know anything about the plaintiff? Are you really going to evaluate and treat him like you would a patient in your medical community who will come back for more appointments and refer his friends and family to you? What if it was your hospital director's wife coming to see you with these same problems? Would you treat her any differently?

Discover the human truth of who this defense expert is at this moment. Don't be angry about it. Find the truth. Accept and embrace the truth. Then ask the expert for the truth on video, and watch him squirm. When the defense expert denies the basic human truths, he will lose credibility. Showing that the defense experts are biased and have no credibility is a chapter to your story. You tell it during your case-in-chief. By the time the defense gets up to tell their story, it is already exposed as false and misleading.

Questions for the Defense Expert

When you are taking a deposition of the defense expert who says your client is not hurt, you can videotape his deposition and tell the story through him. You can tell the story of what you have experienced through your questions, then you can play this to the jury and the jury will see the expert's true colors before he even comes into court. Here are some example questions that could have been from the Tom Valens case:

Q: Dr. Ames, Tom is fifty-six years old, correct?

Q: And he lives in a three-bedroom house on Sycamore Street?

Q: How long does it take Tom to get up in the morning?

Q: It takes him three times as long to get out of bed than it did before he went through three years of being misdiagnosed, isn't that true?

Q: When Tom wakes up in the morning, he wakes up with pain in his back, head, neck, and hands, isn't that true?

Q: He did not wake up that way before three years of misdiagnosis, did he?

Q: He now wakes up that way pretty much every day, true?

Q: Is it true that Tom takes medication to help him when he feels this way in the morning?

Q: His bathroom, which is next to his bedroom, has prescription bottles for pain in the cabinet behind the mirror, correct?

Q: And he goes in and opens the medicine cabinet and opens the prescription bottles and takes his pain medication every morning?

Q: And his treating doctors have prescribed these medications?

Q: His treating doctor, Dr. Charles, has seen him twenty times over the past year, correct?

Q: And you have seen Tom only one time, for less than half an hour after you were given money by the defense to work on their side of the case?

Q: Tom then, two times per week, gets a ride to go to physical therapy?

Q: And, at physical therapy, the therapist, Kimberly, has a master's degree?

Q: Are you aware that Kimberly puts her hands on Tom and examines his range of motion, and then determines what therapy is appropriate?

Q: You read in the deposition of Kimberly that I, Tom's lawyer, have been to physical therapy with him and sat there with him during therapy?

Q: I also came to your office with Tom, correct?

Q: I told you during that visit that I would provide you with anything you needed and that you could talk to anybody you wanted to so that you could evaluate Tom independently, correct?

Q: At your appointment, you did some tests on Tom?

Q: You were doing these tests because the defense lawyers had asked you to do them, correct?

Q: And they paid you money?

Q: But it is your testimony to this jury that your evaluation and report were not influenced by the $20,000 that the defense paid to you, and the $2,000 for your deposition today, correct?

Q: Can you assure us that you are being just as fair to Tomas as you are to the defense, who hired and paid you?

Q: Let's look at your report. You did not mention in your report to the defense how long it takes Tom to get up in the morning. You left that out. You also did not mention [list additional damning evidence]. You left that out, didn't you?

Q: You have written many hundreds of reports like this for the defense, correct?

Q: If Tom had come to you as a patient, would you have seen him more than just one time?

Q: Would you have written a report like the one you did for the defense?

Q: When Tom came to your office, he was not treated as your patient; he was a "litigant" and you were examining him forensically, correct?

Q: The morning he came to your office, what did you believe about him? Did you already have any beliefs or biases about his condition?

Q: Your motive was to earn the money you were paid and then to write a report that you knew the defense lawyers were waiting for, correct?

Q: Did you plan for the possibility of writing a report, to the law firm that hired you and sends you business, stating that every problem Tom is claiming truly exists?

Q: You do hundreds of these reports each year for the defense, correct?

Q: When was the last time you wrote a report to the defense that helped the case of the person who was hurt?

Q: At the time you saw Tom, did you want to make more money doing this job, the job of being a forensic examiner for the defense?

Q: Do you know anything about Tom outside of the records the defense sent to you?

Q: Did you evaluate Tom and treat him like you would a patient in your medical community who will come back for more appointments and refer her friends and family to you?

Q: What if it was your hospital director's wife coming to see you with these same problems? Would you treat her any differently than you did Tom?

Q: If Tom had come to you as a patient, would you have earned $20,000 in income?

Q: And, please tell the jury, you do over fifty of these cases per year, isn't that true?

Q: It is good money, and if it were not good money, you would not do it, true?

You can ask these questions nicely and politely. If the expert rambles on and does not answer the question, just be even nicer and ask the exact same question again. You might be kind enough to reask the question the way my partner John Carpenter does: "Thank you for that response, sir, but my question was a little different. I asked you . . ." Have the court reporter read the question back to the jury if you have to. If the expert gets defensive, he loses credibility, and you are winning. Remember, you only win if you are polite. If you catch the expert not answering questions on video and being evasive, you can kill the expert's credibility before he even testifies by showing the video to the jury.

This is a method to establish a chapter in your story, which is that your client has been subjected to unfair handling by the defense, whose stance is, essentially, "Let's pay you nothing and put you through a bunch of forensic evaluations by paid testifiers we are hiring and paying to do a very specific job." We all know that the experts have a goal in mind once they are hired. We need to establish that these experts have biases and motives, but we must do it kindly and not lose our cool. Understanding where the opposing experts are coming from as human beings is important. What do they have to protect? What motivates them?

Discovering Your Clients' Human Stories

Steve Halteman

Meet the clients. I'll use the *Blunt* case as a framework to demonstrate, for two reasons: the outcome of the case was successful, and it is our most recent case and thus fresh in my mind. As a reminder, Sofia Blunt was three years old and had cerebral palsy. The cerebral palsy was caused by trauma at birth. We believed that both Dr. Haupt (Jennifer's OB-GYN, the delivering doctor) and Sierra Vista Medical Center, the hospital where Sofia was born, caused the trauma. The defendants felt otherwise. Sofia's dad was Andrew, her mom was Jennifer, and her little sister was Charlotte. The trial was in San Luis Obispo, California.

Getting to Know Sofia and Her Family— Gathering Facts[1]

I arrived in San Luis Obispo and showed up on the Blunts' doorstep shortly thereafter. Why their home? I'm interested in people's private faces, not their public faces. The quickest shortcut to that is by meeting people where they are most comfortable and open. And it is the best place to collect facts for the case. For example, the Blunts live in a second-floor apartment. Sofia is wheelchair bound. As I climbed the stairs, a fact popped into my head. Every day, Andrew and Jennifer have to carry a growing Sofia up and down these stairs. Jennifer is a petite woman. How much longer could she keep doing that?

They invited me into the living room, and we made small talk for a while. Within ten minutes, I was greatly relieved to find out I liked them. My job instantly became more attractive. Maybe I'd set a record on the fridge test—how soon are people comfortable enough with me that I could open the fridge and help myself?

What if I hadn't liked them? Well, that would have made my job harder for sure. Still, I believe this: the more you hang out with someone, the more information comes out. Information and facts are always good in a trial. They are like ammunition in a battle; you can never have too much. My job is to bring the ammo. Also, the more time you spend with someone, the more she will trust you, especially if she believes you are on her side in a fight. With trust come yet more information and details. Even if you dislike your clients personally, spending time with them, especially in their homes, will make your cases stronger. Even if your mutual dislike is apparent to one and all, to want to help someone makes that person want to help you. If you don't have the time to spend with your clients, maybe you have too many cases. At a minimum, send someone you trust to visit and listen closely to what they have to say about their experiences.

---

1. The appendix contains details regarding the specific facts of this case.

For example, a previous trial, *Wall v. Miramontes*,[2] involved a young man, Matthew Wall, whose penis had been smashed in a motorcycle crash. The crash happened when Mr. Miramontes pulled out in front of Matthew.

Matthew and I spent quite a bit of time together throughout the trial. We roomed together at the hotel, drank beer, and generally passed the time. One morning, we were going over his testimony. Nick and Courtney Yoder, Nick's co-counsel, planned to wrap up Matthew's testimony that day, then rest their case.

For the hell of it, I asked Matthew, "Help me out here. Is there anything you haven't told me yet?"

Matthew looked away.

I waited. (Patience of India. Just wait.)

Finally, he looked back and said he didn't like to talk about this part.

I waited some more.

"Well, I lost an inch and a half in length after the surgery."

The look on my face must have asked the question that was in my head.

Matthew said, "Well, no one asked me about it and it's not something I like to talk about."

A tough smile to suppress, but pure ammo.

Nick saved it to the end, and Matthew's confession was powerful. I'll leave the jurors' vivid reactions to your imagination. I don't know how much it contributed to the $7.5 million verdict, but I suspect it didn't hurt. Gold stays in the ground unless you take the time and effort to look for it.

Back to the Blunts, as I sat in their living room. I'd dropped as much of my ego as I could. In a radical gesture, I hadn't even brought my cell phone, so there was no twenty-first-century urge to check it. I tried to listen a lot more than I talked. I was receptive. We became more comfortable as the time passed. I hadn't read their depositions, so all was new to me. We were on the same team. I tried to reduce whatever level of intimidation I might have brought into the room

---

2. *Wall v. Miramontes*, case number 37-2009-00068436-CU-PA-EC, Superior Court of the State of California, County of San Diego, East County Division.

by telling them I had just learned it was no longer acceptable to buy my court clothes at Salvation Army. So I had upgraded to Marshalls, but Salvation Army had a better selection. The conversation flowed. We talked about them growing up in the area. I told a little about my background so there was a two-way street. I was building a foundation for their testimony, but on the same foundation, I hoped to create a friendship.

At the same time, I observed and collected facts. I wasn't in a hurry. I noted the apartment's layout, the furniture, the sleeping arrangements. I watched Jennifer and Andrew interact with Sofia. I saw the effort involved. One parent talked with me while the other focused on Sofia. I saw that when they said they would always take care of her, their words had substance. The same was true of their love for both daughters. My job became easier.

When Jennifer, Andrew, and I were comfortable with each other, I moved on to Sofia. When I saw Sofia for the first time, I was struck by two things. One, she was quite beautiful. Two, she had great difficulty controlling her body. Sofia's cerebral palsy was a severe type. It prevented her from eating, swallowing, talking, or walking. Her movements were spastic.

Enough of the medical stuff. She was also endearing, loved Barney, was a flirt, enjoyed roughhousing, and was making progress on her iPad. We played some games. I held her, which was hard going due to her constant movement. She communicated through her eyes. Her intelligence was obvious, but it was imprisoned in her body. With no way to test for IQ, it was a relief to see she was bright. Especially when I knew the defense would say she wasn't intelligent enough to know she was trapped in her body. But more than anything, she was happy. I credit that to her parents' efforts and her innate personality. Eventually, my goofiness won her over and we bonded. I watched Jennifer put Sofia through the junk drawer routine—a home therapy Jennifer invented. Jennifer placed Sofia in her high chair next to the kitchen junk drawer. She focused on a single object, and with time, grabbed the item and threw it to the floor. Then she moved on to the next. She won me over.

Later, as I tried to create Sofia's story line for the trial, I remembered her playing with her sister, Charlotte. Some insight dawned on me. What was it like for Sofia to see her younger sister run in circles around her? To not be able to keep up? I tried to see things through her eyes, and came up with this: It would be hard not to view the world with jealousy. To see your family eat and enjoy food, when your food is poured in through a tube. To watch other kids run and play. More thoughts came from my first visit with Sofia. Andrew and Jennifer slept above the kitchen in a makeshift loft. Charlotte had one bedroom and Sofia had the other. When the night terrors come, as they do for every child, how would Sofia get to her parents? She wouldn't be able to, nor would she be able to call out to them. If we were to ask Sofia when she is most frightened, it would have to be at night in bed and alone. This would be powerful information to a jury.

Later in trial, the only significant difference between the two life-care plans were the amounts of attendant home care Sofia would need. The defense felt four hours a day was sufficient. We believed twenty-four-hour care was necessary. The cost difference between the two added up to millions. The defense ridiculed the idea of someone being paid to watch Sofia sleep. The ridiculing stopped when Nick spoke to the jury about the terror of the night and a child unable to react. And this all came from a visit.

The next time I saw Sofia, she smiled at me in recognition. I was hooked. She gave me all the motivation I needed to be in California for two months and away from my family, in that smile.

Back to the Blunts' living room. I was still getting to know Jennifer and Andrew as a couple.

Sofia's grandma Shelli showed up. We started to talk about what happened on the day Sofia was born. This grandma was also there. She remembered seeing nurses crying in the hallway after Sofia's birth. Another fact for trial.

We figured out that Andrew actually did cut the cord, even though he had never thought about it. Slowly, their personalities were revealed, layer by layer, like an onion. The strains on their marriage that caring for Sofia caused were obvious. I realized that I would feel trapped. Did they? I asked if I could talk with each of them alone to get their life stories free from spousal editing. But first, I headed to the fridge, and I was comfortable enough to help myself. No problems. They passed the fridge test in four hours. It was all going to work out.

Jennifer and I worked together first. We went over her life, her fears, her dreams. We talked about Sofia's birth, the aftermath, and her relationship with Dr. Haupt. Later, I read in her deposition that she didn't get to hold Sofia after she was born. The impact of reading that fact in a deposition is far different than sitting in a room with a mother reliving that she didn't get to hug her daughter until four days after her birth. And even then, not properly, because Sofia was covered in medical devices. These conversations helped me join the flow of the case. Throughout this conversation, I took notes. Jennifer loaned me a painting she did, before the birth, of Sofia in her womb. I saved it for closing. Finally, I asked her about the skeletons in her closet, things that the defense would try to dig up and ambush us with. I warned her of the possibility she would be spied on, videotaped, and followed. It would be a brawl—we just never knew what kind, with what rules.

Throughout my conversations with Jennifer, and later with Andrew, I maintained a baseline role: the thirteenth juror. It was a role reversal, if you will. If I was sitting on the jury, what would I want to hear from Jennifer and Andrew? What would I want to know about Sofia? What was interesting about their lives, and how would I want to learn it? I was listening to the jurors' needs, rather than lawyers telling them what they needed to hear.

And I believe jurors want to hear details, the kind of details that set a life apart. They want to hear stories that make a life unique. I also believe this. When you know details and stories about your clients' lives and use them throughout the trial, it shows something. It shows that you took the time to relate to your client. It shows that you are not a snake: that you care about your client, and not just your fee. The jury will reward you for caring, or at least lean your way. Every little bit helps, as my dad used to say when he pissed in the ocean. Also, the clients themselves are happier when you make them feel important. Everyone wants an emotional connection. Why not give it to them, if for no other reason than they will be less hostile if you lose?

Andrew and I quickly found a topic of mutual interest. I knew Andrew had been in the Marines, but not that he had seen combat in Iraq as a forward artillery observer. We explored the topic as much as he was willing. Andrew was a lot more reserved than Jennifer, but as I was genuinely interested in his life, he gradually opened up. I promised to track down a book for him I recently read about Afghanistan, which I did. (Hard and fast rule: never break a promise to a client.) I found out he played in a basketball league and had a former NBA star on his team. The talk turned to Sofia, and the strength of his commitment to her. We spoke of the challenges of caring for a daughter who would require constant need for the rest of her life. We talked on until the Thai carryout arrived. I looked forward to more conversations with him.

The food was great and the dining was casual. Everyone was relaxed. I worried that Sofia would never taste Thai food. I was losing my neutrality.

After six hours, it was time for me to leave. Now at least I understood what cerebral palsy is rather than simply knowing the definition. I asked Jennifer and Andrew to keep a notebook of anything that came to them that they considered relevant to the case, and to call me anytime with ideas or information that helped. I told them, "My job security is based on your efforts," in case they missed the point. And it worked.

Facts poured in leading up to trial as well as throughout the trial. For example, Dr. Haupt's partner, who delivered Charlotte (the Blunts' second daughter), told Jennifer that he had reviewed Sofia's birth records. He advised Jennifer to get an outside review of those records. That was relevant to this thirteenth juror. Jennifer remembered this on the eve of opening statement.

The Stories

The next day, I read the Blunts' depositions to make sure my notes corresponded. Then I wrote Jennifer's, Andrew's, Sofia's, and Shelli's story lines. These are basically their life narratives. In this particular case, Nick had asked for a "story of hope" from each of the four. He needed these stories to use with the jury to create a feeling of optimism. This was to counter the defense argument that Sofia would die young, and therefore did not need a large damage award. I'll include a condensed version of Jennifer's story line from Sofia's release from the hospital until the start of trial three years later. This should give you an idea of what a story line looks like. I'll follow that up with a sample story of hope extracted from the story line.

Jennifer's Story Line

Sofia spent the first three weeks of her life in a hospital. When the doctors allowed Sofia's release, Jennifer was anxious to get her home and start their lives together. As Jennifer walked in the door, she knew some things and not others. She knew Sofia wasn't able to digest food, and that Sofia was inconsolable. Jennifer didn't know what was wrong with Sofia. No diagnosis had been provided.

As Jennifer sat in her rocker that first day home, holding her screaming daughter, she tried to gather her thoughts. She was a first-time mother. She had no idea why her baby wouldn't stop screaming. But she knew everything was going to be all right as long as she threw herself into raising her daughter. And that is what she did. For the first three months, Jennifer would strap a crying Sofia to her back and march up and down a steep hill behind her home in an effort to calm Sofia. She chose this hill because it was out of hearing range for the rest of the world. At times, Jennifer thought she might lose her mind, but she kept climbing because it was the only thing that lessened the intensity of Sofia's screaming. After three months, Sofia smiled for the first time. Jennifer began to think that both of them might make it.

Around this same time, Sofia's medical situation began to clarify. Jennifer knew that Sofia's birth had been difficult and frightening. Jennifer knew that Sofia was progressing slower than other children her same age. But no doctor had ever sat down and said, "Here is why." Jennifer remembered vaguely that the hospital had told her when Sofia left that "referrals had been made to public health," so Jennifer wasn't too surprised when a steady stream of therapists began calling and making appointments to see Sofia. At first, Jennifer was resentful. She didn't want to appear needy, nor did she understand why her daughter was being singled out for attention. She felt it was overkill and didn't want to be in the "system."

Now, three years later, Jennifer's mind-set is 180 degrees opposite. She participates in every program available in an attempt to improve Sofia's life. Over time, Jennifer saw the benefits of physical therapy for her daughter. She began to trust the therapists. They, in turn, hinted at Sofia's medical condition. Jennifer learned more when she obtained Sofia's medical records as a result of this lawsuit. Research based on the records led her to suspect cerebral palsy. Finally, a neurologist confirmed her suspicions. Now Jennifer knew what she was up against. She knew the enemy.

Because Jennifer is strong willed, she knew she could beat the enemy. If she won, her daughter would be fixed and would play with the other kids. If she lost, that meant she was a lousy mother. The next two years were an emotional slugfest. They had progress and setbacks. Jennifer went through all the stages of grief—pockets of depression followed by periods of optimism. She worked endlessly on the exercises with Sofia that the therapists suggested. When Jennifer learned she was pregnant with her second child, it upset her because having another baby would take away from her time saving Sofia. Jennifer's goal was to have Sofia caught up with other kids by two or three years old. But as each benchmark passed and Sofia didn't roll over or sit up or walk, the reality of cerebral palsy began to set in. No matter how hard Jennifer threw herself at defeating CP, progress for Sofia would be measured in inches, not yards. Sofia's little sister Charlotte's rapid passing of those same benchmarks only confirmed Jennifer's fears. A mother's efforts could only change so much.

Story of Hope

So why is Jennifer so optimistic about Sofia's future? Well, like any parent, she looks forward to, and maps out, her daughter's progress and advancements. Does it matter the size of the steps as long as steps are taking place? And steps she has in abundance, both cognitively and psychologically.

Let's talk about cognitive steps first. Sofia is unable to speak. This is not related to her IQ. Early in Sofia's life, her inability to communicate frustrated her and she cried. Through the help of her mother, father, and therapists, she has learned to use nonverbal communication to indicate what she wants. When she wants her mom to turn the page, she taps it with her hand. When her mom tells her a story, she focuses on her mom. Her attention span is increasing as she gets older. Sofia laughs at the right places when something funny happens. She has shows like *Barney* that she enjoys and shows like college basketball that she does not. Recently, Sofia has begun working with an iPad. Sofia has a fine mind trapped inside an uncooperative body.

Yet even Sofia's body control continues to improve. For the first two years of her life, Sofia could barely lift her head when lying on her stomach. These days, she can roll over. Until her third year, Sofia could not swallow food (she is fed through a gastric tube directly to her stomach). In the last few months, Sofia has begun to eat small bits of food. Small progress for some, but leaps in the eyes of Jennifer. In my last phone call to the Blunts, I learned that Sofia is doing barrel rolls, can lift a bottle to her mouth, and prefers lemon ice cream to peas, with which I am sympathetic.

Jennifer celebrates her daughter's progress and wonders what is to come with the delight and joy that any parent feels. She focuses, as we all should, on Sofia's progress and not on how Sofia's progress compares to other children. She takes pride in Sofia's steps, and wonders if someday these steps will turn into walking.

At the same time, Jennifer finds cause for optimism in the ongoing technological advances that continue to improve Sofia's quality of life. Might one day a machine enable Sofia to bypass her body and allow her mind to control her movements? Might a new surgery do the same? Who knows the future? No one does, and certainly not Jennifer. What Jennifer does know is that the future looks a whole lot better now for Sofia than it did during those months of climbing a summitless hill.

Preparing for Trial

Nick and I begin preparing for trial by meeting the witnesses and learning their stories. Nick does not use a printed list of questions, so instead, we create trip wires to put the story into action.

A trip wire in trial preparation is a written subject or title that triggers a response from the brain. When Nick sees a trip wire, it causes a flood of information on the subject. From that flood, he asks questions on the fly that convey his witness theme to the jury. And hopefully, he entertains them as well.

For example, with Andrew on the stand, the trip wire might be "marines." From there, the flood of possible questions might include:

Q: Andrew, why did you join?

Q: Were you in Iraq?

Q: Do you have PTSD?

Q: Do you have combat experience?

Q: Would you attempt to do a second tour?

We'll have more on the development of trip wires and themes later, I promise.[3]

Throughout the Trial

The *Blunt* trial lasted two months. Throughout the trial, I made a point of staying connected with the Blunts. We swapped books, watched some TV, and ate a lot of tacos together.

One evening, Rod Ritner (co-counsel on the *Blunt* trial) and I went with the Blunts to the San Luis Obispo street market. Observing peoples' varied reactions to Sofia was educational for us. But it was our turn to educate Jennifer and Andrew when we saw them walk right past a giant, inflatable slide. Hey, parents with young kids aren't allowed to walk past a slide. It's a state statute.

---

3. For more information on developing trip wires, see chapter 12.

Jennifer and Andrew were obviously hesitant. Rod and I weren't; we weren't the parents. So we carried both kids up the slide and down we flew together. Sofia's howls indicated that perhaps one slide down was insufficient. Again and again, we went. When Rod and I broke down cardiovascularly, Jennifer and Andrew took over. Who says the law can't be fun? (More importantly, an inflatable slide is already reserved for Sofia's next birthday.)

What's the point? Well, with friendship comes trust. And trust between the clients and legal team in a trial war is a positive. I became the liaison between Nick and the Blunts. In a big trial, Nick is pulled in a thousand directions. I am not. So when the Blunts wanted to know what was going on or had concerns, they'd come to me. If I didn't know the answer, I'd make sure they got it from someone who did. When the defense offered to settle, I could see it was causing sleeplessness for the Blunts. So I set up a meeting with Nick to discuss the pros and cons. This way, everyone was on the same page. Trust and friendship helped me prepare Jennifer and Andrew for their direct exams, as well as readying them to be cross-examined.

Either Jennifer or Andrew attended just about every day of trial. Sitting there by their side, day after day, was an important job. I developed a sense of the rhythm of the trial and was able to anticipate when the defense lawyer was ready to start talking about Sofia's shortened life expectancy. It was my job to keep Jennifer and Andrew calm, and more importantly, from not blowing up during the trial. Sadly, the projections for Sofia's life span grew considerably shorter and grimmer as the trial wore on. When I anticipated the defense beating this drum, I would get Jennifer and Andrew out of the courtroom. No mother or father wants to hear predictions of their child dying young—especially when the premature death is financially beneficial to the speaker. Jennifer and Andrew trusted my advice and usually chose to leave the courtroom. The *Blunt* jury, like all juries drawn to distraction and movement, inevitably witnessed this and noted the departure. The reason was confirmed in the jurors' minds moments later, when the defense, unable to change tack quickly, started asking questions about Sofia dying young.

What were the benefits of this? Well, if you're trying to win the hearts and minds of the jurors, there are a few:

1. It showed we cared about our clients.

2. It showed our side had the upper hand because we pretty much knew what the defense was going to say before they said it.

3. It showed that the hurtful things the defense was saying caused damage to people.

4. It kept Andrew, a former marine, from killing the defense lawyer.

Every little bit helps.

The verdict on the *Blunt* case was $74.2 million. The initial offer was zero.

Now that the trial is over, Nick and I remain friends with the Blunts. This is the true measure of success, although big verdicts are also nice. Some of the nontrial discussions we had have proven beneficial. Andrew is signed up for another try at college. Jennifer is surfing and entering running races again. I hope to see them all in Costa Rica someday soon, where I plan to take Sofia and Charlotte on a zip line. In the end, I know that the next time I pass through San Luis Obispo, I have a doorstep to land on. And, in exchange for access to their fridge, the Blunts know they have a baby-sitter they can count on.

A final gift from the Blunts arrived in an email some weeks after the trial finished. Wanting to get back to Costa Rica, I had left San Luis Obispo right after the end of the trial, before the verdict was reached. In the email, Andrew wrote about how happy he was with the verdict, but also how overwhelming the first few days after the verdict were. He wrote of how nice it would have been to have an ally like me around to guide them through the process. Wow! I should have seen that one coming. How obvious. Learn, and live, as well as improve. What else can we do?

Trial and Dealing with the Worst

The Reverse Fluster and the Thirteenth Juror

Steve Halteman

The *Landeros v. Torres*[1] case involved a young teenage girl, Rosie Landeros, who was brain damaged when a drunk driver struck her car. This was a case where I served the role of being the thirteenth juror. It was also the first case I worked on with Nick following his invite in Costa Rica. I arrived in Bakersfield, California, a few days before the trial and was nervous about my ignorance. (At the time, I was ignorant about the value of ignorance. Today, ignorance is my ally. I'll have more on that later, I promise.)

I walked into a room filled with the legal team. Everyone knew the case backward and forward. Nobody other than Nick knew me from Adam. Nick introduced me and had been talking me up, and it was obvious that nobody was happy about my

---

1. *Landeros v. Torres*, case number S-1500-CV-261305 SPC, Superior Court of California, Kern County, metropolitan division.

involvement with the case. This really pleased Nick; he gets a kick out of stuff like that. Anyhow, I kept my mouth shut and observed. I watched all the interactions. I tried to learn about the case and the members of our team by listening to what they said, but also by listening to what they *didn't* say. It was a safe course of action, because I obviously wasn't going to impress them with my legal brilliance. I thought about my personal goal in all this. That was easy. I'm competitive to a fault. I wanted to win this case like I want to win every race I enter. And I wanted to contribute. Nick seemed to think I would. I wasn't so sure about the others, and I didn't blame them. When I told him, "I don't think the others want me here," his response was: "Fuck those guys. We are doing our own thing."

But I wanted to help out our whole legal team, and I believe that my role as the thirteenth juror enabled me to do that. Here's how. At first, I thought my role as the thirteenth juror was limited to court time and its aftermath. All day, I would sit in court near the jury and listen to what both sides had to say. In my mind, I was seated in the jury box. On my head rode the cap of neutrality. My goal was to have no dog in the fight. My notes would reflect what did and didn't work for both sides, or when I was lost, bored, or overwhelmed. Which side was I drawn to? Who carried the day? Then after court, I'd provide feedback to whichever lawyer on our team was interested, as well as my two cents' suggestions. My feedback and suggestions were free of bullshit because I figured this was a onetime deal, so what did I care about impressing these people?

Pretty quickly, I realized that I could up my contribution by jumping into the fray before the courtroom stage. I told the lawyers on our team, "Run your facts and theories by me before you present them in court. If I understand them, chances are the jurors will too. If I don't, maybe they won't either." In effect, I gave them a wall of ignorance. For example, a lawyer would try some medical testimony out on me. If I didn't get it, I'd say so. The lawyer would tweak it and try a new approach. This would go on and on until I finally understood what they were talking about. Most lawyers are bright. When presented with a wall and a goal behind that wall, they'll figure out how to go around that wall, or how to dig under it, or how to climb over it. Whatever it takes to reach their goal. And that goal is juror comprehension. Perhaps the best compliment I received during the *Landeros* trial was, "Try it out on Steve. If he can understand it, anyone can."

I suggest you find your own thirteenth juror. Jurors are random, as should be your thirteenth. Preferably, this should be someone who isn't obligated to you in any way but whose opinion you trust. Basically, she will be a free one-person focus group. Try running some of your ideas by her and see how they play out. For example, let's say you can't decide whether to go after a witness hard or easy. Try the approaches you're contemplating in front of your thirteenth juror. Listen to her feedback. It might prove beneficial. Same with parts of your opening, closing, and even jokes. Of course, don't violate the attorney–client privilege. It always helps to get what is running through your head in front of the eyes and ears of another.

The Run

As you may have surmised from his introduction, Nick is, shall we say, psychologically complex. The pressures of a long trial only add to his complexity. Throw in Nick's temper, being a brawler and one who is always willing to "take it outside," and I had to find a way to calm my friend. Nick disliked the opposing legal team, and that is putting it mildly. He was upset about the frivolous defenses in the case and the way the defense was treating his client, Rosie. I immediately saw a big storm brewing, and I concluded that a relaxed, controlled Nick would be more effective than a pissed-off Nick. In the first pretrial hearing I saw how the new big gun, opposing counsel Sean Harrison,[2] refused to shake Nick's hand. I didn't need brilliant insight to see where things were headed. So I came up with a two-point plan.

Number one was the run. Every morning, I got Nick's ass up and forced him to run forty to sixty minutes. I did this for

---

2. This name has been fictionalized.

multiple reasons: running reduces anxiety, it takes the edge off, and it centers our mental acuity and brings focus to the day's activities. It reduces aggression, simply because it takes away the excess energy we need to be aggressive. It releases endorphins, which make us feel good about ourselves, our lives, and our cases. I suggest those forty to sixty minutes to anyone in trial, whether it be walking, jogging, or running. No cell phone. No distractions. You need to be alone, to sift through your upcoming trial day, or maybe you need to be with another person to bounce around ideas and make sure you finish your run. Through the weeks of trial, we developed a habit of dissecting issues and fleshing out solutions during these runs.

Because Nick is very competitive, but clearly a slower runner than me, I often forced him to listen to me during our daily run. We developed a synergy that has grown strong and that carries through to this day. I have seen and Nick will tell you that there have been leaps and bounds of improvement in Nick's temper, quickness in decision making, relationships with judges, and health since he started running. So my advice is that if you are going to try cases, hit the paths or do some sort of good sweating cardio for forty to sixty minutes every day of trial, first thing in the morning. Slowly ease into it. I promise that you won't regret it, and it will make you a better trial lawyer.

The Reverse Fluster

The second strategy for dealing with the explosion that I saw on the horizon with the growing hostility between Nick and the opposing legal team was the *reverse fluster*.

From the word go, it was obvious that the nonhandshaker and Nick were going to end up in a hallway or outside-of-court situation. I thought that the opposing counsel genuinely disliked Nick, and he intentionally geared his hostility to get under Nick's skin and disrupt his flow. Nick, who revels in the opportunity to beat the pulp out of big bullies, was waiting for justification to do something that would have put his license to practice law in jeopardy. Sean Harrison would get in Nick's face, and Nick happily told me how he was just waiting for the slightest physical contact to justify a left hook to the temple of big Sean Harrison.

I had to intervene to prevent the inevitable. I designed the reverse fluster, and it has become a foundational part of Nick's life since. During the *Landeros* case, it allowed Nick to deal with the daily personal attacks that the bully lawyer Sean Harrison made.

Basically, the reverse fluster went like this. In response to any personal attack from the opposing counsel, Nick agreed to only respond with one of two statements, which I promised him would be much more effective than a left hook:

1. "I'm sorry you feel that way."

2. "You must be very frustrated."

We didn't have to wait long. On the first day of trial, at the first opportunity, the opposing counsel approached Nick and accused him of something along the following lines: "You are unprofessional, a disgrace to the profession, an embarrassment to your co-counsel, and way out of your league." Worst of all, Sean Harrison insulted Nick's suit, cowboy boots, and tie selection. Sean said all of this to Nick outside the presence of the judge in a rising, antagonistic voice that was clear to all in the peanut gallery.

This angry lawyer was standing up in front of Nick, way too close for comfort, the bailiff was on the edge of his seat, and I held my breath. Proudly, I watched as Nick turned his head to me, smiled, turned back to Sean, and said, "I'm sorry you feel that way, Sean. You must be very frustrated."

Blood rushed to Harrison's face as he exploded. "What the hell does that mean? You're being . . . That's . . . That's disingenuous . . . You are disingenuous!"

Nick stood up, then softly said, "Sean, I am sorry you feel that way. I look forward to spending more time together." Then Nick calmly walked away.

In the end, somebody did actually get under someone's skin. Just the reverse of what Sean intended.

The Thirteenth Juror

As the *Landeros* trial progressed, I began to find my sea legs. Sitting with the jury as number thirteen, I developed a sense of what was effective and what was not, what inspired or bored us as jurors, what I wanted to see and hear, and what moved me as a human. I learned that I disliked technical medical testimony once I believed the person was hurt. My mind wandered continuously when exposed to it. But worse was when our economist testified, with his *present values* and *discount rates* and so on. Judging from some of the jurors' reactions and clock staring, I was not alone. I pitied the lawyers asking the economist questions, and I hated the tediousness of it all. Then it came time for the defenses economist to testify. Right before lunch, their economist dumped a pile of new data on us. It was all left-brain crap.

Before Nick took over the job of doing the cross, he asked me how we could make all this statistical shit understandable to the jurors as well as attack the defense economist's credibility.

I said, "Why aren't the bastards all rich, these experts on the economy?"

"Tell me more," said Nick.

So over lunch, I gave Nick all the questions I wanted to ask the economist as a juror. For what it's worth, here is our short-and-sweet, right-brain cross of any economist. Notice the lack of reference to discount rates and present-value computations.

Q: Let's talk about the field of economics. What exactly is the study of economics?

Q: So you can explain the economic history of the United States using the science of economics, correct?

Q: Also, you can predict the economic future using economic theory, correct?

Q: So right now, you must be a very wealthy man, correct?

Q: You are able to see recessions coming, able to know when to put the money in and pull the money out? When to jump in?

You could see the housing crash coming, right? Buy low, sell high? You took advantage of all that, right?

Q: Why not?

Q: Is the study of economics a hard science or a soft science? For example, a hard science is like chemistry, where when you mix two chemicals, the result is always the same. A soft science would be political science, which is a combination of the study of the history of politics and a guesstimate of how politics will play out in the future. So is economics a hard science or soft science?

Q: So in the end, economics is a soft science, agreed?

Q: [Economics is] useful for taking a guess at the course of future economic events, but [you are] unable to say with certainty what will happen?

Q: Like any course of future events, the economic direction of the United States is subject to war, oil supply, and other unknown variables, correct?

Q: Really, other than predictions, [the] economic future is unknowable with certainty, correct?

Q: Or else, you really would be rich, right?

Q: So you've made a prediction about the plaintiff's future economic needs, correct?

Q: And your predictions might be right, correct?

Q: But your predictions might also be wrong? Correct?

Q: And the plaintiff's economist might be wrong, correct?

Q: Then again, the plaintiffs could be right, correct?

Q: And if the plaintiff's economist is right and his plan is accurate, that would mean your plan is incorrect and inaccurate, correct?

Q: Only the future itself will determine which economist in the end was accurate, correct?

Q: In fact, both plans might turn out to be wrong because Rosie lives much longer than anyone has predicted, correct?

Q: That scenario would leave both plans underfunded, correct?

Q: Rosie might need even more money, correct?

Q: Or what if inflation runs rampant and eats away the value of her award? This could cause Rosie to run out of money when she needs it most, when her parents are elderly and unable to take care of her anymore, correct?

Q: Or Rosie's parents might die early and her needs would change, correct?

Q: So in the end, we leave it up to the jurors to decide Rosie's future economic needs, correct?

Q: And perhaps that is best, wouldn't you agree?[3]

The defense economist came along for the ride and agreed that the economic future, as well as Rosie's future, truly was unknowable. What is known is that the jury came back and found in favor of Rosie Landeros to the tune of $31 million.

The *Landeros* case was a few years ago, and my role and approach have evolved. During our last trial, *Blunt v. Sierra Vista Medical Center*,[4] my job was to:

1. Be the thirteenth juror.

2. Be a walking solo focus group.

3. Maintain neutrality.

4. Remain ignorant about the medical issues, just like the jury.

5. Prepare the clients and lay witnesses.

6. Help select the jury.

---

3. *Landeros v. Torres,* case number S-1500-CV-261305 SPC, Superior Court of California, Kern County, metropolitan division.
4. *Blunt v. Sierra Vista Medical Center,* case number CV 100071, Superior Court of San Luis Obispo County, San Luis Obispo, CA.

7. Help with the opening, trial strategy, and closing.

8. Run.

How did I approach this? How did I prepare ahead of trial? Should I have read a thousand pages worth of documents? The answer is that other than getting a brief outline of the facts of the case, I didn't start out by reading depositions and records. Why? Because I had not met the humans we were there to help yet, and the human story would frame how I looked at everything else. Too much information is counterproductive. On the *Blunt* case, Nick called me and asked me to be on the case. It took about fifteen minutes for Nick to explain the case and for me to decide I was in.

While on the plane from Costa Rica, I reviewed my roles in the grand scheme of the trial and what I needed to do to prepare for them.

1. Be the thirteenth juror.

    Jurors don't prepare, so why should I?

2. Be a walking solo focus group for other members of the team to try out ideas on.

    Again, focus groups don't prepare. Neither did I.

3. Maintain neutrality for purposes of analysis throughout the trial.

    This is something I do rather than prepare for.

4. Remain ignorant about the medical issues in the trial, just like the jury, for as long as possible.

    My ignorance forces the other attorneys and experts to explain the medical issues to me in such a way that I can understand them as a lay juror. Due to my innate inability to grasp technical issues of any kind, the other members of the team have to work very hard to help me comprehend. But once I get it, so will the majority of the jury, and I will tell the team which explanation best worked for me. I embrace ignorance as an asset, and I pity those who don't have it.

5. Prepare the clients and lay witnesses.

I always want to meet the humans before I consider their labels or gather information. That is why I don't read depositions before hanging out with the clients. I want to get a sense of the people first. Later, I can learn about their connections to the trial and the connections between them and the jurors.

6. Help select the jury.

There was no jury pool yet, so I couldn't prepare to select them. And I still didn't know enough about the case to start considering who would be a good juror or bad juror.

7. Help with the opening, trial strategy, and closing.

I couldn't do any of that until I met some folks and learned some more. So I couldn't prepare on the plane.

8. Run.

I'm always up for a run, but not on an airplane.

Checklist complete. I didn't have anything to do until I got to San Luis Obispo. So I ordered a beer.

Focus Groups

Nick Rowley

Focus groups are important, especially if you do not have a lot of trial experience or if you are trying new methods. This is where you get real everyday human beings together, create a mock jury, and talk about your case. We do focus groups to learn about cases, not to advocate our case and win. In the focus groups I do, I want to learn how I could lose my case, and I want to discover the feelings other human beings have about the issues in the case that I am most afraid of. If there are things about which I am uncomfortable talking to a jury, I try it first with a focus group.

The best focus group is what we call a discovery focus group. In this kind of group, you do not tell the mock jurors who you are representing. You give them information and ask for their thoughts and feelings. It could be photographs from the scene of the collision, some medical records you are concerned about, or a videotaped deposition of a witness or expert.

There are a number of ways to do these focus groups. As I mentioned earlier, David Ball has a video called *Focus Groups* that

I would suggest getting.[1] A great man by the name of Finlay Boag out of Pleasanton, California, does focus groups, and he will soon be writing an article on focus groups that will be available for Spence Trial Lawyers College attendees. Finlay was absolutely instrumental in my development and success as a trial lawyer, and he forced me to do more focus groups than I can count.

If you do deliberation focus groups (where you present both sides of the case in an adversarial way and ask the jurors to deliberate and answer a special verdict), present the strongest defense story of the case you can come up with.

Ask your focus group jurors about pieces of evidence, clips of depositions, or anything you are afraid of in your case. How do these make them feel? Then ask them what would make them feel differently? Ask them what scenes or experiences they recall from their own lives when they hear the stories you tell. Test the evidence that you think is helpful and hurtful, and get feedback. You might learn that what you think rocks really doesn't and what hurts really isn't that big of a deal. Look for commonsense themes and common experiences. Ask the focus group jurors to write down their themes of the case. Ask them to pretend that they are writing a book about the case, and then ask them to write down the chapter titles that they would use to tell the story. Look for talking points for jury selection. Ask them to give you their three-minute opening statement or closing argument on your case.

Be open to learning from everyday human beings about what is important and not important. This is what you are going to get with a jury, so listen and learn.

Talk to lawyers who do focus groups, and attend one of theirs. I have done over a hundred of them. The best trial lawyers out there do them regularly. The more difficult and the more valuable the case, the more you need to do some focus groups.

In the *Landeros* case, we did well over twenty focus groups. We were in a conservative jurisdiction where there had never been a large jury verdict for a personal-injury case. I believe the

---

1. David Ball, Debra Miller, and Artemis Malekpour, *Focus Groups: How to Do Your Own Jury Research* (Portland, OR: Trial Guides, 2008).

largest verdict was $3.5 million on a clear liability quadriplegic case. We got a verdict of $31.6 million plus a settlement of $5 million against another defendant.

The goal of our focus groups on *Landeros* was to discover and overcome the bias that the members of the community had against giving money for pain and suffering and against large verdicts in general. Our noneconomic damages verdict ended up being $22 million, a record. The way we did it was by telling stories of love and hope for Rosie's future, and discussing the value of young people in the Bakersfield community. We learned through the focus groups that making noneconomic damages about how grim, dark, and depressing Rosie's future would be resulted in lower numbers, sometimes very low numbers. But when we talked about how Rosie always had a smile on her face and how her life would be great and wonderful if we gave her all the resources she needed, the numbers went up.

7

MINI–OPENING STATEMENT

Nick Rowley

If you can get the judge to let you do a mini–opening statement, you've got to do it. That's my humble opinion. In California, the law now allows lawyers to present brief three- to five-minute mini–opening statements to the entire group of potential jurors before jury selection. I have also done this in Minnesota, Missouri, and Oregon. Judges like it, and I request permission to do a mini-opening in every case no matter what state I am in. I tell the judge how California calls for it in the code of civil procedure, how the judge has discretion to allow it, and how it expedites voir dire and gives us a much better shot at getting a fair and impartial jury.

"How, Mr. Rowley?" asks the judge. "How does a mini–opening statement expedite voir dire and help us get a fair and impartial jury?"

This was my response:

> Let's imagine ourselves as one of those jurors sitting there in the box, Your Honor. If you were to ask us if we can be fair and impartial and follow the law, Your Honor, the brutally

honest answer from each of us would be "I don't know." Ask us if we are fair and impartial and if we are people who follow the law, ask us that in front of fifty other people in our community and in front of a judge up there sitting higher than all of us with a flag next to him and lawyers in uniform watching us, and most of us are going to sound off like the rest of them: "Yes, Your Honor."

Now, if you really want to give us the opportunity to think about whether we can be fair and impartial and do a good job as jurors, and if you want to give the lawyers an opportunity to be able to intelligently decide whether or not to exercise preemptory challenges, tell us something about the case. Give us a taste of it; let us feel in our guts whether our prejudice and bias start to stir.

The mini–opening statement does just that: it gives the jurors a preview of what the case is about. It stirs up the humanity inside of the jurors. That is what they need in order to decide whether they can be fair and impartial. That is why states are not only allowing the opening statement, but have codified it and said that lawyers should do this before voir dire. We are always trying to improve our system, and the mini-opening is one of those improvements.

If Your Honor is against it because it is new, I have some judges whose phone numbers I could give you who would tell you that they felt exactly as you might feel right now, but how they have truly found that mini–opening statements help the voir dire process.

That is what I would say to the judge in a jurisdiction where mini-opening is not allowed. What I use the mini-opening for is to do exactly what I tell the court: to give the jurors a preview of the case so they can decide whether they each want to be part of a team of justice for my client.

Here is an example of a hypothetical mini–opening statement in Sofia's case. I don't go through a bunch of formalities—"Good morning, thank you, blah blah blah"—I jump right into it.

Brutal honesty. Brutal honesty is something I am going to ask each and every one of you to give us here in a bit when we get to talk to each other. I am going to start by being brutally honest with you.

I am here suing your local hospital, Sierra Vista Medical Center, a hospital that this community is very proud of, a hospital that saves lives and that many of you rely on. I am also suing one of the most popular doctors in your community, Dr. Haupt. Dr. Haupt has been in this community helping families for thirty years. He is a doctor that delivers babies.

We are suing them both—Sierra Vista and Dr. Haupt—for many millions of dollars. We are suing them for negligence. Again, for many millions of dollars. We are going to ask you to sign off on this after we prove the case.

Brutal honesty. What does that stir up inside of you? Does hearing this upset you? Does hearing any of this turn you off? What feelings and thoughts are stirred up inside of you just by hearing what I have said so far? I am going to ask you to give us your brutal honesty and tell us how you feel about a case like this.

Sofia has a bad brain injury, a permanent brain injury: cerebral palsy! We are blaming the hospital and the doctor for that. It is going to cost many millions to give her compensation for what she has suffered. We are going to ask for a lot of money in pain and suffering damages.

Should I be afraid of having you as a juror on this case? I am going to ask you to tell me if there is any reason for me to be afraid of having you as a juror on this case. You see, my goal is to find twelve people who will give us a fair shot at winning. We are hoping to find twelve jurors who won't go out of their way to side with and help the doctor and hospital win the case. We are looking for twelve people who are not turned off by the case and who are willing to sit as jurors being equally fair to Sofia. Also, I want to be clear, we are not looking for twelve people who are going to side with Sofia before we prove our case. I believe in a fair fight. And it is not a fair fight if people are coming into the case as jurors already siding with one side or the other.

Thank you for listening. Please hold on to what you feel inside listening to what this case is about and ask yourselves with brutal honestly if you can give us that fair fight and promise that you are not turned off by the case or already siding with the doctor and hospital.

The jurors now know what the case is about and can honestly tell us whether they are turned off by the case and are unable to be fair and impartial jurors.

This is a short chapter because mini-openings are short. There is not a lot to talk about, but I want you to think about the mini-opening separately. Imagine getting to give the jury a preview of the movie, asking them if they would like to see more, and finding out whether they are going to like the movie or not. A problem with voir dire is that the jurors know nothing about the case and cannot decide whether they are biased or bad for you. With a mini–opening statement, they get to feel the case in their gut, maybe hear some of the ugly parts of the case. You will see who makes up their mind quick and learn a lot more about your jurors than you would if they just had some dry, boring statement of the case read to them.

Nick's View of Voir Dire

Nick Rowley

Now it is time to talk about how we are going to find our group of open-minded, caring human beings, our jury.

Josh Karton is responsible for how comfortable I am in front of juries. Approximately nine years ago, he had me conduct voir dire to a group of over fifty people using the voice of Daffy Duck (which made me very upset). To make things worse, he had me hold hands and maintain eye contact with each mock juror I was speaking with. I moved through the room, holding hands with each "juror" as I spoke to them. I was so embarrassed that my eyes filled with tears. I wanted to run away and hide. Somehow, Josh helped me break down a wall that stood between me and the humans I was trying to connect with. Josh forced me to feel, connect, and shed the professional layers that I had built around me over many years. Through many focus groups, a lot of hands-on practice, and more work with Josh and other staff at Spence's Trial Lawyers College, I have learned how to create a connection with just about anybody. I have successfully taught others to connect.

What I have learned is not manipulative; it is about being real, open, and honest, and truly listening to and caring about the humans I speak with. It cannot be fake. It must be real. And it comes from inside of me. While I am going to try to put what I have learned into words, if you want to get better and master the ability to connect with people in a courtroom, you must attend regional seminars at Spence's college.[1]

With that said, the primary purpose of voir dire is to establish a human connection, to build a team of open-minded, caring humans who care about justice and who will work hard to see that justice is delivered. It is the most important part of the trial because it is the beginning of relationships.

WE START BY REJECTING

The core of the standardized jury-selection process is rejection. While we might say we want to establish connection, the first thing most of us do when the jurors walk into the courtroom is reject them. This is how we start our relationships with jurors, and it is the most horrible way to begin.

Here is an example of how I, and maybe some of you, have started our relationships with jurors in our minds:

> Shit, I don't like the way this jury pool looks! They look white, old, and conservative. Where are the black, brown, beaten-down, angry-at-the-system people who I really want on my jury?
>
> That guy is an engineer; that other guy is a white retired accountant. I wish I could press a button and make them both disappear.
>
> That woman looked at me and smiled. I think I'll talk to her.

Rejection, rejection, objectification, stereotyping. This is how we start our relationships with jurors. Many of us do this and continue to do it. We reject them from the start, and yet we want them to like us, connect with us, be open with us, and trust us.

---

1. The website is triallawyerscollege.com. Go to the website and pick a date. You won't regret it.

It is what is within our minds and guts that rejects the jurors, and this damages our relationships with them. Smiling and acting nice does not fix this. Jurors distrust us, and if we reject them in our minds and guts, they feel it. You transmit energy, your body language shows it, and the jurors feel it. When we talk and act differently than we feel, distrust starts to build.

Instead, imagine a relationship beginning where you look at and appreciate every juror. You are happy that every one of them is in the courtroom. You are truly thankful that they are there, because without every one of them, we would not have a jury system. Just by showing up, they are helping you.

INCLUDE AND ACCEPT INSTEAD OF REJECT

I want you to try something different, something that I have found truly does work. From now on, the moment we see our jurors, every one of them, we are going to love, appreciate, and accept them. We are not going to reject any of them. They all came to help us—even those who don't want to help us will in fact help, as long as we love and appreciate them and take the first step. Many jurors may not end up on our jury—they may not be right for the case or what we need in a juror—but they can all help us and themselves.

We are going to select our jury by including them. We are going to build a team of caring justice seekers, rather than kicking people off whom we have unfairly judged.

We will do this by honoring and caring for our jurors, by being brutally honest, and, most importantly, by learning how to shut up, listen, and feel. I say "our jurors" because they truly are ours. They are there for us. We have called them and asked them to be there for us and our clients. It is our command, our demand for a jury trial, that has brought them to court. They responded to our call, and despite the subpoenas, they had a choice whether to show up or not. Start with this, and be thankful and appreciative. There's a chance that if we were in certain other parts of the world, nobody would come. The members of the community would not be there to help. We would have no case and no justice to pursue.

When it comes to talking to the jurors, have the confidence that it really does not matter what you are talking about as long as you are connecting. My dear friends Joseph "Joey" Low IV and Grover Porter say it best: "We connect 'gut-to-gut,' not 'head-to-head.'"

The goal of voir dire is to connect gut-to-gut: to care about each juror and honor him, no matter what comes out of his mouth. Some people teach students to talk to the jury about their fears. That is one part of voir dire, but it is an advanced one. First, you need a strong foundation and the ability to truly listen and be comfortable with whatever a juror says. To do this, you have to learn how to become human and speak the language of humans to our jurors. If you start out by identifying your fears, you will go right into your attorney head. You skip the foundation necessary to even begin talking with your jurors.

A New Way of Listening

Listen! To be great trial lawyers, we have to be great listeners. Keep these points in mind:

- Listening means really caring and taking in what a person is saying.

- Listening is not preparing what we are going to say while the other person is still talking.

- Listening is not allowing our minds to race into thinking about how to advise a person, analyzing what she said, finding the next place to go in the conversation, or leading the speaker closer to our agenda.

- Listening requires imagining ourselves in the skin of the person who is speaking.

- Listening means we shut our mouths, turn our left brains off, and stop making conclusions about what we are hearing.

In voir dire, if we are preparing what to say next rather than listening to what the juror is saying, other jurors won't talk. We need to let silence and our open, accepting body language validate each juror. If we don't do this, the next juror won't talk because we have betrayed earlier jurors by failing to really listen. The same goes with the people we love, our family and friends.

Failing to truly listen is counterproductive to winning. If we are not listening, we won't learn the true story. We have in our own minds what the story is, and that very well might not be the truth.

The human being we are talking to is more important than the message we want to give, or where we want to "direct" the juror. This relentless endeavor of validating the jurors' feelings and making our nonverbal connection is more important than what our left brain is telling us. This is what we must learn in order to master voir dire.

Going deeper. *Reflective listening* means truly hearing and taking the speaker's words into our mind. *Reflective feeling* is a phrase I take credit for coming up with years ago. It is something much deeper than reflective listening. Reflective feeling is connecting with the root emotions that are behind and underneath the speaker's words, taking those feelings into our core, and giving a verbal or nonverbal communication back to the speaker that shows them that we understand and care about their feelings.

As humans, we have all experienced reflective feeling because it is instinctual. When another person we care about cries and we see their eyes full of tears, tears come into our own eyes. We are reflectively feeling for them. When one person gets angry and in response we feel anger, that is reflective feeling. Riots are a product of reflective feeling.

Attorneys struggle with voir dire because they suck at reflective listening and do not understand or know how to turn on their ability to reflectively feel. In law school, we learn to be cold and become analyzers of facts. We learn to talk and talk, to be in control, to be in control of the words, and to get people to say things that we want them to say. The problem with this is that in a trial, we do not win or lose with words. Rather, we win or lose with emotion.

When it comes to voir dire, we have no connection and no control over our jurors. More importantly, we have no credibility.

Often, we do not have time to get up and talk about our fears. If you are stuck in a jurisdiction where there is no voir dire, then you must still find a way to connect. Do this by *reversing roles.* Connect with your eyes and your body language, your voice, but most importantly, your gut.

Be in the moment. Breathe. Realize where we are, and feel the feelings we have in the courtroom. Remember, "It all begins with you."

Care about the jurors. Look at them and truly care, truly feel, as a human being, what they are saying and why. The jurors have taken time away from their lives. Many don't want to be there—and even if they are content with serving their civic duty, they do not want their time wasted. We want to address the things that concern us about the case. We want the jurors to care as human beings about what concerns us. In order to do that, we must care about them.

We must care about what is going on with the people we are seeking to connect with. We want to address the things that concern us about the case. We want the jurors to care as human beings about what concerns us. In order to do that, we must take the first step of caring about them. The jurors are giving us their precious time. We must honor them, and we do that by caring about them. Reverse roles with the jurors. Imagine what it is to be them. They're sitting there, listening to the judge, listening to us, being told when to sit, when they get to use the bathroom, when they get to eat, and when they get to go home. They are no longer in control of their own lives. Most of them do not want to be there.

Without reversing roles (putting ourselves in their shoes), we have no foundation to begin establishing connections. If we can start our jury selection by putting ourselves in the seats and shoes of our jurors, we will see a different perspective.

Here is a method of reversing roles with the jurors that I learned at the Trial Lawyers College many years ago, from Gerry Spence, Joey Low, Jim Nugent, and others. I will sit down in the jury box and consider the answers to these questions before a trial and during a trial:

Breathe . . . and imagine yourself as a juror.

Where are we?

What is important to us?

How does it feel to be here in this courtroom?

As a juror, why should I care about this case?

What am I skeptical about?

How does all of this affect my life and what I care about?

Breathe . . .

Why am I here as a juror?

What do these lawyers think of me?

What are my feelings today and why?

What would I like to see happen today with this case?

As lawyers, if we are talking more than 10 percent of the time during voir dire, we are talking too much. If we are talking, we cannot be listening. If we are not listening, we can't feel anything that is going on. If we are thinking of our next questions before the juror finishes talking, we are not listening, and the jurors will know it.

GET VOIR DIRE STARTED

You need to have tools and methods to get voir dire going and accomplish the specific goals that you set. Let's talk about some of those tools to prompt jurors to talk, share, and connect with you, and the process. You also need them to talk among themselves and form a group. I am going to give you a step-by-step way to get voir dire rolling—what to say and how to set a cadence to your communication with the jury.

1. You say: "In order for me to do a good job right now, I need to learn as much as I can about each of you so I can decide whether or not to have you as part of the jury. The only way I get to learn about you is if you will be talkative."

2. You say: "I am hoping you will be the most talkative group of people that ever sat in this jury box. Would you all promise to please talk to me?"

3. You say: "Brutal honesty. *Brutal honesty*. What does that mean to you? Would somebody please talk to me?"

4. You say: "Thank you, I need your brutal honesty to learn as much as I can, and I am going to ask all of you to not hesitate with what you have to say. Don't be afraid to hurt my feelings."

5. Talk about whatever you want to talk about: "Money. In this case, the end result we are fighting for is a money verdict. May I have your permission to talk to you about money? I will be asking you to be part of a verdict that gives money for pain and suffering, millions of dollars for pain and suffering. Does that bother you at all? Brutal honesty. Is there any part of you that would not want to be part of a jury that gives money for pain and suffering?"

Jury selection is the time when you have to force yourself to shut your mouth and listen. Use your eyes and your hands to invite the jurors to tell you what *brutal honesty* means to them. Have at least three jurors respond to this. Listen to their responses. Feel their words inside of you as a human. Care about what they say. Show them you care by thanking them. Slow down. Don't be afraid of silence. When there is silence, the room fills with human feelings. This is setting the cadence or rhythm for the rest of voir dire and your trial.

There will be times when jurors are brutally honest, and what they say isn't exactly a ringing endorsement of your thoughts on the case. This is an example of voir dire from Sofia's case:

Q: You work in a hospital. Do you feel troubled to be in this case?

A: Yeah, yeah. No doubt.

[I need to know more.]

Q: Would you tell us why? Brutal honesty.

A: I just don't like lawsuits to blame a professional for their trying to do what they're trained to do. There is no guarantee, and they're not miracle workers. I just have a hard time blaming a professional for mistakes.

[When someone is honest, and expresses an opinion like this, in broad terms, about lawsuits and defendants, the likelihood is that many jurors feel the same way. In this case, I wanted to clarify her response and ask the other jurors what they felt.]

Q: I'm going to see if I heard you right, and if I can project it a little bit. Tell me if I'm wrong, or if I misquote you at all. You don't like the idea of a lawsuit against a medical professional when they're not miracle workers, and suing them when they're trying to do good, to help? Is there anyone else who, brutal honesty, feels the same way? I see Mr. Lee and Mr. Young.[2] Please talk to us.

MR. LEE: Well, exactly what you said. I mean, somebody is giving their all, and there's only so much you can do at a certain point. You got two choices, and with his education, he's making his choice, or whoever it is, no matter what profession. It could be the judge, whoever. He is going to make a choice. It might be the wrong one at that time. People aren't perfect.

[This juror hit the nail on the head. People aren't perfect, and they sometimes make the wrong choices. This happened in Sofia's case. The wrong choice cost her a normal life. Now the jurors have heard this perspective from another juror, who is one of their peers. To validate him, I say:]

A: I agree with you. Thank you.[3]

---

2. Juror names have been fictionalized.
3. *Blunt v. Sierra Vista Medical Center*, case number CV 100071, Superior Court of San Luis Obispo County, San Luis Obispo, CA.

Another example of brutal honesty from the voir dire in Sofia's case starts with me cutting right to the chase:

Q: Sitting right here, what side do you favor?

A: The hospital.

[I repeat the answer. It's a simple way to get the juror to say more.]

Q: The hospital?

A: Yeah. I think they did the best they could. They're not miracle workers, and things happen . . . I hate to see someone like him throw his studies and his career away because the circumstance is beyond their control, beyond all their control. It sounded like a lot of people were in there trying to save that baby. But to throw away all of their lives isn't going to bring that baby back. And I just don't see justice in that.

[*This* is brutal honesty. It's not a position that would seem to help Sofia's case, but she's honest, and this is what I need to hear. I respond, sincerely, by saying:]

Q: Thank you so much. Thank you so much.

[By showing that I care about this juror, as a human, no matter what her beliefs—by showing I respect and honor her brutal honesty—she continues to be even more honest.]

A: It's embarrassing.

[I need to let her, and the other jurors, know that their honesty is important and not something to be ashamed of. They're not bad people for holding whatever beliefs they have. They are to be commended for opening up themselves to the process. I affirm her by saying:]

Q: You don't have to feel bad saying that. It means a lot that you're willing to say it.[4]

Slow down. Let the silence become close to uncomfortable at times. Give pause to your words. Don't jump in with a lawyerly

---

4. *Blunt v. Sierra Vista Medical Center,* case number CV 100071, Superior Court of San Luis Obispo County, San Luis Obispo, CA.

question within a second of a juror's response. Bite your tongue, keep your mouth shut, and truly listen to the responses. Invite other jurors to respond by saying something as simple as, "Mr. Johnson, how about that?" or, "Ms. Smith,[5] what thoughts or feelings does hearing what Mr. Johnson said stir up inside of you?" Or, in response to a juror who has just said something, say, "Thank you sir. Please say more about that."

These are short cues to get jurors talking.

- "Please tell me about that."
- "Please say more."
- "What else?"
- "How so?"
- "Would somebody please talk to me?"
- "Who else feels this way?"
- "Mr. Johnson, how about that?"

If you want to learn about a person, you need to listen to her and care about what she is saying.

PLANT PARADIGMS

Now we are going to talk about a method known as *planting paradigms*. This technique forces people to take a position, and gets them to explain their feelings and beliefs in a nonconfrontational manner. This is a way to identify who the leaders on your jury are, who the dangerous people are, and how firmly prospective jurors are committed to certain positions. You can use this technique for money for pain and suffering, prejudice, feelings about police, suing the local hospital, burden of proof, feelings about lawyers, homosexuality, and money for wrongful death. You name it, and you can plant a paradigm and get discussion on a topic going with a jury.

---

5. Juror names have been fictionalized.

A simple example of planting a paradigm begins with a statement: "Some people feel tattoos are artwork, while some people don't like tattoos. I want to know how each of you feels." Or, "Some people feel that it's OK to get money for medical bills and time lost from work, but not for pain and suffering. What do you think about that?"

Move from one side of the jury box to the other, using physical movement and positioning your body to identify a place where each opposite end of the paradigm exists. For example, this is what I do in my cases. Walk through this with me:

[Center yourself in front of the jury.]

> Money for pain and suffering. We are going to be asking for millions of dollars for pain and suffering in this trial.

[Go a few steps over to the right.]

> Some people feel that money for medical bills and time lost from a job because of an injury is OK to get compensated for, but not pain and suffering.

[Walk to the other side of the jury box.]

> Some people say if there is a lot of pain and suffering, that might be worth a lot of money.

[Go back to the center.]

> Would somebody please tell me how you feel about money for pain and suffering as compared to giving an award of money to cover medical bills?

[Listen, honor, and follow up.]

> Thank you, please say more.
>
> Mrs. Moreland, what are your thoughts?
>
> Who else feels this way?
>
> Mr. Hart,[6] how about you?

---

6. Juror names have been fictionalized.

Who feels differently?

Q: Mrs. Moreland, knowing that we are asking for money for pain and suffering and this is a pain and suffering money case, should I be afraid to have you on this jury?

MRS. MORELAND: Yes, you probably should be. I don't believe in money for pain and suffering. You wouldn't want me as a juror.

NICK: Thank you for having the courage and brutal honesty to tell me that. Could you tell me more, why that is?

Discuss the subject openly and honor the jurors by using reflective feeling and accepting whatever their views are. Some jurors will excuse themselves for cause. Sometimes I explain to jurors what a cause challenge is. For example, I might say:

> Thank you for being willing to be brutally honest about your feelings and beliefs. A challenge for cause means that a juror gets off of being on a jury because they can't give both sides a fair fight. Some people, good people—this might not be the best case for them to be a juror on. There are things in all of us that we just can't put aside, and if that is the case with you—if you have some belief or opinion that should make me afraid of having you sit as a juror on this case, please let me know. Your honesty will help all of us have a fair fight. So please let me know if there is a reason I should be afraid of having you on the jury.

PRACTICE REFLECTIVE FEELING

Try to reflectively feel what the jurors feel. This means you take your own words into yourself and feel what you just said. Reverse roles with the juror, and reflect it back. Stay with the juror until you establish a connection.

In one of my recent cases, I had a juror who was a police officer. We discussed his job and some of the situations he's had to face in that role. To reverse roles with him, I said:

> I'm imagining what you do, and it's tough to imagine being in that tough situation you were in. It just seems very scary. But at the same time, I remember when I was in a uniform serving and dealing with scary situations. I was proud of my service.

[By acknowledging how he feels and sharing something about myself, I've created a connection.]

You can also make a connection by thanking jurors for sharing their thoughts with brutal honesty, whether their opinions seem to help or hurt the case. In another case, after a juror opened up about his opinions, I responded:

> I think it takes a lot of courage to talk about our own issues. Thank you for telling me that. Thank you very, very much. And don't feel bad about it. We all came in with who we are and who we're trying to be and become.

The jurors *must* feel that you honor them and who they are, opinions and all, whether they support your case or not. Show appreciation for brutal honesty and for them being willing to open themselves up. It's not easy to share personal things, especially with strangers, in open court. *Any* honesty, whether you deem it good or bad, helps your case. Applaud this, acknowledge it, respect it, and cherish it. This honesty brings you closer to the jurors, and brings them closer to your client. It can only help.

Do not leave the juror too quickly, because that will cause an incomplete termination. An incomplete termination is leaving a juror after he's responded, without truly acknowledging his response. Incomplete terminations affect your new beginning with the next jurors.

I see this all the time, when a juror gives an answer to a lawyer in voir dire, and the lawyer snaps his head to another juror and does not honor the communication he's just received. This is rude, and it will affect communication with the other jurors. You can prevent this by pausing after each juror responds and saying a simple, but sincere, "thank you." With eye contact. If what the juror gave was something profound or personal, give it a bit of silence. Honor the gift. Silence is OK. It invites this juror and other jurors to share more.

If the juror does not say more, and you want more, then stay with the juror. Imagine casting a lifeline out. The line will not come back until you establish the connection and reflect the juror's feelings. Simply open your hand and ask the juror to say more. You could also say, "Please tell me more about your thoughts about that."

For example, imagine a client who is a tattoo artist. You are addressing the concerns about overbearing prejudices against tattoos and artists. When a juror says, "I don't like tattoos," you could say, "Could you tell us more?"

The juror says more about it. "My son came home with a tattoo when he was seventeen and still in high school. I wanted to know who did it. It caused major problems in our home. Now he wants it removed. It is ugly."

Stay with this juror. Try to feel what the juror is feeling, identify the feeling, live that feeling, and feel the shock the juror felt. You can do this in your head, thinking:

> My idiot son just ruined his body for life, marking it with this shit. How could he have done this? Is it my fault? Did I not teach him what's right, what I expect of him? He's going to regret this for the rest of his life. How could he have been so stupid? What's everyone else going to think of him? What happens when he wants to get a real job, like I want him to?

Or you can validate the juror by sharing the feeling you've experienced, putting yourself in the juror's shoes. Whatever it is, repeat back slowly the words: "That must have been very upsetting." You have now validated the juror. Don't leave that juror just yet, however; do not allow an incomplete termination to occur. With your eyes, your body, and your humanity, send the feeling back to the juror and validate him. Then, only after the connection is complete, and you have validated the juror's feelings, slowly turn and ask other jurors if they have felt the same way at any point in their lives.

I do this by saying, "Who else here knows that feeling?" There is no script. Rather, the method of reflective feeling and honoring the juror is something I do mostly without lawyerly words. I use my eyes, I ask other jurors to share, I say thank you. I go slowly.

If you say thank you, then it must be real. You must truly feel thankful and even explain why you feel that way.

For those of you who say, "We only get fifteen minutes for voir dire!" or "What about when we don't get voir dire? In Utah, there is no voir dire!", I have a response for you: whether you, the opposing lawyer, or the judge conducts voir dire, your job is to listen, feel, reverse roles, and connect on a human level.

Remember, connection is your goal. Even when your opponent is doing voir dire, your job is to connect and reverse roles! The only way to connect is to *feel and reflect*. If the judge only gives you ten minutes, which gives you less than forty seconds with each juror, *connect*. Find a way to connect! It does not matter what you talk about.

Sometimes, I ask the question, "If you could be anywhere right now, on a perfect day, whom would you be with, and what would you be doing?" That question isn't really related to the case, but it shows the juror that I'm interested in him, as a person. I also sometimes ask, "If your best friend asked you, 'What side of this case would rather have you as a juror?' what would you say?" This question is aimed at getting the juror to get in the mind-set of talking to someone he knows and trusts, and being brutally honest in a quick manner.

Don't be surprised if the jurors are being kind with and connecting with your opponent too. You have created an environment of trust and caring. Be OK with the jurors trusting and liking your opponent. Don't worry. Later on, when your opponent betrays the jurors' trust, the jurors will punish your opponent.

Voir Dire from the *Blunt* Case

The following are selections of my voir dire on the *Blunt* case. If you read this, remember these are just words. Voir dire is a feeling, an art. You need body language, eye contact, an open heart, and a softness that does not show on a transcript. I started out in my usual way:

> Good afternoon, everyone. I'm hoping that somehow I can figure out a way to get you all to become really talkative. That's maybe instinct, to be really quiet and not say too many words when a lawyer is asking you questions, but this is the only chance I get to ask you questions, and the only chance I get to learn as much as I can about you, and which twelve of you are going to be up for this job. It's going to be a long haul. It's going to be a long case.

[Right up front, I mention brutal honesty. Then I'm brutally honest with the jury. I know this case is going to be long: lots of experts and testimony, lots of medical issues to deal with. They need to know this up front, and they need to see me being honest right away. No sense pretending that it'll be a three-day trial. That's why I say, "It's going to be a long haul. It's going to be a long case."]

> I'm wondering if all of you will promise to be talkative and talk to me. Is that something that you can promise to do? Will you all promise to talk, and maybe be the most talkative jury panel that's ever been in this courtroom?

[I say this with a sincere smile, hoping someone will say something. Someone always does, but even so, my heart beats a little bit faster, fearing that I will stand here for an eternity, looking at a group of strangers, all staring at me, saying nothing.]

JUROR 1: Depends on what you're asking.

[Finally. Thank you, Juror 1.]

NICK: *Brutal honesty.* What does that mean?

JUROR 1: I'm brutally honest is what I am.

NICK: OK. Brutal honesty, what does that mean to you all? Can someone talk to me?

[It's always good to have the jurors phrase things using their own vocabulary. Whether it's their beliefs, their definitions of legal jargon or medical terminology—it's best they state these things out loud, and then I can modify what they say or ask questions as necessary.]

JUROR 2: It's the truth, even if you don't want to hear it.

NICK: Mr. Smith, don't be afraid to hurt my feelings, OK? I promise you that I would much rather know, right now, how you feel about being a juror on this case about certain issues, than I would after the trial, to hear you say, "Well, you know, why did you even select me as a juror anyways?" I'd hate to find that out at the end of the trial, so I need to learn as much as I can now.

[Throughout this voir dire, I keep giving the jurors permission to be honest. I allow them to be open and address their fears—most people don't tell the *whole* truth, because they don't want to hurt someone's feelings. I address that fear, and keep prodding them to tell me as much as possible about themselves.]

. . .

[After other jurors have expressed the opinion that people aren't perfect, Juror 3 chimes in.]

JUROR 3: My son will be taking his state boards to be a nurse this Friday, so I have that connection. I also worked at a state hospital for fifteen years as the Protestant chaplain, and I have some religious concerns about suing as a way to settle issues. And so, in addition to what other people have said, my feeling is that everything should be done that is humanly possible to solve the problem before bringing the issue into court. The money issue is a big one also. Was it $50 million?

[Better clear this up really fast.]

NICK: No, sir.

JUROR 3: No?

NICK: It will be around fifteen.

JUROR 3: Fifteen.

NICK: It's not fifty.

JUROR 3: I don't hear too well out of one ear.

NICK: I heard fifty, but I said fifteen. At the end of the day, I promise you all I'm not asking for $50 million. But, nonetheless, I'm asking for a whole lot of money for this little girl.

JUROR 3: With all due respect to the family, that's my opinion.

NICK: And how would that affect you? At the end of the day, and it came time to add up the money on a case like this, would it be a struggle for you, because of your beliefs that you just so brutally honestly shared with us, to be a part of a money verdict?

JUROR 3: It would be difficult.

[This juror is being honest. I need to know if that difficulty will prevent him from giving Sofia the fair deliberation she deserves.]

NICK: I'm the lawyer on this side here, and I'm representing this family. At the end of the day, I've been up-front with you, and I'm asking for money. That's the justice that we can get. Should I be afraid of having you on the case as a juror? And I hope I'm not offending you.

JUROR 3: No, you're not. No, I don't think you need to be afraid of me. I mean, I would do the best that I could to follow all of the rules and guidelines, but there is that issue with me.

[Hmmm. That's still not a clear answer. So I need to get this juror to clarify his position even more.]

NICK: Do you think, sitting here now, that the issue would cause you to favor one side versus the other?

JUROR 3: I really don't know.

NICK: Well, thank you. The thing is, if we have a feeling, or a belief, or what could be a prejudice inside us, we need to talk about it. I think the best thing we can do is own it and bring it out to the surface, so we can deal with it. I really thank you for that.

[That was an example of acknowledging a juror's brutal honesty, creating a connection, and having a complete termination.]

[Speaking to the next juror:]

NICK: Do I have any reason to be afraid of you? Brutal honesty.

JUROR 4: I don't know. I think I would have a hard time. I mean, I don't like the circumstances, but I still just—

[I'm just going to cut to the chase.]

NICK: Sitting right here, what side do you favor?

JUROR 4: The hospital.

NICK: The hospital?

JUROR 4: Yeah. I think they did the best they could. They're not miracle workers, and things happen.

[I've included more of this juror's thoughts above, in the section "Get Voir Dire Started." Basically, I just keep respecting her honesty, while getting her to spell out more of her thoughts.]

• • •

NICK: If, at the end of the day, I prove my case, and I prove these medical professionals messed up, and they ran through some stop signs, and that this baby was brain damaged because of that, would you be able to—at that point, if I proved that case—would you be able to side with us?

JUROR 5: If you proved your case.

NICK: And you would give me that chance?

JUROR 5: Sure.

NICK: Thank you.

[Turning to the next juror:]

NICK: Mr. Johnson. How about you?

JUROR 6: Prove your case, I'll side with you. If you don't prove your case—

NICK: Side with them?

JUROR 6: Yeah. I mean, I think life is precious, and not guaranteed for anybody.

[That's true. I agree.]

NICK: I agree.

JUROR 6: And two hundred years ago, that child would have died. The fact that it's still alive says something for the medical staff. But if the condition of the child right now is due to negligence, then by all means, the family is entitled. But if it just is one of the tragedies of life—

NICK: It happens—

JUROR 6: —not being guaranteed, you can't really blame anybody for that.

NICK: If this is just a tragedy of life that, you know, bad things happen to good people. If, at the end of the day, this is just a bad-things-happen-to-good-people case, and this baby was just going to end up brain damaged, even though everybody did their job the right way, then that means we go home with nothing.

We're not here for sympathy. We're not here to talk about sympathy. We're not here for this much sympathy. Not sympathy at all. But if we prove our case that this staff didn't meet the standard of care, that they did drop the ball and missed things they should have caught, you can side with us?

JUROR 6: If you prove that case, yeah.

[This guy keeps talking about "proving the case," which makes me wonder if the jurors truly understand what needs to be done for me to "prove the case." This might be a good time to explain the burden of proof.]

NICK: And in talking about proving that case, in a criminal case, you can prove a case beyond a reasonable doubt. In a case like this, a civil case, you just have to prove that it's more likely true than not true. I mean, all we have to do is, if you take all the reasonable doubt on this side, and all the reasonable doubt on that side, if we just tip the scales, and show that it's more likely true—not beyond-a-reasonable-doubt true, but more likely true that the doctor was negligent, that the hospital staff was negligent—we just show it's more likely true, that means we win. It's the easiest burden of proof in the courtroom. It's not the clear-and-convincing standard, the beyond-a-reasonable-doubt standard. It's more likely true than not true.

Some people feel, "Well, if you're suing medical professionals, then it ought to be a higher standard. I don't really like this more-likely-true standard, and I wouldn't want to follow it." Some people say, "Well, the law is the law." I need to know where you're at with that.

JUROR 6: I don't feel good about that balance being so minute, no. I think that it should be a little more weighty. We're going to listen to experts tell us things. I have no idea what they're talking about. Number 4 here says I have to be the sole judge of their believability. Well, I have to be able to believe them. I can't listen to a guy, and throw out what he says as being a bunch of bull. I have to be able to believe him. So, yeah, it just should be more than just a little, in my opinion.

NICK: I expect that it will be a lot more.

JUROR 6: Like I said, your first question, if you prove your case, yeah, I'm with you. But, you know, it's not something that I take lightly for either side.

NICK: Thank you. I know you're in the hot seat now, and I'm asking you these questions. At the end of this case, you'll actually hear an instruction that you don't have to accept an expert witness's opinion. I mean, if an expert came into a courtroom and said that smoking doesn't cause cancer, or pouring arsenic in the river doesn't harm your children, do you believe that, just because they're an expert and they get to say, "I've got a degree" or "I'm from Stanford"?

JUROR 6: Well, if we can't believe them, then why are we listening to them to begin with? That's my issue, I guess. I mean, why are they here?

NICK: All experts for both sides, as you heard from counsel, make money. There's a difference between an expert witness and lay witnesses in litigation cases. Anyone can go hire an expert. It goes for both sides.

Would you leave room for the possibility that experts for both sides could be biased? That I could call in an expert that might just be completely full of it? He's taking the money to testify. The defense could call in an expert, and they get paid, and they're willing to do anything they can to help the hospital and the doctor get off? Would you leave room for the possibility that in our country of human beings, that might be true? Anybody? Mr. Thompson, what are your thoughts on that?

JUROR 7: I know a lot of forensic medical doctors. Sometimes they know what they're talking about; sometimes they don't.

[Exactly my point. This is what the jurors need to hear. It's best coming from another juror, their peer.]

NICK: Say more, please.

JUROR 7: Well, they're just doctors with some forensic training is all they are. So, you know, they know a little bit about the law, and they know about the specialty they've been trained for.

NICK: So, if I tell you that I have a doctor from Stanford, or from the University of Pennsylvania, or from Johns Hopkins, and they're going to come in and tell you X, Y, and Z, are you going to believe it, just because it comes out of their mouths?

JUROR 7: No.

NICK: No?

JUROR 7: No.

NICK: Well, why? They're experts.

JUROR 7: They're not always right. They know what they've been trained on. Sometimes they've been trained improperly.

NICK: Can experts be biased—

JUROR 7: Of course.

NICK: —to try to help the side that they're trying to help.

JUROR 7: As long as they're being paid, they can be biased.

[*Yes. Exactly.* Now the jurors have heard my emphasis, again, through the mouth of their equal juror. He's made my point: expert witnesses can be biased, so lay witnesses are more credible. This is why you want to prove the story through lay witnesses. Amen, brother.]

* * *

NICK: Mr. Isaacs?

JUROR 8: As I understand it, this case concerns negligence.

NICK: Yes, sir.

JUROR 8: And determination of that.

NICK: Yes, sir.

JUROR 8: And I have no problem with that.

[This guy seems intelligent and knowledgeable. I don't have a lot to ask him, but I need to connect with him somehow. Might as well talk about his background.]

NICK: You served in criminal cases before, three in Oregon, as I recall.

JUROR 8: Yes.

NICK: Whereabouts in Oregon?

JUROR 8: Portland.

NICK: How long have you been down here?

JUROR 8: I'm a third generation.

* * *

[He hasn't given me a lot of insight into himself—his thoughts, beliefs, prejudices. I haven't connected on that deeper level yet. I need to keep trying.]

NICK: The thought of a lawsuit for money—do you have any brutal honesty, beliefs, or thoughts on medical malpractice lawsuits? What do you think I may want to know if I'm going to decide whether to have you as a juror on the case?

JUROR 8: My only bias, or predisposition might be a better word, is that I'm a long-term school trustee. One of the things we have to deal with, which is always difficult, is the special education situations, and the special treatment and financial burden that the district and the rest of our community bears as a result. It's something I'm fairly oversensitized to. But, as I understand it, this is a negligence case, and the future of the child in question is a separate issue. What we're dealing with here is the negligence.

[Bingo. We're not here to talk about any other issue. Just negligence. He's hit the nail on the head. Now I want to know a little more about him as a person.]

NICK: Yes, sir, it is. Thank you.

Maybe this is a question you might not expect. I'll ask some more of you this question, but if you had a day in the world to be wherever you wanted, doing whatever you wanted, with whomever you wanted, what would that day be like? Where would you be?

• • •

[Turning to the next juror:]

NICK: Mr. Smith. Where are you at with all this?

JUROR 9: Well, I wish I wasn't on this jury. It's going to be too long and emotionally charged. I wish I was articulate enough to talk myself out of it.

But I understand the case. It's going to be difficult. We are all cursed with biases and blessed with a sense of fairness, and

I'd like to believe that most of my life, I've been blessed with a sense of fairness.

[Wow. That's well put.]

NICK: Thank you.

At the end of the day, I mean, you may think that everyone involved is a good person.

JUROR 9: Right.

NICK: Dr. Haupt isn't a bad man, and isn't a man that did anything intentional. You may think my clients are great people. Even though you feel people are good people, will you be able to focus on how what went down this day was the wrong thing?

JUROR 9: It's the understanding of the situation—you are not asking us to judge people. You're asking us to judge the situation.

NICK: Judge what happened.

JUROR 9: What happened.

NICK: Yes.

JUROR 9: And I think I understand that.

[Again, a juror saying exactly what I want the jury to know. This is what happens when we ask jurors to be brutally honest, and when we make a connection.]

NICK: Thank you.[7]

IDEAS FOR VOIR DIRE: MEDICAL MALPRACTICE CASE

Medical malpractice cases brought by wrongfully injured plaintiffs are considered the second most difficult cases to win and see

---

7. *Blunt v. Sierra Vista Medical Center,* case number CV 100071, Superior Court of San Luis Obispo County, San Luis Obispo, CA.

a success rate on average of roughly 7 to 10 percent. (See the next section for the number one most difficult type of case to win.) Many of the cases I have tried are medical malpractice cases.

One of the most famous and influential civil plaintiff's lawyers in history, Tom Girardi, is somebody who has been my friend and mentor since law school. Tom made a name for himself trying medical malpractice cases, cases other lawyers were afraid to take and could not win. Tom told me as a young law student that lawyers who only take the big, easy cases are cowards. That to be a real trial lawyer, I need to be willing to take the toughest cases and be able to pick myself up after losing. What I respect most about Tom is his fearlessness. He still, to this very day, in his seventies, takes on, puts his money and resources into, and personally tries the most difficult cases. He is a true warrior for justice who has become among the most successful ever by living the motto "fight for the little guy and never give up."

Attached to this book is a disc with the transcript of my voir dire on the *Blunt v. Sierra Vista Medical Center* case. My primary goal in voir dire was to connect with the jurors and get them to promise us that there was no reason for me or Sofia's family to be afraid of having them as jurors on the case. I asked them if they would go out of their way to side with the hospital and doctor or help the hospital and doctor be the winners of the case. The transcript speaks for itself, but beneath the words exist human connections that we made. After three days of voir dire, when our jury was selected, we all felt good.

We knew our jurors as human beings, not just labels and objectively on paper through questionnaires. The defense had a questionnaire and a jury consultant who made decisions based on paper. I didn't even read them. We had an engineer, an accountant, an Iranian man, an emergency dispatcher, a bluegrass musician, a white woman from South Africa, and a woman who worked for the post office and delivered mail. The jury was conservative except for the musician. That didn't matter. They were a group of people who cared and were willing to listen. I believe that is because I listened to them first.

IDEAS FOR VOIR DIRE: CIVIL RIGHTS CASE

Experts consider civil rights cases[8] among the most difficult cases to win. These cases rarely survive the myriad of motions for immunity and summary judgment. Those that do survive are met with hostile jurors who are often prosafety, which means that they are willing to forgive the police, whom they see as protecting "us," while they think the case was filed by the proverbial "them."

These cases only succeed approximately 4 to 6 percent of the time. Even when they do succeed, the jurors are hesitant to find against the police for large sums of money. Often, the attorney's fees far exceed the actual damages that the juries award to plaintiffs.

I am handling these cases now, and I am going to win them. This is the beginning.

My Mentors in Civil Rights Law

I am going to share with you what I have learned from three phenomenal trial lawyers who successfully try and win these most difficult cases: Joey Low, Gary Dordick, and Garo Mardirossian. I want you to know who it is that I am turning to for mentoring and advice on these cases.

First, Joey Low, who started his adult life serving us in the Marine Corps, is one of the best trial lawyers I know. Like me, he is a product of Gerry Spence's Trial Lawyers College. He has been one of my most influential teachers for the past eleven years I have practiced law, and I am proud that he is also one of my best friends. His fame so far has not been as a rich civil lawyer, but rather as a lawyer who volunteers his time to pay forward what he has learned. He trains public defenders and lawyers who are dedicated to handling civil rights cases. He is a man who comes closest to being selfless as any trial lawyer I have ever met. With his skills and record, he could easily be spending his time making

---

8. 42 U.S.C. Section 1983

millions doing personal-injury work, but instead, he takes on more pro bono cases than anybody I know. At the drop of a hat, he buys his own plane tickets and flies across the country (and other countries) to defend helpless soldiers who are being prosecuted in military courts.

Second is Gary Dordick, who is a humble man from humble beginnings. Gary is an unusual phenomenon. This man went straight from high school into an unaccredited law school, never having gone to college. He took the first year law student exam, which is required in California (and is known as the baby bar), and passed, finished law school, passed the bar, and started trying cases within his first few weeks as a lawyer. Over the past twenty years, being the voice for the underdog, Gary has become known and continuously recognized as the top trial lawyer in California. Meeting him, you would never think he is a trial lawyer. He is soft spoken, wears blue jeans, and is covered in tattoos. He prefers to spend his time being a father, playing guitar, and riding horses, but he continues to find himself in courtrooms. He is unable to say no to calls for help from other lawyers. I met Gary my first year out of law school and went to watch him in trial as often as I could. He has become a big brother to me, and apart from my own family, he is the person I spend the most time with.

Garo Mardirossian is somebody you might regularly see on CNN. His parents were survivors of the Armenian Holocaust, and he has the anger of injustice and righteous indignation running through his veins. He was raised to be a hard worker, running a gas station with his father. He started working in elementary school. As a young lawyer, Garo worked his way to the top by taking police brutality cases that no other lawyer would touch. Freedom, life, liberty, and protection from oppression are themes that he speaks of with great passion. Garo continues to set precedents with money verdicts in civil rights cases and cases against automobile manufacturers. He is known nationwide as one of the top civil rights and product liability trial lawyers. I am proud that he is one of my best friends and a mentor who has invested himself in helping me become successful.

Money and Civil Rights

So now that you know where I am getting my ammunition to do these cases, let's talk about getting money and justice for people whose cases are based on the wrongful taking away of civil rights.

First, how can we ask for money for taking away someone's civil rights? How do we relate to ordinary civilians and get them to understand and value what a loss of freedom is worth? After all, it is not the loss of an item or a loved one, which are common experiences. It is the loss of a civil right, something that most of us never think of. In fact, most citizens struggle with being able to recite what their civil rights are, how they got them, and what they cost. Studies show that a large majority of U.S. citizens are willing to waive some of their rights in order to feel safe. So how do we change jurors' perceptions of what the value of their civil rights is—if they think their rights have any value at all?

Discussing Civil Rights in Voir Dire

Assigning a dollar value to the taking of a civil right is difficult. Most of us take civil rights for granted because we have always had them and have never been without. Joey has a way that he overcomes this difficulty in voir dire, and with his permission, I am going to share it with you.

Recently, while trying a case in U.S. District Court, Central District of California, I heard a U.S. marshal said to Joey, "Mr. Low, we believe that the police were unfair to your client, but we have not seen a plaintiff's verdict here in over twenty-four years." A week later, the jury came in for Joey's client. After the defendants appealed, they paid the plaintiff $1.4 million. I asked Joey how he did this.

His response was, "It all began with voir dire." This is because every juror has to have a personal experience with the loss of freedom, but they do not remember it in these terms.

First, we start with a discussion of the importance of justice and liberty. We do this with a metaphor so that the jury can personally understand and value the loss without anybody ever violating the golden rule.

Then ask the jury questions about their own experiences so that you can learn more about who they are and what value, if any, they place on civil rights.

For example:

Q: When I was in the service, they told me that I had to get the anthrax vaccination. At that time, I believed that for every ten thousand people that received the shot, one would actually contract the deadly disease and would die. I thought to myself, *No way am I willing to get this shot.* However, being in the service, you don't get a choice. I was not free to refuse this vaccination. Like everyone else, we were ordered to shut up, line up, and man up as we got shot full of the experimental liquid.

Has anyone here ever had a time in their life where the choice was made for you and you felt that you were not free to disagree?

Here the jurors reflect on their own life experiences. When called upon, they will talk about those times in their lives when they were not free to decide what they would eat, where they would go to school, who their teachers would be, when they went to bed, or whether they would go to church. They will inevitably talk about their parents, their teachers, their spouses, their kids, and their bosses. Get them talking about it and keep them talking. Then ask the next question.

Q: I want to talk to each of you about freedom and civil rights. Have you or anybody you care about ever been wrongfully arrested, convicted of a crime, or put in jail?

Let this question sit. There will probably be silence. Look at the jurors individually. Embrace and feel the silence in yourself. Identify the feelings. Be still with the silence. With silence, there is feeling. Jurors will begin to remember or imagine and feel what it is to have their freedom and civil rights taken away.

Continue with the next questions:

Q: Some people would rather die than be wrongfully imprisoned. The patriot Patrick Henry said, "Give me liberty or give me death." Have any of you ever thought of what the value is of having freedom and civil rights?

Q: At the end of this trial, I will be asking for millions of dollars as the dollar value for the freedom and civil rights that were wrongfully taken away from Joseph. *Does that bother or offend anybody here? I need your brutal honesty.*

Allow some silence and hopefully somebody will speak. When they speak, listen and feel. Ask others to share. Make sure to go through every juror and ask, "Does that offend you, that I will ask you to put a dollar value on the loss of freedom and civil rights?"

Q: Who here believes that our rights exist for all of us or none of us?

Repeat, "All of us or none of us," and start calling on individual jurors. Slowly but powerfully, say:

Q: All of us or none of us, Mr. Hays?

Listen, feel, reflect.

Q: Mrs. Brown,[9] all of us or none of us, what are your feelings?

Q: Why?

Having to explain *why* causes us to feel and believe even more.
After leading a group discussion on this, we want jurors to understand and agree that freedom and civil rights have value, and promise to be willing to do the difficult job of equating those rights with money. The following is one way to do this:

Q: Some people believe that civil rights, freedom of speech, freedom of religion, freedom from unfair prosecution, freedom of life, liberty, and the pursuit of happiness, are gifts. These are gifts that have been paid for by the lives and limbs of those who knew what it was like to live without these rights. *Has anyone here had a loved one serve us in the military?*

---

9. Juror names have been fictionalized.

Listen and let the people share. Feel. Thank them. The last question to ask is:

Q: Who here feels, even a little, that it is offensive to put a dollar value on civil rights and freedom in a civil courtroom, which is the job we are going to ask you to do in this case?

Let them share and feel and thank them for sharing.
You continue with:

Money is the only way to place a value on civil rights in a courtroom. It is the only way to prosecute a case where a person has had his civil rights and freedoms wrongfully taken from him. In this case, after I prove the wrong that was done to my client Joseph, we will be asking you to figure out dollar values. We need to be sure that nobody is bothered by this or unable to do the job.

Quickly, scan and go through each juror (with open hands) asking, "Is there any problem with that? Does this bother you even a little?" Ask this a few times and make sure to make eye contact with every juror, giving them a chance to tell you if there is a problem. If the juror's eye contact or body language tells you there is a problem, ask him or her softly if there is a problem and what it is. You must be brutally honest with the jury in order to receive the same in return.

We can boil voir dire down to a few things: connection, brutal honesty, validation, and respect. This is your first time to connect with the jury. Start connecting by being brutally honest. You need them to talk to you, so you say that. You're nervous? Say that. By showing them your vulnerabilities, they'll show you theirs in return. By being brutally honest, you show that you're willing to expose something intimate about yourself, and that makes you just a little more human, rather than just some lawyer in a suit. Validate their feelings. Don't judge, and don't reject. Make them feel that whatever they say is OK, even if it doesn't help your case. Respect them for being willing to share something scary. They are human, and humans naturally want to hide their problem spots. Validate and respect the jurors who step into the light, baring their souls, sharing their fears, their biases, and their true beliefs. What an honor that you are trusted enough to hear these things. Reward this honesty with respect. Honor the connection you've formed with each juror by sincerely thanking them for their thoughts, and only moving on to the next juror when it feels right. Connect with the jury, and you may have already won your case by the time you're ready to start opening statements.[10]

---

10. For more about this, please see my DVD *Connecting with the Jury* (Portland, OR: Trial Guides, 2013).

9

Steve's View of Voir Dire

Steve Halteman

The importance of jury selection is obvious. The method on how to do it is not. Every attorney has his or her own style. Certainly Nick does. In fact, I'd say Nick's voir dire is his strongest suit as a lawyer. In every case I've worked on with Nick, we've come out of voir dire with a significant lead over the defense. Nick best explains the methods he uses to achieve this. My goal here is to explain my role in the selection process, how I started out looking at the process, and what I have learned as an outside observer.

Abandoning Stereotypes

I started out the way many have, which is thinking things like: "What do we think of juror number nine? Should we overlook what juror number two said about tort reform? Juror number five is an accountant; we don't want him. Whom should we kick off?" I would make lists of desirable and undesirable attributes to look for in potential jurors. "Because the plaintiff is X, we want jurors who are Latino stay-at-home dads who make $75,000 in the stock market, vote Democrat, and whose hobby is flying vintage aircraft." Really? Why did I make the lists? Did I really think that I would find any jurors who would meet the qualifications I wanted, that these people would magically appear in the jury pool and decide exactly the way I predicted?

In the early days, yes, I did believe that (or at a minimum, that each of the qualities they matched would bring them a step closer to deciding in our favor). Now, I believe differently, and I have subscribed to a method that is unique to anything else I have seen.

Humans do not fit into boxes. Labels and stereotypes mislead us. Humans are the sum total of their life experiences, public and private. That sum total defies any category, label, or easy discovery. We kid ourselves if we think that we can learn enough about each human in a public voir dire to predict how each one will decide our complex matter, weeks or months down the road in the privacy of his or her mind.

So why did I make those lists? In retrospect, three reasons:

1. To establish parameters in a process where there are none.

2. To make me feel like, and look like, I knew what I was doing: "I created this list, I am now looking for the people on this list, and when I find these people, I will have been successful in my work."

3. I was being lazy and falling back on stereotypes.

Because none of the above, in my mind, was a ringing endorsement for the use of lists, I stopped making them. But I still held on to my stereotypes. Though I've worked through my life to rid myself of stereotypes, most of my successes have been overseas. I've held on to my North American prejudices. I brought them to the table when helping pick juries. It turns out, they didn't help much. Actually, they've let me down. Specifically, there are two groups as potential jurors that I traditionally opposed: accountants and engineers. Like many, I believed that they are always against big money plaintiff's verdicts, they live in their left brain, they are not good jurors for plaintiffs, and they are too fascinated with numbers. I told this to Nick and he smiled. I was thereafter proven wrong, to Nick's delight. Two recent cases have proven Nick's position that accountants and engineers are humans just like anybody else, and we should not stereotype. So I've given up on stereotypes as a reliable indicator.

So why shouldn't we use stereotypes? A few reasons. One, they are often wrong. Two, even if they are right, there are always exceptions. What percentage makes up the exceptions: 51 percent to 49 percent? 99 percent to 1 percent? Who can say with accuracy? Three, a notion or image of a group or individual does not accurately predict what decision a person will reach after hearing a body of evidence and having the opportunity to do something that is not stereotypical.

By the way, what *are* stereotypes, exactly? According to the people who write definitions, a stereotype is "a fixed, commonly held notion or image of a person or group, based on an oversimplification of some observed or imagined trait of behavior or appearance, whether positive or negative." It doesn't sound like the definer was too fond of stereotypes either.

Of all the stereotypes I can think of, job stereotypes are the weakest, primarily because many people don't identify with their jobs and often resent them. Still, long after I should know better, I fall prey to them. As a recent example, on the *Blunt* case, a gentleman in the jury pool said he was a pharmaceutical sales rep. I jumped to an immediate conclusion. A guy selling drugs to doctors. Prodoctor. Prohospital. Bad for business if it gets out he was on a jury that delivered a verdict against the local medical establishment. Conservatively dressed. Don't want him. I assumed he was a defense juror and wrote an X next to his name. I moved on.

Much later, in response to a question about plaintiffs asking for $15 million (the amount we were asking for at that time), the sales rep spoke eloquently. Of course, I was barely listening because I had already made up my mind. However, I had to do a double take when I heard him talk:

> Well, you see, my sister has cerebral palsy. Right now, my father is taking care of her, but one day, it will be my

responsibility. And frankly, I don't think $15 million is enough for a lifetime of care for someone who has cerebral palsy.

Beautiful manna from the skies and a nice comeuppance to boot. This came from a juror who on paper, by the way he dressed and looked at us, along with his occupation, would have been a sure kickoff of the jury. The truth is that we all are much more complex than our stereotypes.

IF NOT STEREOTYPES, THEN WHAT?

So if not lists of desirable attributes in potential jurors, and not stereotypes, then what can we do to prepare for jury selection? I thought about this quite a bit before the *Blunt* case. I have to use my left brain some of the time. There are two things I came up with.

The first thing was that I had to figure out if I had any preferences at all about potential jurors ahead of jury selection that did not relate to stereotypes. I came up with one preference. In gender-specific injures, I prefer the gender injured to be on the jury.

Thus, for *Wall v. Miramontes,*[1] in which Mr. Wall, who was twenty-three years old, suffered a smashed penis, I preferred the following: males young enough to be sexually active, but old enough to understand the value of money.

In the *Blunt* case, I preferred women on the jury who had given birth, due to the traumatic birth, and men who were involved with the labor and delivery of their children.

Second, I learned what I could about San Luis Obispo County juries. What I learned wasn't promising: they were traditionally conservative, hostile to big verdicts, and with no significant med mal plaintiff's verdicts in more than twenty years. This turned out to be a broad stereotype, subject to falsity and exception.

When the jury was selected and sat down in the box, did these people know they were supposed to be conservative and hostile to big verdicts? Did they know there had been no significant med

---

1. *Wall v. Miramontes,* case number 37-2009-00068436-CU-PA-EC, Superior Court of the State of California, County of San Diego, East County Division.

mal verdicts in San Luis Obispo County in more than twenty years? My guess is that they were unaware of their supposed stereotypes. Nor did they know the respective histories and reputations of the lawyers involved in the case. I believe they were a newly constituted village of sixteen, part of the greater San Luis Obispo community, but a completely separate entity when it came to decision making.

We saw them as wonderful people: powerful, capable of setting a community standard of medical care for San Luis Obispo, and ready to be convinced by two competing advocates.

How We Pick a Jury

So how *do* we pick a jury? We do it by sticking to our bedrock philosophy, which is laid out in two goals:

1. Do not look to exclude potential jurors. Instead, seek out jurors to include and make part of a caring team for the community.
2. Emotionally connect with each potential juror so that they in turn care for our client.

Thus, what we need to say to any potential juror is, in essence:

Hey, we want you on this jury. We care about you. You seem like a cool person, so ask any questions you want because there are no bad questions. Let's chat. Tell me what you're thinking and feeling. Does any part of what you know about this case and what we want to accomplish upset you or turn you off? Please let us know if you are going to cause us trouble.

If the potential juror doesn't want to be a part of your jury, she will let you know.

How to apply this philosophy of inclusion? Well, let's take a look at the process.

People from the community are told to show up on a given day for jury duty. I think it is safe to say that some people welcome the disruption in their lives while others resent it. After parking, waiting, filling out forms, and more waiting, they will shift toward resentment. Finally, the potential jurors are brought into a large room, where they listen to the judge's speech and maybe a mini-opening. Then someone calls some names, and voir dire begins. All of this occurs at glacial speed. It is worse than waiting in any line you could imagine, and to make matters worse, the jurors are not allowed to have their cell phones on and are not allowed to even read a book. Not much fun.

In the *Blunt* case, we needed three days to pick the jury. With dawning awareness, everyone in the peanut gallery began to realize just how long this was going to take. Any enthusiasm dwindled quickly. People got bored and pissed off. I never sit at counsel's table during voir dire, as I prefer to remain in the peanut gallery. This way, I can feel the hostility and hear some of the commentary. I hear things like:

"When I get up there, I'll let him have it."

[This rarely happens, as when people actually do get into the jury box, they are somewhat subdued by the atmosphere.]

"This is such bullshit!"

"Another break? You've got to be kidding me."

"Our tax dollars at work."

What happened next?

Well, Nick stood up and slowly walked toward the potential jurors. The jurors waited with a mixture of anticipation and boredom. He stopped about six feet from them, introduced himself, and had a bit of a chat. The chat was about how great it would be if they could be the most talkative jurors ever.

"This is the only way we are all going to get to know each other," he said. He talked about how scared he was that no one was going to talk to him and how terrible he would feel. He asked them for their help, a basic human request.

"Would you all just please promise to talk to me? And best of all would be if you all could talk with each other. Will you help me out?"

The nods indicated they were on board. The whole time, Nick was moving laterally along the jury box, back and forth, making eye contact, being calm.

Next, he said, "Brutal honesty. What does that mean?"

Nick said he wanted them to be talkative, and he immediately gave them the opportunity to do just that—talk. Somebody piped up and answered. Nick responded: "Thank you, Mr. or Ms. So and So [he memorized all their names]. Can you tell me more?"

The conversations began. *Conversations.* Not question-and-answer sessions designed with an agenda. We let the other side do that. You'll get to hear their answers. We want a general conversation about themes and lives and how they relate to this case. We want to know what troubles people and whether we should have any reason to fear having them on the case. We want to know if they are willing to be part of a team. We want all of them to be acceptable jurors. We show all of them appreciation and love.

Parts of Nick's Style

Let's see if Nick's style is right for you. I don't think many of the jurors were expecting a conversation. I think they were expecting more of a gentle interrogation. Something along these lines:

The lawyer gets up and goes to podium. The lawyer has a list of questions and a list of jurors' names corresponding to the seating chart. She asks questions from the question list to juror one. She cracks a couple jokes, everybody laughs, and the lawyer feels like her voir dire is great. She glances down each time to catch the name of the next juror she will ask a question to. Sometimes she moves in numerical order. Either the lawyer or her colleagues take notes on each juror's answers. The legal team collects information and makes left-brained decisions based on that information.

Some quick, personal observations.

1. **Don't use the podium.** When a lawyer goes to the podium, I groan. It reminds me of church. Someone's about to preach at me. Sorry, Dad. So I check out. Nick never uses the podium.

2. **Memorize potential jurors' names.** To not do so shows a lack of respect to that juror as well as your client. Luckily, Nick does his best to memorize the names of potential jurors.

3. **Move around.** Asking questions of jurors in numerical order is predictable and therefore boring. Asking questions to one, then two, then three, allows number eleven to check out. Luckily, Nick is not predictable, nor are his conversations, which tend to jump around.

4. **Don't take notes.** I'm uncomfortable when people take notes about my answers. It makes me feel like I said the wrong thing. Luckily, Nick doesn't take notes in voir dire.

OK, off my pulpit and back to Nick's style.

When Nick conducts voir dire, the conversation is ongoing. Nick is just a participant, which humanizes him in the eyes of the jury. His objective is to talk as little as possible. The more the jurors talk, the less he talks, and the more information comes out. I've actually seen extended conversations between multiple potential jurors, with Nick not even in the picture. When Nick is in the picture, it is in one of three ways. If he is addressing everyone in the jury box, he tends to stand about six to eight feet away, making general eye contact. When he wants to bring the peanut gallery into the discussion, because we're all in this together, he pulls back geographically and obviously raises his voice. But, when a conversation is one-on-one, Nick moves close, just a couple feet away from the potential juror he is speaking with. He listens and concentrates. All eye contact. He lowers his voice. Nothing in the world is more important that this conversation right now. He shows how he cares about the juror and the conversation, and he's open to the emotional connection if they are. Nick is the proxy for his client. Nick is saying: *I care about you; please care about my client.*

Nick told me once that he imagines a lifeline between him and the potential juror. It is easy to break, but important not to do so while the conversation is ongoing. When the conversation is over, the lifeline continues and the juror is connected with Nick while he talks to other jurors. He transitions gently by thanking them for talking with him. He really means it when he thanks the juror. He even connects with jurors who say things that hurt the case and who don't want to be helpful. Nick does not move on to the next conversation until he has symbolic permission from the juror he is conversing with.

STEVE'S ROLE AS THE THIRTEENTH JUROR

My job in all this is to observe and listen to the ongoing conversations. I also try to read the body language. Watching and listening to a conversation that you are not involved in will yield a lot of information. Try it sometime, mainly because the possibility of interjecting is impossible. Thus, you are not thinking about your own clever contribution while the other person is talking. So I'm all eyes and ears. At the end of each conversation, I do a gut check. Are we connected? Would they care about our client?

My criteria are different depending on the role I see the juror fulfilling. If I perceive the juror as a follower, I don't need to be overly certain about his answers to the two questions above. It's enough that the potential juror appears to be a decent, caring person. However, if I perceive him to be a leader, my gut has to be certain. It's just too risky to allow a leader on the jury that you are not certain of. Leaders have a tendency to become forepersons or quasiforepersons. As an illustration, on the *Wall* case, a potential juror had a forceful personality and responded strongly to questions. I was sure he was a leader and followed his conversations with Nick closely throughout voir dire. My gut told me he was very receptive to our case and would fight for us in the jury room. I presented my opinion to the rest of the legal team. Others were not so sure. In the end, we kept him. I said he would be the foreperson. Turns out, he was elected as the foreperson. Luckily, the outcome was good, or my gut might have been retired to Costa Rica.

My other job is to reverse roles with the jurors during voir dire. I try to figure out where they are coming from and how they perceive Nick's approach. Are our themes resonating? This helps me advise Nick during the breaks about how things are going.

For example, I might say, "I think you need to check back in with juror X. You let her go too soon and she had more to say," or "You missed juror X's point," or "Why don't you ask juror X about . . ." Basically, I'm just another set of eyes and ears in the courtroom, dedicated to the cause. If there's trust, it can't hurt.

Answering Hard Questions

What about the hard, tough questions? The scumbag-lawyers, ambulance-chasers, insurance-rates-go-up, doctors-can't-practice, coffee-in-the-lap, millions-for-nothing, frivolous-lawsuit questions? Well it seems to me that if you really want to try to include everyone on your jury and if you really care about potential jurors, then there are no bad questions, nor bad answers. It's just a conversation.

"I am suing your local hospital for tens of millions of dollars. Does that upset you? I need your brutal honesty," said Nick to each juror.

Sometimes jurors ask questions. Nick is very good at handling tough questions. But to illustrate my point that there are no bad questions or answers, here is a typical exchange.

A potential juror says, "All plaintiffs' lawyers are scumbag ambulance chasers."

Nick's response:

> Well, I know I've met a few scumbag plaintiffs' lawyers in my time. Especially the ones that advertise on TV late at night. Yucky. But would you leave room for the possibility that there are some good plaintiffs' lawyers out there too, trying to help people and who care about justice, who are willing to take on the big corporations and HMOs, the hospitals that cover up mistakes and destroy records, and the doctors who hurt their patients? Would you leave room for that possibility? Would you give me a chance to prove I'm one of those lawyers?

The potential juror will let Nick know with his answer whether he wants to be on the jury. Nick will take this topic of conversation and ask the whole jury to talk about it. He will accept all answers lovingly. If a juror is set against Nick, Nick will smile, look the juror in the eye, and say, "I wish I could change your mind."

But Nick has done so much more with his answer than just find out whether this potential juror would be a good fit. He's tried to connect with a potential juror who probably doesn't like him by stereotype, but who nevertheless might end up on the jury. He's shown vulnerability to the potential juror as well as the entire jury pool. He's classed himself as one of the good guys. Finally, he's planted some of the upcoming trial themes about hospital cover-ups and destroying records in the jury pool's minds, without directly mentioning the case. I believe that you can turn every situation that arises in voir dire to your client's advantage. Whether you can pull it off is a different matter, but the potential is always there.

A good example happened in the *Blunt* case. A gentleman was called from the jury pool as a replacement for a juror who had been dismissed. The judge went through the standard questions and then asked if there was anything the gentleman wanted to say. "Yes, there is," he replied. "I have a problem with Mr. Rowley." He then went on to say that he didn't like anything about Nick and what Nick stood for. I dubbed him the "Nick's a dick" juror. The judge dismissed him for cause before Nick could talk to him, and the day came to an end.

Afterward, Nick asked me, "What was that about?"

I said, "I don't know, maybe it's the Perrier you were drinking and the cowboy boots you were wearing."

The next day, voir dire continued. I believe many lawyers would let the incident pass and hope that the jury pool would forget about it. Instead, Nick looked to turn it to his advantage. The first thing he said the next morning went something like this:

NICK: Well folks, yesterday, a gentleman got up here and said he didn't like anything about me. I was shocked. I've never had that happen before. He hadn't even met me yet. It really hurt my feelings. I feel terrible. I asked a friend of mine why he thought the gentleman didn't like me. He said probably because I was wearing cowboy boots and drinking Perrier.

[The jurors have a good laugh at this point.]

Well folks, I've been wearing cowboy boots since I was a kid growing up in Arizona. And the Perrier.

[Of course at this point, Nick is holding a Perrier bottle, as well as wearing cowboy boots.]

Well, sometimes when I'm standing up and talking in front of jurors, I get nervous, which causes my tummy to get upset.

[He actually said *tummy,* which suggests he's a dad.]

This Perrier water has little bubbles in it that calm my tummy. I hope you don't hold it against me.

[Some *no*s.]

But more importantly, is there anybody here who feels the same way as the gentleman did yesterday, who just . . . doesn't . . . like . . . me?

This time, everyone in the box said, "No, you're fine." With vulnerability comes advantage and bonding.

Our conversation with potential jurors continued over the hours and days of jury selection. Nick slowly worked his way through his conversation topic trip wires.[2] Over time, a sense of each potential juror emerged.

If Nick does his job well, all the potential jurors feel like we want them on this jury, they feel like we care about all of them, and we've established at least some connections with every prospective juror. There may even be prospective jurors that already care about our client.

---

2. For more information about developing trip wires, see chapter 12.

When Nick exhausted all of the conversation topics, he sat down. We gathered round, we went with our gut, and we talked about who we could include on our team of justice.

Two Struggles

At the same time that actual jury selection was taking part on the surface, two struggles were taking place below it. I would argue that the outcome of these two struggles were as important to winning the case as the eventual makeup of the jury.

The first struggle was a competition of sorts. Remember your favorite teachers, and think of three traits they shared. This is what I came up with:

1. They cared about their students and their jobs.

2. They were funny. I laughed a lot in their classrooms.

3. They knew our capabilities as students and taught us accordingly. This is what I would call maximizing our education.

Keep those traits in mind. Now I would like to suggest that the jury box is a classroom. In it sit students of varying backgrounds and abilities. They are new to the class and the subject matter they need to study. Each of the lawyers is a teacher. But here's the twist, one that every student or former student would appreciate: these two teachers are competing for the same job. You want your students to look forward to your presence and your class. If you win this competition at voir dire, and the jurors select you to be their teacher, then your message will be their education throughout the trial.

The second struggle involves selling your case throughout voir dire. Basically, which lawyer is more successful in planting his or her themes in the potential jurors' consciousness? Through your conversations with potential jurors, you introduce your case. Talk about the amount you are asking for right away. Own that number. That way, the amount is old hat by the time trial is under way. Incorporate your trial themes as trip wires. In the *Blunt* case, conversation trip wires included cover-ups, destroying records, bad medical care, bad birthing experiences, brain damage, and cerebral palsy, to name a few. The jury's education begins in voir dire. Win the jurors' hearts in voir dire by emotionally connecting with them. Win their minds in voir dire by educating them on your case themes. See if the jurors are open to being part of the case or are set against it for personal reasons or beliefs.

If all of the above doesn't work for you, then you could always follow our co-counsel Rod Ritner's sole rule for picking a jury: does the juror pass the barbecue test? In Rod's words: "If I would invite a juror to a barbecue at my house, I will probably be OK having them on my jury. If I wouldn't, I don't."

The following bullet points cover some additional ideas I try to live by in voir dire:

- Perceptions often dominate our initial observations. In short, we prejudge or size up people before we meet them or hear them speak. If we observe someone before we meet them, we make snap judgments, both positive and negative. These observations often dominate our initial interactions with that person. For example, we observe a well-dressed young woman walking with a Bible. Most people would feel comfortable developing an opinion about that woman without ever having met her. Same with an attorney holding a Perrier and wearing cowboy boots.

  There isn't much you can do with your jurors' initial perceptions of you, other than dressing well and not shouting at your co-counsel. But as to *my* initial perceptions, I work very hard at dropping my preconceived ideas about any potential juror. I don't want an opinion about jurors until they are seated and interacting with Nick. Then I begin to draw my conclusions. Their opinions often conflict with their appearance. I'm often surprised.

- Always go with your gut. Believe in your gut. It is your instinct screaming. Your gut is your ancestors advising you on how to proceed. Work on trusting your gut and making decisions based on it. This will help your descendants to carry on and prosper. If you've worked hard to keep an open mind and have waited to develop an opinion about a potential juror until after she starts speaking, and your gut is telling you something about that juror, follow the advice.

- Stereotypes are for lazy people. Don't reject or include a potential juror based on your own stereotypes. It is easy to take that shortcut, but you are not doing right by your client. Hear each potential juror out. Look the person in the eye and listen beyond the stereotype. Surprises are in store.

- Observe without judgment. Try to watch and listen to your potential jurors without concluding whether you would personally like or dislike them. Just ask yourself if they would be a good fit for this jury and be open to your client's plight. An asshole can still fight for your client back in the jury room.

- People have a public and a private face. People may have extreme private opinions, but they will temper those private opinions to make acceptable public statements. They will especially do this in an uncomfortable public forum like jury selection. I believe the private face is revealing while the public face is an accommodation. Trying to see the private face behind the public one is a skill I still need much improvement in, but it is a worthy effort.

Finding a Leader

During the short breaks in the jury box, who is the hub of conversation? Who is not quite outspoken, but commands respect and holds his or her head high? Who in the jury seems to be in control of themselves and in control when you are asking questions? Identify leaders by who they are in the community, their positions in life, their careers, and how they interact with the other prospective jurors. Identify leaders, followers, and neutral people. Leaders are more likely to be your foreperson. Interestingly, I've often found the future foreperson to be seated in the geographical center of the jury box. Perhaps that location makes them the hub of conversation by default.

If a potential leader is somebody you don't feel connected with by the end of voir dire, and who you believe might side with the defense, let her go. The trend and energy you feel with a juror, and how she interacts with other jurors, will continue throughout trial and in the jury room. Potential forepersons are often jurors with forceful and assertive personalities, and who get along well with others. We all know when we meet a powerful person, if we listen to and honor her. And if we validate that powerful person, she might in turn want to help and validate us.

Voir Dire Is Like a First Date

To this point, I've spoken about the process of voir dire and how we go about it. But in summing up, I'd like to talk about what voir dire actually is. Some would say voir dire is the process of selecting potential jurors by obtaining information from them through questions and answers. I say voir dire is like a first date, and we should treat it as such.

We all know the difference between a good and bad first date from experience. Anyone going on a first date wants to have a good one, just like any lawyer wants to have a good voir dire. We want to impress our date. We want our date to hear our story while we learn his or hers. We want good conversation and chemistry. We want him or her to like us, to be attracted to us, and to want to see us again.

Voir dire is the same. It should be a conversation that isn't dominated by anyone. You need to make a good impression. You want to get your story and themes across while you learn the jurors' stories. You want them to like you and want to see you again. You want good chemistry.

Now apply a traditional voir dire technique to a first date. First, you keep your date waiting until you are ready to speak with her. Then you talk about yourself and your story for a while. When you're done, you pull out a list of questions and start asking. "What do you think of doctors?" "Have you ever been involved in a medical emergency?" "Do you want to have kids?" "How many?" All the while, you're taking notes on her answers. At the same time, you're thinking, "Wrong answer and she's out of here," or "You're not ideal," or "My stereotype is confirmed." This isn't exactly a recipe for a successful first date. In fact, it's downright rude, on a date or in voir dire.

Some ideas to live by in dating and in voir dire:

- Perceptions often dominate initial observations.

- Dress well for your date or your jurors.

- Try to look beyond their appearance and hear what they are saying.

- Always go with your gut. What does your gut say about the juror or date after you've heard him or her out? Follow that.

- Stereotypes are for lazy people. Don't stereotype your juror or date before all the facts are in.

- Observe without judgment. Watch and listen with an open heart and mind. The time for judgment on a juror date should come after the conversation.

- People have a public and a private face. Apply yourself to examining the private face, for a juror or a date.

Voir dire is a lot more than just an information grab. Voir dire and first dates are both forms of seduction. People have fallen in love on a first date as well as completely lost interest. Similarly, jurors have fallen in love with a lawyer and her client during voir dire, as well as completely lost interest. Hard questions have been asked and answered on first dates and during voir dire, and their answers influence outcomes. Lawyers evaluate potential jurors, and jurors evaluate lawyers in voir dire. The same happens on a first date. The goal is also the same in voir dire and first dates—to get to the more comfortable second date and continue the relationship. In a trial, the second date is the opening statement, which just happens to be the next chapter.

10

OPENING STATEMENT

Nick Rowley and Steve Halteman

NICK'S THOUGHTS: OPENING STATEMENT

This is the time to show the jury that you have the credibility they started to believe in during voir dire. You are calm, not overly emotional. Start out slow, with undisputed facts, then weave in themes of the case, and then expose the frivolous defenses. You are going to be brutally honest with the jury and not oversell your case. You are going to take the main defense themes, address them, and crush them. By the time the defense lawyer gets up, there will be nothing new that he will have to say. His opening will be boring and ineffective. This is your goal, along with firming up your connection and relationship with the jurors that you started in voir dire. By the end of opening statement, your jury will be emotionally invested in the case because it is a case that is important to the community, and important to humanity.

Opening statement is not a time to start out with a sad sobbing story about how bad your client is hurt and damaged.

The jurors don't quite care yet. The jury needs to care about the importance of the case to their community before they care about your client.

By the end of the opening, we want the jury pissed off at the defense for their frivolous defenses. We need to accomplish this before we even begin to talk about our client, injuries, and damages. The jurors need to know that we have been left no choice but to come to court and ask them for their time. We have been left with no fair choice but to ask them to equate pain, suffering, and misery to amounts of money.

The themes of the opening statement must be important to community safety, integrity, and how there has been a gross betrayal in the community. Frivolous defenses have made that gross betrayal even worse.

When you sequence the story, put the defendants' bad conduct right up front and center. Break it down slowly, without embellishment. Present the rules that the defendant broke one by one, explain the purpose of each rule, and explain the consequences of breaking them, consequences that affect the public at large.

Rick Friedman and Pat Malone's book *Rules of the Road* is a must-read for learning exactly how to sequence an opening statement. Rather than plagiarize what Rick and Pat have said much better than I can, I am going to ask that you read *Rules of the Road*[1] and Rick's *Polarizing the Case*,[2] not just because Rick is my friend, but because I have read them both cover to cover many times.

On the subject of damages, David Ball (the messiah of money damages) and his writings lay out a brilliantly sequenced approach to getting comfortable talking to jurors about money in voir dire, opening all the way through to closing.[3] I have read every book that David Ball has put out cover to cover and repeatedly.

---

1. Rick Friedman and Patrick Malone, *Rules of the Road: A Plaintiff Lawyer's Guide to Proving Liability*, 2nd ed. (Portland, OR: Trial Guides, 2010).
2. Rick Friedman, *Polarizing the Case: Exposing and Defeating the Malingering Myth* (Portland, OR: Trial Guides, 2007).
3. David Ball, *David Ball on Damages* 3rd ed. (Portland, OR: Trial Guides, 2012).

I want to give you a feeling. I want you to have fire burning inside of you when you get up in front of the jurors. I want the passion to be something that slowly emanates from you bit by bit through the first half of your opening, with your beating heart and soul exposed by the time you stop, at which point the jury is with you, feeling you, loving your client, and looking at the defense lawyer with skepticism. By the time your enemy gets up to speak, there should be no surprises. You will have said everything he is going to say, shot it down, and shown how ridiculous and misleading the defense case is. There is no better feeling than seeing the insurance defense lawyer get up and have no connection—he is alone in the room, and he feels it. The act begins, but everybody—including the defense lawyer—knows that the defense act is a fraud and further betrayal of the truth.

Betrayal

Betrayal is a powerful theme that you must make a part of every case. Each human in that courtroom has felt the knife of betrayal. Show them the betrayal, bring it into the courtroom, and place it on the defense table. Hold the betrayal in your hands, take it over to the defense table, and tell the jury you want the defense to take it back. You want the defense to own it: to feel it for themselves and make sure it doesn't ever happen again.

I am going to tell you to do something that most other teachers say not to do. This concerns the opening statement and points that the lawyers say are "not evidence." That is something the jurors hear so much. Other teachers say, "Never tell the jury that what you are saying is not evidence." Instead, here is what I want you to do. The first thing you say in opening is this:

> You have heard from the judge, and you will probably hear many times throughout this trial, that nothing I say is evidence. That is true. But that scares me. It makes me fear that some people might think that what I have to say, what my beliefs are in the case, are not important. Please listen to what I have to say and hold me to it. Everything I say will be backed up by the evidence. It is just like when you go back into that

jury room, what goes through your minds and souls during this trial and what you say to each other when you are back there deliberating: *nothing you say to each other, your feelings, nothing that you believe, is evidence.*

But you know what? Your feelings, your voice, your belief in this case are the most important things we have, and at the end of the day, it is all that matters. It is the only thing that can make a difference. So, please listen carefully to what I am going to say during this trial. I promise at the end of the trial, you will see the credibility in what I say and what I believe. It will be backed up by the evidence.

The *Pulp Fiction* Opening

It is *Pulp Fiction* time. The *Pulp Fiction* opening is something that Finlay Boag, Steve Halteman, Courtney Yoder, and I developed and practice. The movie *Pulp Fiction* was a masterpiece, as was *Reservoir Dogs,* because they jump from scene to scene going backward and forward in time. These films keep the observers on their toes.

To illustrate this method, we are going to use a mild traumatic brain injury case as an example. This case resulted in a $7 million verdict/judgment in downtown San Diego. Our client, Steven White, was accused of drag racing and rolling his vehicle after colliding into the vehicle that his friend, whom he was racing, was driving. The offer was close to zero, and then at the time of the trial, the offer was $250,000. Liability was fully disputed.

We started a *Pulp Fiction* opening with a good piece of the defendant's conduct. Don't label it, don't oversell it; just state the facts. For example:

> Now we get to tell you why we are here and why we need your help. On June 8, 2005, the defendant broke the law by driving a vehicle on a highway while he was intoxicated on drugs and alcohol. Here is what happened.

[Show one or two pictures of the vehicles.]

> Here is what happened to Steven.

[Show picture of Steven's brain scan.]

[Stop. Let that sink in.]

> We have litigated this case for three years, more than 1,000 days, and the defense [pointing to the defense] has refused to accept responsibility.
>
> If we were to go back in time to June 8, 2005, we are at the local grocery store in Fallbrook, California. Two young men are standing at the cash register waiting in line; the smell of marijuana and the bloodshot eyes and the slurring speech are obvious to everybody. And, guess what? They have the munchies. They are buying candy. Candy and beer. They have keys to the vehicle in their hands, and after they get through the cash register line, they are going out to get into a half-ton pickup truck, put the keys in the ignition, and go look for somewhere else to keep partying.

[Stop. Let that sink in.]

> Steven White is seventeen years old. He is a hard worker. He has a summer job. He has worked a long day roofing, and he is such a good worker that they trust him to lead the crew at times. He is giving his coworker a ride home.
>
> Because of the choices that the defendant made, and the decision to get intoxicated and drive, and then get even more intoxicated on drugs and alcohol and drive some more, Steven ended up with an injury to his brain when he was ejected from his truck. The defendant left him lying on the pavement and drove off and went to a party and drank more beer and smoked more marijuana.

[Stop. Let that sink in.]

> In order to understand what happened to Steven's brain, let's talk about how the brain works, and how it makes us the human beings that we are.

[I then go on to talk about the brain and make myself a neuron in the brain, the jurors neurons in the brain, and the judge a neuron in the brain, in order to offer a visual demonstration of how the brain works; I show visuals; I spend fifteen to twenty minutes talking about brain anatomy. During this time, I do not talk about Steven's brain.]

* * *

Now let me tell you what happened to Steven's brain.

[I go on to talk about what happened to Steven's brain and the different injuries and the experts and the testing. Then, back to the defendant and his conduct and his lawyers.]

* * *

The defendant refused to help Steven. He left him there on the pavement, bleeding—left him there to die. Drove away. Did not even call 911. The pavement was cold. Steven was lucky to not get run over by another car. The defendant went to a party. There was no way for the police to arrest him for driving under the influence because of the time that had passed by the time they finally caught up with him. His mother and father took him home, but bought him a new vehicle the following week. Then they got their lawyers involved.

[Next, move on the defense case.]

The defense lawyers went out and hired expert witnesses who they had hired many times before to help them defend Steven's case. First, they blamed Steven, and said that the car collision was his fault. Then, they hired experts to say that his brain injury really isn't that bad. Those experts are Dr. Jones, Mr. Smith, and Dr. Harper.[4]

Steven's life since his brain was injured. From the time he left work that day to the time the paramedics picked him up off of the pavement, Steven's brain changed, and it changed forever. His personality is different. He was an outgoing young man, on the water polo team. People describe him as talkative, funny, smart, hardworking. Now, Steven spends most of his time sitting alone in a dark room. He is lonely; he does not like to be around people. He cannot hold a job. He

---

4. These names have been fictionalized.

has become a problem to his family. People with the type of brain injury that he has often end up homeless, living under bridges, or in prison. The frontal lobes of his brain have been injured and the injury is a forever injury.

[Then, talk about money.]

I am going to ask you to sign your name to a verdict for many millions of dollars to represent the fair-trade dollar value of Steven now having to live a brain-injured life. He won't be the father that he would have been; he is a different person now. He is a burden to his family rather than a solid young man who they can depend on. He will be brain-injured forever. The evidence in this case is going to show that the many millions of dollars I will be asking you for is reasonable, and I hope you decide to give more. Let me tell you how it breaks down and what the evidence will show.

[I go through what the defense is going to say and how the evidence will show how that is wrong.]

I end my opening statement by thanking the jury and telling them how important and powerful they are. I tell them I will try to make the trial go quickly to honor and value their time. I invite them to ask questions. I tell them that if anything makes them uncomfortable, to please let us know. I care about the jurors and I show them I care. I do not get angry during opening. I might show some sadness or disappointment, but I keep a very even temperament.

The First Two Witnesses

I make sure to set up the opening so the next two witnesses are very strong. I need witnesses who will allow me to destroy what the defense says in their opening, and cause the jury to distrust the defense lawyer. One lay witness and one expert is the way I like to do it. Do *not* start the case by calling your client. Sometimes starting the case by calling the defendant is a good way to go. Call the defendant and then maybe the cop. Or call the defendant doctor in a med mal case, and then call the best liability expert you have, followed by a lay witness. Basically, have a full day of testimony set up to validate your opening statement and crush the defense opening. Primacy is important, and once the jurors distrust the defense, it is very hard for the defense to turn that around.

Demeanor during Opening Statement

The downloadable content that accompanies this book includes opening statements from various cases where you can see the different ways I have approached openings. When reading transcripts, I want you to imagine in your mind what I am doing. I give every word and sentence I deliver to a specific juror, I make eye contact, I go slow, and I allow silence to fill the courtroom because with that comes feeling. I make sure that the juror receives my message, every piece. Then I slowly transition to another juror. I spend time with the jurors, keep the connection, and foster the relationship.

Maintain eye contact, and feel that umbilical cord between you and each juror during opening. Opening statement has to have cadence, rhythm, a solid delivery of humanness. Do not yell, do not point, and do not raise your voice. Be as soft as you can but still be strong. Again, do *not* oversell any part of your case.

Connecting with Your Client and Using Role Reversal to Improve Opening Statement

It's difficult to connect with our case story while our left analytical brain is hard at work with formal discovery. How often do we want to get into motions to compel and into fits over discovery? Yet how much time do we spend stepping back and examining the human story, rich with feeling and details, to see what the case is really about?

You can never spend too much time in your client's life. To prepare for opening statement, go to your client's home, work, and neighborhood. Take a ride with her. Have her show you her life story with pictures, videos, letters, and whatever she has. Now spend a day with her. Imagine the day of her injury. Go through the day as if you are she. What do you feel being her? Take time and really feel what it is like to be in her skin. Now put scenes into action from her life. Get some friends and colleagues together and re-create scenes from her life—experience the scene from as many roles as you can. Be her husband, daughter, friend, and coworker. Use your creativity to feel and understand.

Have someone play the defendant. Have a talk with the defendant. Ask the defendant hard questions. Become the defendant and see how it feels when someone asks you these questions. Try to go beneath what you imagine the defendant saying on the surface, and get in touch with what really must be going on inside him. If you have been doing your own personal work with your own feelings, you may begin to have a better understanding of what is going on with the defendant or any other person.

Maybe you've seen a therapist in the past, or maybe you're seeing one currently. Whether you feel you have issues to deal with or not, therapy is a good way to learn more about yourself, and, in turn, learn more about your clients, defendants, and witnesses. I highly recommend it, not only for personal growth, but to become a better attorney. If therapy just isn't your thing, at least focus on the questions I posed at the beginning of this book. Look inside yourself. Who are you? Really work on this. Take time exploring your thoughts, beliefs, and fears. Again, this will not only help you grow as a person, but it will help you grow leaps and bounds as a lawyer.

Just reverse roles with that person and imagine being them. It is good to do this with the judge and defense counsel. Using this technique of role reversal with various parties is very valuable.

The First-Person Opening

There are some lawyers who are familiar with what has become known as a "first-person" opening. It is where the lawyer becomes the client in the opening statement and speaks to the jury as the client telling his own story. Personally, I believe this a good way to practice being the client, but use it with caution in the opening statement. You may come off as too emotional too soon. It may appear to be an acting trick to jurors, who are already suspicious of lawyers using emotion to manipulate them. I recommend doing the first-person storytelling as part of preparation, but use it with caution in opening.

They way to properly use first person is *not* to say, "I am Andrew," and then start talking as Andrew. The way I would do this is to stand in one place in front of the jury and say:

NICK: You will hear from Sofia's parents during this trial—

[Take a step to the side or forward and step into Sofia's parents' shoes, and now speak as one of Sofia's parents.]

—and her father, Andrew Blunt, will tell you:

NICK SPEAKING AS ANDREW: I love my daughter. She is badly hurt and severely disabled but she brings so much happiness and love to our home. I really didn't want to have to come here to court, but the defense has left my lawyers and my family no choice. My daughter shouldn't be this way; she deserved a better life than what she has been dealt.[5]

The defense may object, and all you have to do is say, "The evidence will show and Andrew will testify . . ." and continue on with what you were saying.

Another example:

PLAINTIFF'S ATTORNEY: You will hear from Dr. Rothman:

[Step to the side and step into Dr. Rothman's shoes.]

SPEAKING AS DR. ROTHMAN: I am an expert witness. I make well over a million dollars per year testifying for the defense industry. I have made over $17 million doing this job. I make more money testifying than I do helping patients. This is good business for me. I will tell you what I tell most all juries, which is that the medical bills in this case are unreasonable and that there is nothing wrong with Steven.

[Step out of Dr. Rothman's shoes now.]

PLAINTIFF'S ATTORNEY: Dr. Rothman will—ever-so-nicely, and ever-so-professionally—call Andrew, me, and the doctors that treated Steven liars and frauds and cheats. He is a paid testifier.

---

5. *Blunt v. Sierra Vista Medical Center,* case number CV 100071, Superior Court of San Luis Obispo County, San Luis Obispo, CA.

DEFENSE: Objection.

PLAINTIFF'S ATTORNEY: The evidence will show that Dr. Rothman will sing, to the tune of the many millions of dollars he makes as a defense expert.

DEFENSE: Objection.

PLAINTIFF'S ATTORNEY: Dr. Rothman makes millions of dollars calling people who are hurt liars and fakes. The defense has hired him before; they will hire him again. Dr. Rothman is this defense firm's go-to guy when they don't want to pay on a case. You will see that when I cross-examine him. Thank you. The next thing I want to talk to you about is . . .

STEVE'S THOUGHTS: WHAT THE JURY NEEDS IN OPENING

One of my tasks during trial is to help the lawyer or lawyers (there never seems to be just one) be human beings while communicating a human story. Human stories seem to work with jurors. Human stories tend to come from the right brain. I've found that a right-brained human story will work with both right- and left-brained jurors. I've found that a left-brained logical presentation will work with left-brained jurors but leave right-brained jurors cold and sometimes lost. At least, they leave this thirteenth juror lost.

Another observation: many, many attorneys seem to be left-brained, so I often end up being a liaison between left-brained lawyers and right-brained jurors. How? I show up at the last minute and am ignorant. Usually by then, the legal team has the case and roles and witnesses assigned. I show up, ask questions, and make the lawyers explain the complicated medical stuff to me. Let's be honest: I'm not acting when it comes to complicated medical terms—I really *am* ignorant. So I make them explain it to me again and again until I understand it. It helps them. It helps me. And it will help the jury in the not-too-distant future. And maybe, in the process of explaining it, we can also humanize it and upgrade the interest level.

Trial by Humans, for Humans

An aside about legal teams. Two brains are better than one. One brain is insufficient to conduct a medium to large trial. A second brain gives you something to bounce ideas off of and to tell you what you missed or forgot. Three brains are an improvement over two. Four brains are the best of all, especially if there is a distribution of rights and lefts. Five brains are not better than one. With five brains, you have too much input, and efficiency congeals. The process of decision making becomes unwieldy. Each additional brain after five only adds to the confusion. Note: I didn't say lawyers, only *brains*. These should be people you have confidence in; their job titles are secondary.

So the legal team is assembled. They are creating the opening. The team debates story lines and themes. People are stressed. Nick doesn't want to get up and run in the morning. The machine is kicking into gear. There is too much work and not enough time. When I'm working with Nick, time especially seems in short supply because attorneys often call him on to their cases at the last minute. If you asked someone on the legal team what all this activity is, they would probably reply, "We're preparing for trial." I feel that the legal team often forgets about the jury at this point. No one will say, "We're preparing for a jury." Or better yet, "We're preparing for a specific jury." The jury has been picked. Maybe it is a good idea to take a breath and consider what your specific jury wants to hear. What will appeal to them?

Who Is on Your Jury?

To know what will appeal to your jurors, you have to know who is on your jury. Who is sitting in your jury classroom waiting to be educated? Part of determining who is on your jury is figuring out how intelligent they are. Think back to classrooms in high school. Is it me, the goof-off in the back row of average intelligence? Is the future rocket scientist from the front row there? Or is another kid from my high school there? I'll call him Bob. Bob had a severe speech impediment. It was instantly recognizable. It sounded like his mouth was full of saliva when he talked. Bob worked in the same fast-food place for five years after graduating. One day after his shift, he went home and decided he needed more money in his life. So he grabbed a mask and a pistol and returned to his place of employment. The manager looked up from the till and froze at the sight of the masked gunman.

He heard, "This is a stickup. Give me all the money."

The manager replied, "What are you doing, Bob?" Bob's speech impediment was unique.

"Damn it, I'm not Bob and I don't work here."

Bob's life on the run with wealth lasted approximately seven minutes, as the police beat him home. The point I'm trying to make, other than to entertain a bit, is that there will be a wide range of intellectual capability on your jury. How will you appeal to all of them? How do you figure out just how smart your jury is? These are tough questions, and important ones. You need to tailor your presentation to a specific range of intelligence.

Let's take a look at intelligence. Many people judge intelligence by level of education. My experience has been that education is not a good indicator of intelligence. Is IQ? It might be, but that's not something you're likely to find out in voir dire. So how do you measure intelligence? I came across a quote when I was very young. For some reason, it stuck in my head my entire life: "Do not be arrogant because of your knowledge, but confer with the ignorant man as well as the wise." For years, I thought the quote meant don't be stuck up about being smart and only talk with other smart people. Go ahead and talk with the dummies too.

But then something happened in India that made me revise my definition. I was hanging out with a camel herder in the Thar Desert, which is part of Rajasthan. I was following that quote, in a way. I thought that I, with my college education, might learn something from a simple camel herder. I came to find out that the herder spoke five languages and knew everything there was to know about camels. Suddenly, the shoes switched. Now *I* felt ignorant, and *he* was following the quote. Then one day, my camel-herder friend asked me how long it would take him to ride a camel to America.

Who was the smart one? Who was the ignorant one? Who had the right to claim arrogance? In the end, we were both a little of each. And that is true of all of us. No one walks through life brilliant in all bodies of knowledge, nor ignorant in all. There is just too much knowledge in existence today. To be a Renaissance person is impossible. There are so many different kinds of smart: book smart, machine smart, emotionally smart, computer smart, street smart, handyman smart. The list goes on. Even Bob probably has his areas of brilliance.

What does this have to do with your jury? Well, the full range of intelligence and ignorance will be sitting on your jury, shifting between one and the other, depending on the subject at hand. The jurors will have a range of abilities to understand the evidence you provide. At times, some jurors will be sitting in percentages of darkness, while others will be enlightened, like in any classroom. What can you, as their chosen teacher, do about it?

You can do a couple of things. First, prepare. You've had multiple conversations with all your jurors throughout voir dire. Write up a biography on each juror. Include what you know, what you can safely infer, and what your gut tells you about each of them. Try to fathom what will appeal to them and what will put them off. Look for trends among the group. Think about tailoring your themes and messages so that they will have the broadest appeal. In the *Blunt* case, we ended up with twelve jurors and four alternates. Eight of the twelve jurors were women. All four of the alternates were women. My gut told me, after listening to their conversations, that this jury would be receptive to strong emotional messages, that their emotional intelligence was at a high level. It was an emotional case and we focused on that. Comments the jurors made after the verdict indicated that they received our emotional messages well. The case hit them hard, emotionally.

Second, realize that as the jurors' teacher, you have to engage in some classroom management. One of my backgrounds is in teaching. Early on, I realized that no matter what, every class has a hierarchy of abilities—a top half of the class and a bottom half when it came to learning. This is the reality of the educational world. If you direct your efforts at the top half only, you will lose the bottom half. This is a recipe for chaos in the classroom for a teacher, and a disaster for a plaintiff's lawyer who needs nine out of twelve in California, or more in some jurisdictions. If you direct your teaching efforts at the bottom half, you will slow down and sometimes bore the top half, but at least you will bring everyone along. For those of you who say direct your efforts at both halves at the same time, I reply, you're a better teacher than me. My suggestion is to adjust the complexity of your message to the bottom half of your jury classroom. In a med mal case, this means making the medical testimony comprehensible to *everyone* sitting on the jury and in your classroom. Otherwise, the informed half will hold the balance of power back in the jury room, which might or might not be a good thing. Likewise, will the uninformed half simply go along with the informed half, or will they dig in their heels with resentment at the imbalance and be contrary on principle? I propose that it is safer for all jurors to be informed when reaching their decision.

We're Ready to Start

The opening statement is the movie finally starting after a long wait of previews and announcements. There is a relief. Everyone is ready and excited to get going. The jury is fresh. There is good atmosphere in the courtroom. The jury is familiar with you from voir dire. They like you. Hopefully, they've chosen you to be their teacher. (If they haven't, here is your chance to win them back.) Their note pads are out. They are ready to learn. They want to see the big picture, but they also want to be entertained. They want some Hollywood.

While on a break during Nick's opening statements in the *Blunt* trial, I was going over my notes. The person sitting next to me, who had been watching the opening, made a call. "You've got to get down here. It's just like the movies." Kudos to the lawyers.

Don't disappoint them. Justify their having selected you as their teacher. How do you do that?

Be Ready

First, be ready. Don't underprepare—or worse, overprepare. You're the best judge of when you have done either. Nick is horrible when he overprepares, but he is rarely in danger of that. Have your trip wires down and be ready.⁶ No notes, no podiums, no reading. For example, the second half of the *Blunt* opening took up forty-nine pages of trial transcripts. The trip wires, which are basically a boiled-down outline of the subjects to cover, would look something like this:

- Decelerations and accelerations
- Dr. Haupt's arrival
- Delivery
- Alternatives to delivery
- Baby delivered looking dead/Apgar scores
- NICU team
- Cord blood gas test
- Gunk in lungs/respiratory therapists/code white
- Respiratory failure
- Hospital cover-up

Usually the trip wires are in chronological order for flow purposes. They are written out in big letters on a sheet of paper. The sheet of paper sits on counsel's table within Nick's view. As he moves about the courtroom, he will pass by the table and catch the next trip wire. If things go according to plan, the trip wire will activate the information associated with it. Nick will then pass that information on to the jurors in a coherent and entertaining manner. At least that's the plan. I see trip wires as the next step below memorization, without the tedious appearance of an eyes-staring-upward memorized speech, but with the advantage of a lawyer so well acquainted with the topic that notes are unneeded.

---

6. See more about developing trip wires in chapter 12.

Tell a Good Story

Second, be ready to tell a hell of a good story, starting out slow and with much credibility, reeling everybody in, one by one if you have to. It should be the kind of story your grandpop told you, or at least should have told you. Expose the jurors to your message and themes without them being aware of it, because the story is just so damned good. This should work like product placement in a good movie. Keep the story moving along. Don't let it die in parts. Use unpredictability and even some soft humor (if you're funny naturally). Nick talked about the *Pulp Fiction* opening. Unpredictability is how I characterize that. Telling the story in chronological order puts people to sleep. Jump back and forth in time and set scenes if you can. Bring life to the courtroom.

Use Breaks to Your Advantage

Third, be aware of breaks and use them to your advantage. Around a break time, bring your story to a dramatic point, then suggest to the judge that now would be a good time for a break. The judge will go with your flow, especially if she is enjoying the show. And it gives the jurors something to ponder as they down their coffee. When you come back, reaffirm what you told them before the break, then keep going.

Draw In Your Audience

Fourth, start the opening with something that draws in your audience. Prepare and rehearse what you are going to say to start it off. Nick often opens with something along these lines:

> Now I really get to talk to you! [Pause.] I'm excited. We finally get to tell people what really happened. The Robertson family has waited three years, more than a thousand days, to have their story heard by members of your community.

This hints at secrets to be revealed, that Nick has been held back by unseen forces so far, but now the justice is about to start and the jurors get to be part of it.

Use Props and Audiovisuals

Fifth, please prepare to use props and audiovisuals. Nobody can be interesting for two hours straight if they're just talking. In this age of ever-shortening attention spans, you need to spice it up. Don't make the jurors listen too much—let them see some things that will stick. Maintain their attention.

Remember the pure joy back in high school when you heard this: "OK, class, today I'm showing a movie"? The subject matter was irrelevant. The change in routine was what captured our attention. Our AV guy, Pat Logan, is a genius. He creates pictures of Nick's words and themes, what he calls magnets for the jurors' attention. Visuals linger in jurors' minds, and, when you combine them with words and themes planted at the right time, they can stick and grow deep roots.[7]

Argue Your Case

Sixth, argue your case as much as the judge will allow you to. It shows the jury passion for your client and the righteousness of your cause.

Own the Dollar Amount

Seventh, own the dollar amount you are asking for. Don't hide from it. Believe in it, or your jurors won't. Of course we're asking for that amount; who wouldn't? You've brought it up in voir dire, hopefully—or at least the concept—and ensured that jurors are not prejudiced against large jury verdicts for pain and suffering. It's old hat now. Bring it up again. Be up front and honest with the jurors about what you are asking for so it is not a big surprise in the end.

Steal the Defense's Case

Eighth, steal the defense's case from them, as well as their attack on yours. Lay out the brilliance of opposition counsel. Talk about

---

7. For more information about audio and visual presentations, see William Bailey and Robert Bailey, *Show the Story: The Power of Visual Advocacy* (Portland, OR: Trial Guides, 2011).

his or her incredible skill and ability to distort facts and obscure the truth. Explain what their experts will say and lie about. And explain why they will lie. Then teach your jurors how to expose the lies and how to avoid being conned by the trickery of opposing counsel. If you are very successful at this, the defense will bypass their own story line and spend their opening trying to refute yours.

Don't Speed Up the End

Ninth, don't speed up at the end when you are running out of time and still have a lot to say. By the end, the jurors are tired. By speeding up, you reduce the jurors' comprehension by trying to jam a multitude of ideas into their brains in a short period of time. What is more important: what you feel you need to say, or what the jurors will remember? Why not pick out the most important thing you have to say at the end and say it *slowly?* This makes it dramatic and more memorable, and you appear organized.

So, as the thirteenth juror, I ask you to please plan to do all of the above—not only so that I am interested and entertained, but also because at the end of your opening, I want to feel, "Let's just give the money to their client now and be done with it. They obviously deserve it."

11

Bring Life to the Courtroom

Nick Rowley

First, bringing life to the courtroom begins outside of the courtroom and long before trial. It may seem like this book should move on, chronologically, to either the defense's opening statement or to calling our first direct witness. However, let's take a step back to the scene where your case first began.

Let the Scene Tell the Story

You want the scene of the tragedy to be vivid in the jurors' minds. The chances of the judge allowing the jury to visit the scene are slim to none, so you will need to re-create the scene for them, in the courtroom. To do this, you first need to go to the scene of the tragedy as you prepare your case. If it is a hospital room, walk into the hospital, sit where the patients are, and sit where the families wait. Eat the hospital food in the cafeteria. Take in the smell of it all. See how the doctors walk on by and the power that they have. See the difference between the doctors (the decision makers), nurses, account managers, and patients, waiting with their loyalty, hope, and submission to the people with power whom they have to trust, because their HMO gives them no choice.

Go to the admissions department, which is the gate to getting in as a patient. See where the patients are shaken down for their money and insurance cards before they are allowed to get care, or are otherwise turned away if their insurance is not good enough or nonexistent. Feel what your client felt. Was it rejection? Embarrassment? Fear?

You have the power to convey these scenes—these sights, sounds, feelings, experiences, and emotions—to the jury through voir dire, opening statements, closing arguments, and witness examinations. The only way you can truly know the scene is to go there. Maybe more than once. Become as familiar with the scene as your client or the witnesses.

WALL V. MIRAMONTES[1]

The *Wall v. Miramontes* case involved a penis injury from a motorcycle versus van accident. In this case, the defense offered zero and disputed liability. The plaintiff, Matthew Wall, was serving active duty in the navy. He was a twenty-four-year-old kid and he drove a motorcycle. He had everything in life going for him, and he was going to use the G.I. Bill to go to school to be an engineer. His past medical bills were only $51,000, and the defense offered nothing, claiming that Matthew was completely recovered from his injuries and was also at fault for causing the collision because he drove fifteen miles per hour over the speed limit around a blind curve and drove directly into a car dealership's shuttle van.

Because this was a vehicle collision, we needed to develop our story by actually going to the scene and spending some time there. We turned off our cell phones. We imagined that we were

---

1. *Wall v. Miramontes,* case number 37-2009-00068436-CU-PA-EC, Superior Court of the State of California, County of San Diego, East County Division.

there at the intersection, that we were driving the defendant's shuttle van, and that we were riding the motorcycle. We had to put ourselves in the roles of everybody involved in order to feel and understand what happened and find the truth.

What is your message? What did you see the day that Matthew got hurt? If you were a bird perched up on a telephone pole, and you were looking down at everything that happened, what would you have seen? What would you have heard? What emotions would have gone through you as you watched this collision occur?

We went to the scene with Matthew and relived the collision by going over it second by second, from the point of starting the drive around the curve to the point that the ambulance took Matthew away. Doing this, it became obvious to us that Mr. Miramontes (the van driver) was not paying attention, and that there was no way that Matthew negligently caused the collision.

In depositions and in trial, we could then re-create the scene by modeling the vehicles, establishing a point of impact, and bringing everything to life rather than simply asking confusing questions. Use the courtroom and establish in the beginning where north, south, east, and west are. Establish a place in the courtroom in front of the jury as the point of impact. The point of impact should have the defendant's vehicle coming directly at or from behind the jury so the jurors are able to understand and experience the truth of what happened.

By doing this, we made it tough for defense witnesses to lie. Defense witnesses will lie if they can get away with it. In cross-examining Mr. Miramontes, we brought him down off of the stand and had him show us how he looked before he pulled out into traffic. In reliving and reenacting what he did, he said he looked "left, right, and then pulled out." He did not look left again. He admitted he was looking to the right when he pulled out and that Mr. Wall was coming from the left. We all know the rule: when we make a left turn, we should look left-right-left. Mr. Miramontes showed the truth of his negligence when we put him in the position of driving the van in the courtroom. There was nothing his attorneys could do to stop the truth from coming out.

Tell the Story with Medical Records

With regard to medical records, we want to hear the voice of the author of the record speaking to us. Give the medical record a voice; get the witness you are cross-examining to acknowledge that this is the voice of the doctor or nurse speaking to us, telling us what was going on at the medical clinic or in the surgery room at 4:15 a.m. on April 19, 2009.

Diagnostic tests have a voice and life to them. If it is an MRI, it is the machine telling us what it does, how it finds things that are abnormal in the body, and what it finds.

Here are some examples of how to do this in deposition and even in court.

The Story from an MRI Machine

Q: An MRI machine tells us things about what it sees inside a person's body, true?

[Every expert will agree.]

Q: If we put a voice to this MRI machine and you were that voice, tell us what an MRI machine does.

A: It takes pictures of things inside the body that we cannot see on the outside.

Q: Doctor, we have this MRI scan you have reviewed of Sofia's brain. What does this MRI scan tell us it found? Does it tell us whether there is any blood in her brain from trauma?

A: Yes, it does tell us that.

Q: What else does it tell us? Does it tell us if her brain is alive or dead? It does not, does it? The MRI machine and its films that you have shown the jury do not tell us if Sofia's brain is alive or dead, does it?

A: We know she was alive!

Q: My question is a little different, sir. *If* she had stopped breathing and her heart had stopped beating—the MRI machine films you have shown the jury do not tell us whether Sofia's heart is beating, true?

A: That is true. The MRI does not tell us whether the heart is beating.

Q: So, looking at the film now, years after it was taken, by only looking at the MRI picture, we cannot know whether or not the heart was beating. We have to look at other records, true?

A: Yes, that is true.

Q: The MRI only gives us one picture in time, true?

A: True.

Q: The same goes [for] breathing, true?

A: True.

Q: And if we were [to] ask the MRI machine or its operator why these pictures do not tell us what the breathing or heartbeat of the baby is, we would be told that the pictures do not tell us that, correct?

A: Correct.

The Story from a Fetal Heart Monitor

If you are discussing a fetal heart-monitor tracing, it is the baby inside the mother telling us how she is feeling and whether she is OK or in danger. If you are examining a witness, you are speaking with a human being who has a human story.

Q: This fetal heart monitor—this is the way that baby Sofia is speaking to us with her heart while she is inside her mother's tummy?

A: Yes.

Q: Sofia's little heart communicates to us through this monitor, true?

A: True.

Q: She tells us through her heartbeat whether she is tolerating the labor or not and if she is in danger, true?

A: True.

Q: See this portion of the fetal monitoring strip at 6:00 a.m. to 6:15 a.m.? We are being told, if we were there paying attention to this heart tracing, that Sofia's heartbeat is dropping for 70 seconds by 90 beats per minute, true?

A: True.

Q: We are being told that Sofia might be in serious danger, true?

A: True.

Q: We are being told by Sofia's heartbeat that every time there is a contraction, the flow of oxygenated blood to her brain is being cut off, true?

A: True.

Q: There is still time to save Sofia right now, at this time at 6:05 a.m., if we listen to what the machine is telling us, true?

A: Yes.

Q: For the next twenty-three minutes, what do the doctor and nurse do to get Sofia out and save her? They do *nothing*. They don't do a Cesarean, no episiotomy, no change in anything—they just sat and waited and told Mom to keep pushing. They do *nothing* different than that, isn't that true?

A: True.

Q: But all along, we are being told by Sofia's heartbeat, through the machine, that she is in danger—her heartbeat is dropping with every contraction—isn't that true?

A: That is true.

Q: And the machine tells us that this is happening for more than thirty-five minutes, isn't that true?

A: That is true.

Q: Each time it happens, Sofia's brain is being deprived of oxygen?

A: True.

Q: And the machine tells us that when the contraction is over, her heartbeat shoots up to tachycardia, true?

A: True.

Q: That tachycardia is because her heart is trying to pump faster, true?

A: True.

Q: And it pumps faster to get more blood circulating to make up for the time when the heartbeat had dropped?

A: Correct.

Q: And to make up for the oxygen that was deprived?

A: Yes.

Q: And in between the contractions, the monitor tells us she had textbook fetal tachycardia, isn't that true?

A: That is true.

Q: Fetal tachycardia followed by abrupt drops in her heartbeat and loss of her heartbeat for over thirty-five minutes, isn't that true?

A: That is true.

Q: And during these thirty-five minutes, the doctors and nurses did nothing other than massage her mother's vagina and push drugs into Mom's body to force Sofia out, isn't that true?

A: Well, they got the infant warmer ready, Dr. Haupt was coaching Mom through labor . . .

Q: Other than massage Sofia's mother's vagina for the thirty-five minutes of that fetal monitor record that we went over, you watched the video, you didn't see Dr. Haupt do anything other than massage Mom's vagina for that thirty-five minutes, did you?

A: I didn't see anything else; that is true.

The Story from a Blood Test

In Tom Valens's case, the cells in Tom's blood told the story of the levels of oxygen, acidosis, or iron. The test speaks to us and tells us what it finds inside the blood.

Q: When the blood is tested, does it tell us something about what is going on inside Tom's body?

A: Yes, the blood is telling us it is filled with iron and that it is becoming toxic.

Q: So the blood test told this to the doctors?

A: Yes.

Q: What did the doctors do? They did nothing in response to what this blood test told them. They did nothing, did they?

A: The patient did not return for a follow-up visit.

Q: There was no follow-up visit scheduled, was there?

A: That is true.

Q: Did the doctors at least tell Tom what the blood tests told them so Tom could protect himself? Did the doctors call him, send him something in the mail, tell him what the blood test had told them?

A: No.

Q: So for two years after, the blood tests told the doctors there was a dangerous amount of iron building up in Tom's blood, and the only people who were told by the blood test chose not to tell Tom?

A: I don't think they chose not to tell him.

Q: Oh, they just forgot, overlooked it?

A: Yes.

Q: Are you telling us that the doctors didn't read the laboratory test results, or that they heard what the lab tests said and chose not to say anything? Do you even know what happened?

A: No. I don't know.

Q: You agree that Tom had a right to be told about those lab test results, don't you?

A: Yes.

Q: And now Tom has a hand that is like a claw because of the oxidative damage to his joints and soft tissues?

A: I don't know.

Q: You said his injuries were just soft-tissue injuries in the workers' compensation case, true?

A: Yes.

Q: As it turned out, you were right; his soft tissues were damaged and they kept getting damaged for another two years because of the metal building up in his blood cells and all the tissues in his body.

A: I don't know about that.

Q: You don't know about that because you didn't look at the records until just now, and you might completely change your opinion if you had an opportunity to sit down and listen to Tom and look at the iron accumulation in his blood for over two years. You would like that opportunity, wouldn't you, sir?

A: Yes.

Q: If lab tests told you what the lab tests told Tom's doctors, whom you are here defending, you would have let Tom know, wouldn't you?

A: Yes, I would have let him know.

• • •

The basic point is that we need to bring life and energy into the courtroom with each piece of evidence and each witness. The courtroom is the stage to bring the chapters of the story to life. Make it human.

Witness Examinations

Steve Halteman

I'd like to start out with a plea for simplicity.

I once met a man near the borders of Sudan, Kenya, and Ethiopia. On his left wrist, he wore a knife bracelet. It's easy to imagine: the outer edge was sharp, and it had a leather protective covering. On his right wrist hung a piece of wood shaped like a capital *I*. The bottom and top of the *I* were flat. It measured about eight by eight inches. A leather strap attached the *I* to his wrist. He had a stick wedged behind his ear. On his back, he carried a bow and arrow. Around his waist was a gourd. That was it. Nothing else. No clothes, nothing. Over the course of our conversation, he explained his life approach and accessories. The conversation took some time, as we had no language in common, but here was the gist of it.

The bow, arrow, and knife were for food and self-defense. The *I*-shaped wood was for comfort—a chair in the day, a pillow at night. The gourd carried water. The stick was his toothbrush. People use a branch from a certain tree throughout central Africa as a toothbrush. You basically rub the end up and down your teeth. That was the sum total of his possessions. With these things, plus his brain and body, he was ready for come-what-may in his corner of the world. I went crazy trying to think of something that he wouldn't be ready for. Dinner, nightfall, getting lost, sex, traveling. There wasn't anything he wasn't prepared for. It blew my mind. By keeping his life so simple, he had actually increased his efficiency and possibilities into infinity. I shuddered to think at what I would need to haul around to match his capabilities.

In Japan, I ran across this once more. Many Japanese houses have one room with nothing in it. Just tatami mat floors and four walls. Some would say the room has no function. I disagree. The room's possibilities are endless. It has perfect efficiency. By being simple, there is nothing the room cannot be. Bring in futons, and it is a guest room. A table, and it is a dining room. Bring in a desk, and it is a study.

Simplifying Testimony

I think these illustrations apply to a trial. Who are the most important people in the courtroom on any given day? Who knows the least about what is going on on any given day? The jury.

Nobody likes to feel stupid, including jurors. On many days of medical testimony in the *Blunt* case, I did feel stupid. Perhaps some of the other jurors did also. The more you simplify the testimony, the more you clarify it, the easier it becomes to understand. The easier it is to understand, the more the jurors digest it. And as I understand it, testimony is a trial lawyer's method of getting his or her message and version of the case to the jurors. The more the jurors—especially the bottom half of the class—digest your versions of events, the more they buy into your message. And that is how you win. By simplifying your message, you maximize the impact.

How do you simplify testimony? With lay witnesses, this is generally not an issue. They have a story to tell, and in the course of conversation, the story will come out. *People* magazine doesn't need clarification or footnotes; neither should a lay witness.

Three Reasons Jurors Can't Follow Expert Testimony

Expert testimony is a far different piñata. Why is that? Experts are still humans. They have a story to tell. A conversation needs to take place between you and the expert. Yet so much expert testimony is lost on the jurors. Why? For three reasons, as far as I can tell, or three things to blame, better yet.

1. The Experts

The first reason is the experts themselves. No one has ever accused me of being an expert about anything, so I haven't walked miles in those shoes. But I suspect being called an expert is a bit of a burden, especially in a courtroom. It creates an expectation among those who hear it. It also creates a suspicion. How do people prove they are experts? Looking at a person, it is impossible for a juror to say, "Hey, that person is an OB-GYN expert." Likewise, the juror will never see the OB-GYN in action delivering a difficult baby. So the jury will never see the expert demonstrate his expertise. What is left? Both the jurors and expert only have words. The experts say them; the jurors hear them. "I went to every school on the East Coast, I held many positions, and here is what happened in this case."

All of that is fine except when it comes to the last part. So often, the words the expert uses to explain what happened in the case also have a dual purpose. The expert wants to establish himself as an expert in the jurors' eyes, ears, and brains.

> Look, I'm using big, specialized, technical words to explain complicated situations. I am not using them because I am insecure. I am using them because I am an expert in this area. These big words justify me being paid $750 an hour to be here. Respect me, hear me, and rely on my words as the truth.

To simplify every term of art so that the jury comprehends what the experts are saying, I suspect most experts believe, would remove the veneer of their expertness. "If I just talk like everybody else, the jurors won't pay attention." Exactly the opposite. The jurors would be educated at their own level of comprehension, which is how learning takes place. It's your job as a lawyer to convince experts of this, as well as hold them to it. Why don't many lawyers do this?

2. The Lawyers

The second reason expert testimony is lost on jurors is lawyers. Lawyers are also humans, contrary to popular opinion, and are subject to the same vanities as everybody else. They prepare extensively for trial. For example, take a med mal case. A plaintiff's lawyer has put in hours learning the relevant medical material. They know they need to, especially when going head-to-head with the defense expert. And this is where vanity creeps in. The defense expert thinks the plaintiff's lawyer doesn't really know medicine. The defense expert thinks that the plaintiff's lawyer just learned enough to ask questions, exploit weaknesses, and pull one over on the jurors. So the defense expert tests the plaintiff's lawyer's knowledge. It quickly degenerates into a pissing match between the plaintiff's lawyer and the defense expert about who knows what. Who gets forgotten? The jurors. And it's not just in a test of wills. Throughout conversations with both sides' experts, lawyers on both sides throw around the big words. Whether it's to impress the experts, the jurors, or just show that they've done their homework, the result is the same: the jurors have a harder time comprehending the testimony.

Why not try a different strategy? Remember who the most important people in the courtroom are. Remember they *want* to understand. Remember you are their teacher, and you are responsible for their education. The experts are invited guests in your classroom; they're there to enlighten your students and you. Ask questions at your students' level, not at the invited guests' level. Your experts will get the hang of it quickly, because you're paying them. The defense experts will get progressively more annoyed if you turn them into educators. For example, use these phrases:

- "What do you mean by that?"
- "Can you explain that word?"
- "Are you saying . . . ?"
- "Did everyone on the jury get that?"

When experts get annoyed, they make mistakes, which is what you are waiting in ambush for. Try it out. You are not there to score points for or against expert witnesses. You are there to educate your jurors in a way that benefits your client.

3. The Words

The third reason expert testimony is lost on the jurors are the words themselves, which I have hinted at above. Take an example from the *Blunt* case. Pretty early on, Nick and one of our experts started talking about "occlusion of the cord." They went back and forth for a while on it, and then moved on to another topic. As the thirteenth juror, I was trying to figure out what they were talking about. Cord. Right away, I knew they were referring to the umbilical cord. But *occlusion*? No clue. The closest word I could think of was *exclude*. That didn't help. (My guess is that 80 percent of Americans don't know what *occlusion* means.)

OK, forget *occlusion*, what does the umbilical cord do? I'm a dad; I should know this. It brings food to the baby, obviously, because it connects to the baby's stomach. Does it bring oxygen too? I don't think so, because the lungs aren't near the stomach. But a baby has to breathe, and it can't breathe through its mouth because it's floating around in a bunch of juice. I wonder why the baby doesn't have another cord going to its mouth? Hell, I could design a better system. Do babies poop when they are in there? I gotta look this stuff up on the Internet when I get back to the hotel.

While this internal monologue was going on, I was missing everything about the ongoing testimony. So I didn't understand parts, and I missed other parts. Both would be cured by simplifying. Nick clarified what "occlusion of the cord" means after I pointed out during a break that I didn't understand what he was talking about:

Expert: . . . and the occlusion of the cord occurred . . .

Nick: Hold on, Doctor, help us out. What is "occlusion of the cord"?

A: Well, cord is the umbilical cord.

Q: Right, what does it do?

A: The umbilical cord brings oxygen and protein that the baby needs from its mother to survive.

Q: OK, got it. Now what about *occlusion?*

A: *Occlusion* means blocked. So something inside or outside the cord is blocking the passage of nutrients and oxygen.

Q: OK, got it. From now on, can we just say *blockage* instead of *occlusion* so it's clear to me?

A: Sure.

Q: Thanks. Let's talk about how the cord got blocked.

There are benefits to this approach. Nick shows vulnerability by in effect saying, "Teach me." The jurors are thinking, "Cool, he took one for the class, 'cause I didn't know what that *occlusion* thing meant either. I don't feel so dumb." And it sets up the defense expert, who looks like an ass when he insists on using *occlusion* instead of *blockage* because it is the proper medical term. But if the expert does consent to using *blockage* after you point it out for him, then it's a point for you. If you're still keeping score.

How do you determine what words you need to simplify so that they are not lost on the jurors? Have a nonlawyer friend take a look at a list of medical terms you expect to come up at trial. If she wants to see an explanation in parentheses after the term, then it is a strong hint that you should simplify the term and that your expert needs to clarify it to the jury. For example:

> Sofia suffered hypoxic brain damage interpartum (the oxygen to Sofia's brain was cut off while she was still inside her mom, and that caused brain damage).

Or, if you want to try something new and completely different, just use the words inside the parentheses to begin with. Drop the medical term altogether. The simplified version takes longer to say, but it more effectively communicates your message, which saves time in the end. A confession: I must have heard *acidosis* fifty times in the *Blunt* trial. I'm still not exactly sure what it is. Was I alone?

More Notes on Expert Witnesses

I have a few more things to say about expert witnesses.

First, it is prudent to ask potential experts how other lawyers have successfully attacked their credibility in the past. Maybe even do a little research on your own. Surprises during trial are rarely pleasant. For example, we once had an expert witness in a trial who had not been completely truthful about the rank he achieved in the military, his college major, and the existence of his middle name. Because these discrepancies came to light during cross-examination, the jurors didn't have a good impression of his substantive testimony, and they may even have ignored it.

Second, acknowledge (if this is the case) that you've worked with your expert before, eaten together, talked about the case, and paid her, and that you'll use her again. Steal the defense's thunder. Jurors aren't shocked at working relationships, so why shouldn't you tell them about it?

Third, try to alternate your expert and lay witness. One expert after another tends to grind down the comprehension level of even the most enthusiastic juror. Use the human angle as relief.

Lay Witnesses

Now I'd like to talk about lay witnesses. Lay witnesses, or *normal people* as they are otherwise known, are usually my responsibility in a trial. I hope I never have to move up to expert witnesses. By the time we call lay witnesses to testify, we should be well acquainted, perhaps even friends. Nick and I have laid out their trip wires, boiled down from their story lines. I go over the trip wires with them a day or two before their testimony, emphasizing what is important. I avoid overpreparing them or asking them to memorize answers. When we're planning on a conversation based on trip wires, memorization is impractical anyway. Our idea is to have a natural conversation. Few things in trial are as irritating as overly coached witnesses and obviously staged events.

If time permits, we'll work on ways the defense might attack their credibility and their responses. Then on the day of their testimony, Nick runs through their trip wires with them and I have my final chat. We go someplace quiet. They are nervous about the big day. And I say:

> Just be yourself. That's all you have to do, *unless* it violates one of the six golden rules:
>
> 1. No hostility toward either side.
> 2. Don't talk too much.
> 3. Be truthful. That way, you can't screw up.
> 4. Testifying will be three times as emotional as you think it will be. Just don't cry too much.
> 5. Be humble.
> 6. Look at the jurors as much as possible when answering. They are the ones you are really talking to.

It seems to have worked so far.

Implanting Witness Themes

Then Nick gets up and has a conversation with the lay witnesses. The goal is that our theme for the witness is implanted in the jurors' minds.

Take Sofia's dad, Andrew. Our one-sentence theme for him was basically:

> Iraq War veteran, married, has first child at local hospital, where both doctor and hospital screwed up, leaving dad holding the bag.

Here is the theme in action, broken down by trip wires and goals, followed by its corresponding testimony in the *Blunt* trial.

First Trip Wire: Iraq War Veteran

The goal of this trip wire was to establish that Sofia's dad (Andrew) saw combat, was cool under fire, and would not panic when he saw the blood of someone close to him. We wanted to show that Andrew did not fall apart when his daughter came out looking dead, but was, in fact, a calm observer of the attempts to get Sofia breathing. Thus, when Andrew said he didn't see any gunk or goo pulled out of his daughter's airway, the jurors would trust him.

This testimony is Nick questioning Andrew.

Q: Now, did you serve our country?

A: I did.

Q: In the military. What branch?

A: I was a marine.

Q: Where?

A: Here in California.

Q: Did you also serve us in Iraq?

A: I did.

Q: And in Iraq, did you learn how to resuscitate?

A: We were all trained on basic CPR triage.

Q: Were you taught how to use a bag, and bag a patient?

A: Yes.

Q: Were you taught how to put in an airway?

A: Yes.

Q: And do CPR?

A: Yes, I've seen quite a few patients.

Q: And were you also taught to suction?

A: Yes.

Q: And did you see—were you able to ever see soldiers who had so much fluid or stuff—

Mr. Bertling, defense attorney: Objection; relevance.

The court: Overruled.

Nick: Were you able to see situations with soldiers where medics were trying to get air into soldiers to help them breathe, but where there was liquid or secretions coming out that made it hard for them?

Andrew: I've seen quite a few people wounded. I've seen a lot of clogged, and I've seen a lot of kids trying to—trying to get breath in them.

Q: You saw some of the casualties in Iraq as well?

A: Sure.

Q: Not just the people from our side, but the unfortunate casualties on the other side?

A: I'd say more so, more civilians. More—

Q: Did you participate in helping with the civilians in Iraq as well?

A: Of course.

Q: The children?

Mr. Bertling: Objection, Your Honor. Relevance.

The court: Sustained.

Nick: When Sofia was born, were you able to stand there and watch—

Andrew: Yes.

Q: —them resuscitating her?

A: Yes. I didn't leave her side.

Q: Can you—I'd like it if you could come down off the stand and show me, if Jennifer is giving birth, and if she's back here, and Dr. Haupt is here and caught, took the baby, took Sofia, where does Dr. Haupt, what does he do with the baby?

A: He—

Q: He hands her to a nurse?

A: He hands her to where I am [indicating], and she was just—

Q: Tell the jury, what do you see when Sofia comes out? What do you see?

THE COURT: Hold on.

MR. HIEATT, DEFENSE ATTORNEY: We can do all that from the stand.

THE COURT: I think so, Mr. Rowley.

NICK: We're going somewhere next, as to the scene.

THE COURT: OK, but I want this limited questioning right here about the placement, all right? Overruled.

NICK: When Sofia comes out, are you standing?

ANDREW: Yes.

Q: And what do you see?

A: Just saw a dead baby.

Q: And he asked you to cut the cord?

A: He did.

Q: Where does Sofia go next?

A: To a nurse.

Q: Where in the room?

A: Um, here. [Indicating]

Q: Go model where that area would be if Mom is here. [Indicating]

A: She took her, and there was an incubator.

Q: So if we were to turn the incubator and have it facing this way [indicating], where would you be standing when Sofia was being resuscitated?

A: If the incubator was sitting here, I was here. [Indicating]

Q: And you are able to see Sofia?

A: Yes.

Q: How many people are there at first?

A: Just a semicircle. Maybe—I don't know, three.

Q: Were you able to keep your eyes on Sofia the whole time?

A: I was. I watched her the whole time. I was surprised that I couldn't hear her ribs breaking from the chest compressions.

Q: At any point, from the time she came out to the time she goes over to the incubator, do you ever hear her cry?

A: No, she didn't. She didn't cry. She didn't move. She—when they took her out, she looked the same as when she was born.

THE COURT: Mr. Rowley.

NICK: I agree that we agreed this is limited.

Sofia is here. And if you can go back to the stand. And you're watching over the shoulders?

ANDREW: Yes.

Q: Are you panicking? Are you making noise?

A: No.

Q: Screaming?

A: No, I was—I just stood there.

Q: You had been taught to be cool when you need to be cool?

A: There wasn't—you know, I figured they knew what they were doing. There was no need for me to—I mean, I wasn't going to freak out or anything.[1]

Second Trip Wire: Married

The goal of this trip wire was to establish that Andrew is a normal, everyday guy who has stayed with his wife through this difficult time.

This testimony is again Nick questioning Andrew.

Q: Do you plan to be a part of this community for a long time?

A: I do. And I'm—I don't want to be here at all, and I think that, you know, during the jury deliberations, we saw how people—

MR. BERTLING: Objection, Your Honor. Move to strike?

THE COURT: I think I would strike that last comment, but—

ANDREW: I don't want to be here, not one bit. I don't like this any more than the defense likes this, any more than the jury likes this. I mean, yeah, we've got better things to do than this. This isn't something that—I just would rather not be here.

NICK: So why are you here?

MR. BERTLING: Objection, Your Honor. Relevance.

THE COURT: Overruled.

ANDREW: Because I'm her father, and I don't want my wife in here.

NICK: You and I, we have spent a lot of time together? All these questions, this conversation we just had—is that something we went over before?

---

1. *Blunt v. Sierra Vista Medical Center,* case number CV 100071, Superior Court of San Luis Obispo County, San Luis Obispo, CA. Andrew Blunt testimony, page 140, line 8, to page 144, line 19.

ANDREW: We didn't go over it like I explained right now.[2]

Third Trip Wire: Has First Child at Local Hospital

Our goal for this trip wire was to establish that Andrew followed the normal path by having his baby locally, and that it was his first child, so he was inexperienced. He trusted this hospital to do a good job. They didn't, but he went back to this hospital for his second child because in the end, they had brought Sofia back from the dead.

This testimony is again between Andrew and Nick.

Q: When she comes out, and you told us what you had seen, you said it looked like she was dead. Did you believe at that moment that you hadn't got the care that you were entitled to?

A: Yes.

Q: And so, contemporaneously, at the time that she came out, you were aware of what was going on. You already explained that to us.

A: I knew we were in trouble.

Q: I want to go to that. When they took Sofia out of the room that you and your wife were in—well, what did you do? What happened to your body?

A: I just sat on the floor, up against the—

Q: And did what?

A: Cried.

Q: How much time did Sofia spend at—

A: About three weeks.

Q: Is she able to start—Can she hold up her head now and turn?

A: Her head gets heavy, but she gets better every day.

---

2. *Blunt v. Sierra Vista Medical Center*, page 155, line 9, to page 156, line 8.

Q: Why would you go have another child at Sierra Vista Medical Center?

A: I don't see how that's even a big question. I'm not going to do it at home, by myself. And if I—I didn't tell you this, Mr. Rowley. I hope this is OK, but I've been thinking about it. If I go get—

THE COURT: Hold on just one second, Mr. Blunt.

MR. HIEATT: The question has been answered.

THE COURT: I can't remember. But, Mr. Rowley, do you want to ask another question?

NICK: Do you have an answer to my question that I just asked, that I haven't heard before?

ANDREW: I do. If I go to Fantastic Sam's and get a haircut, and it's a bad haircut, a month later, I'm not going to go, you know, to Rite Aid and buy some clippers and try to do it myself. I'm going to go back to Fantastic Sam's and go to a different barber because that's what they are there for. I'll continue to go to this hospital, because I don't—that's what I'm supposed to do. I'm not going to take the risk of going anywhere else, over going to French.[3] You know, ultimately, the NIC unit at Sierra Vista saved my daughter's life. So, you know, when they may have put her in that position in the first place, but I wouldn't go to any hospital without an NIC unit, no way.

Q: The experience at Sierra Vista, with the second child, was it different?

A: I think that—

MR. BERTLING: Objection, Your Honor. Relevance.

THE COURT: Overruled.

---

3. "French" refers to a competing hospital in San Luis Obispo that did not have a neonatal intensive care unit at that time.

ANDREW: I think they knew. I think the hospital was aware of what happened the first time, and it wasn't just a different delivery with the baby coming out, but it was a different experience.[4]

Fourth Trip Wire: Doctor Screwed Up

Our goal for this trip wire was to establish that the doctor whom Andrew put his faith in let Andrew down. We also wanted to establish that Dr. Haupt never discussed alternative forms of delivery with the Blunts.

The testimony is again between Nick and Andrew.

Q: The first time that Dr. Haupt walked into the delivery room after your wife had begun pushing, what was he doing?

A: He was eating something. It looked like a powder doughnut.

Q: Did he come in and come talk to you and say, how's it going, or come talk to your wife?

A: Dr. Haupt and I didn't communicate that much. I'm not really a big talker, and I don't believe he is either, which is— that's fine with me.

Q: But coaching you through labor, we saw that on the video, he was coaching through labor. Did he ever tell you why it was taking so long?

A: No, he didn't.

Q: Did he ever talk to you guys about an episiotomy? C-section?

A: No

Q: Did he offer to talk to you guys about a—

A: No.

Q: Did he offer or talk to you guys about using a vacuum?

---

4. *Blunt v. Sierra Vista Medical Center,* page 150, line 16, to page 152, line 12.

A: If he would have offered any of those suggestions, my wife and I are pretty reasonable, and we would, towards the end, I would have taken anything. I would have taken anything than—I mean, she was just—

Q: It's your first delivery, your first child. In your gut, could you feel that it was taking too long?

A: I knew it was—I knew something wasn't right.

Q: Why didn't you scream and do something?

A: I'm not the talker.

Q: Did you know that the heart monitor, for over thirty minutes, had been losing the baby's heartbeat? Do you know what that was?

A: I knew what the heart monitor was, but I wasn't aware that that's what was happening. I wish I did know. It just seems like an easy fix, and it just really messes with me.[5]

Fifth Trip Wire: The Hospital Screwed Up

Our goal with this trip wire was to establish that the hospital was also responsible in Andrew's eyes for what happened to Sofia, that the hospital violated Andrew's trust in them, that the hospital messed up plenty after Dr. Haupt turned the baby over to hospital staff, and that the hospital created the goo blockage, after the fact, to cover up their negligence.

The testimony is between Nick and Andrew.

Q: I want—you've heard this talk about when Sofia was born, there was all this stuff coming out of her nose and her mouth, and it just kept coming, that prevented all the medical staff who were there, with all the medical skills that they had, from being able to get air to Sofia's brain, oxygen to her brain. Have you heard a lot about that?

A: Yes.

---

5. *Blunt v. Sierra Vista Medical Center*, page 153, line 16, to page 155, line 1.

Q: During this trial?

A: Yes.

Q: What, if anything, was ever told to you by anybody and Sierra Vista Hospital, or anybody like Dr. Haupt, about Sofia having the problems that she now has because she had so much secretions coming out of her nose and mouth when she was born?

A: They never—the first time I heard that was when we—it was much later. It wasn't while we were at the hospital.

Q: It was after the lawsuit?

A: It was. Well, that was the first time that we even—that we started getting communication from the hospital, was after the lawsuit. I mean—

Q: Did you ever have a nurse or any doctor come up and say we couldn't resuscitate your daughter because there was just so much gunk?

A: No, they didn't.

Q: There was coffee, there was spaghetti, there was cheeselike substance. Breathe.

A: There wasn't.

Q: It was so thick, we couldn't help her.

A: There wasn't anything like that.

Q: Did anyone ever say anything like that?

A: No.

Q: When did you first see that her face was purple?

A: When she came out. When she was still in, actually, when her body was still in and her head came out, her head was purple.

Q: And what was the color of her body when she came out?

A: It was the same color. She was all—she was the same color.

Q: Did you see when her head first came out?

A: Yes.

Q: And just the head was delivered?

A: [Nods head.]

Q: Did Dr. Haupt have to pull out strands of cheese or toffeelike or thick substance?

A: No.

Q: Did you ever see any such substance being taken out of Sofia while she was in the incubator?

A: I never saw—I never saw anything that has been described here. And I don't know—I don't know where that would even come from, to be honest.

Q: And no one ever told you anything like that?

A: No one ever said anything like that.

Q: As a parent with a child who ended up with a brain injury, if that is why your child couldn't be resuscitated, would you expect to be told something like that?

Mr. Hieatt: Objection.

The court: Basis?

Mr. Hieatt: Speculation.

Mr. Bertling: Leading.

Mr. Mean, defense attorney: Lack of foundation.

The court: Overruled.

Andrew: Can you ask me again, Mr. Rowley?

Nick: If the reason why your child couldn't be resuscitated was because there was gunk or stuff like that clogging up her airways, was that something that as a parent, as a parent, you would expect somebody to tell you?

Mr. Hieatt: Same objections.

The court: Well, it is leading. Sustained as to the form.

Nick: What would you expect to be informed of as the parent of a patient, if your baby couldn't be resuscitated because of the reason that there was so much gunk that just kept coming out of the nose or the airway, what would you expect as a parent and as a guardian to be told?

Mr. Hieatt: Same objections.

The court: Overruled.

Andrew: I'm sorry. I keep losing my train of thought.

The court: Do you want it read back?

Nick: Yes, please, Your Honor.

The court: Let's hold it, and the objection continues for the record.

Mr. Hieatt: Thank you.

The court: But I'll overrule it. Go ahead.

[Record read.]

Andrew: I would expect to be told anything. I mean, obviously, the truth. I'd like to know the truth, but no one would give us an answer as to why we were in that position. No one said anything to us, ever.[6]

Sixth Trip Wire: Dad Is Left Holding the Bag

Our goal with this trip wire was to establish that Andrew will live with the medical establishment's mistakes for the rest of his life. He is an upstanding guy and is willing to do it. But Dr. Haupt and the hospital created Andrew's situation, and now they are looking for convenient ways to dispose of the mess.

---

6. *Blunt v. Sierra Vista Medical Center*, page 139, line 1, to page 140, line 7; page 145, line 1, to page 147, line 13.

The testimony is again between Nick and Andrew.

Q: So you just heard some talk and some questions by the defense lawyers here, asking about—well, putting your daughter, Sofia, in a home or a place where other children with disabilities, limitations in life. And you heard the term "warehousing." Is that something you [have] given thought to, thought about?

A: No, it's not. We saw a documentary, I'd say it was about a year ago, about institutionalization, and it's not an option.

Mr. Bertling: Objection; lacks foundation. We are talking institutionalization.

The court: Overruled.

Nick: It's not something where you're going to let your little girl end up?

Andrew: No, it's not.

Q: You heard the other day in opening statement, and you've heard this talk about—well, in this courtroom, that Sofia is only going to live for a certain amount of time. Do you remember during opening statement, that coming up?

A: I do.

Q: Had any of your treating doctors, any of the doctors involved with the care of Sofia, did anyone ever mention to you that she eventually is going to die early?

A: No.

Q: When was the first time you ever heard anything said to you like that?

A: When Mr. Bertling said that the other day.

Q: Since you've heard that, have you made some decisions about anything different that you're going to do with Sofia?

A: No.

Q: At the time Sofia came out blue, did you believe something had gone wrong?

A: Yeah, I thought something—I thought something was wrong before she came out. We were into the twenty-third hour of the labor. It didn't seem like it should have gone on that long, and then, you know, from the time I saw her head, until she came out, was a long period as well, and I just—she just didn't look like she was coming out. And so I wasn't surprised. And I wish I would have—I mean, if I had known to look at the fetal heart tracings, I think we would be in a different position today.

Q: Do you feel guilty?

A: Yeah, I do.

MR. BERTLING: Objection. Move to strike.

THE COURT: Overruled.

ANDREW: I do. And that's a lot of the reason that she's not going to be in an institution or a home, or anything like that. If Jenny and I are here, she's going to live at home with us.[7]

Trip Wires and Themes

We aimed most trip wires at getting that theme I mentioned earlier into our jurors' minds. Let's face it, the jurors will be hearing from a lot of witnesses in a long trial. Details will flee from their memories. Impressions will remain. A theme should frame an impression, and hopefully anchor it. Every witness, expert or lay, our side or theirs, receives a theme. Our goal with each witness is to promote our theme. On the *Blunt* case, a number of jurors spoke with our side after the verdict. When we asked the jurors about specific witnesses and their opinions of them, they repeated our themes back to us a number of times. Something must be working.

---

7. *Blunt v. Sierra Vista Medical Center*, page 134, line 16, to page 135, line 23; page 148, line 8 to 27.

After our witnesses' testimony, I congratulate them and thank them. With the Blunts, I continued to speak with them, as either Andrew or Jennifer were in court every day. This reflected well on our side, as Dr. Haupt stopped attending the trial a few weeks before its conclusion. We had some good conversations about the pressures of the trial, the increasing press coverage, and changes to their lives depending on the outcome of the trial. I try to remember that to the clients, this is not a job but an upturned life.

Children in Court

What about Sofia? No one could accuse her of malingering. Her disability at three years old was clear to one and all. She couldn't testify. But her very presence was a form of testimony. We introduced Sofia to the jurors shortly after the start of opening statements. Nick held her, while talking to her and the jurors. After a few minutes, he gave her back to her parents. It worked quite well and the jurors were all smiles. Then Sofia stayed away from court for a number of days. Overexposure is an unrewarding strategy. We wanted to remind the jurors of who the victim was in this case, but not deaden them to it. We wanted each appearance to be powerful.

One visit was especially so, through no plan of our own. Maybe Sofia planned it. Usually Sofia, when at court, would wait in the hallway so she could play. For some reason, on this particular day, Sofia was in the courtroom. She began to grunt. The grunts were making people uncomfortable. They were making me uncomfortable. Andrew asked me if he should take her outside. I was about to say yes, when it hit me: let's see if anyone has the guts to ask her to leave her own trial. Nobody did. I believe it heightened the jurors' awareness of Jennifer and Andrew's lives. But more important, the jurors did get to hear Sofia testify. She had her day in court. Feedback from the jurors, postverdict, was that most of them had a very difficult time seeing Sofia in the hallway. They wanted to cry or smile or just hug her. No doubt, Sofia can work a crowd.

Trial Strategies

Turning now to trial strategies. This section will be a grab bag of tactics that I have observed to work in and out of the courtroom, or suggestions I may have.

Lawyers' Conduct

When you ask most people about their feelings toward lawyers, the responses are not generally warm and fuzzy. *Assholes* tends to come up a lot. But, as with generalizations, peoples' perceptions tend to change when it comes to a specific case. The people are now also jurors. They see the effort, amount of work, and passion the lawyers bring to trial. Suddenly, these lawyers are human beings doing a job. These lawyers become exceptions to the stereotypes. These lawyers are special. But what kind of conduct do the jurors want to see from the lawyers? By *conduct*, I mean your interactions with witnesses as well as with other lawyers. I became aware of this from juror comments after a trial. They went something like this:

> We were disappointed in the way the lawyers acted toward each other. It was all so civil. "After you." "No, after you." A lot of joking and friendliness. It seemed like you didn't really care about your clients. If you did, you would have fought harder. We wanted to see some passion and some brawling. You guys were supposed to be enemies, not friends.

Wow, OK. I thought about it. A brawl, huh? Well it is true that Nick is a much better lawyer when he can't stand the opposing counsel. But that is different than displaying his animosity to the jurors. In the end, what I came up with was that some people go to a car race to see a race, some to see wrecks, and others a mixture of the two. A trial is the same. Some jurors want to see a brawl, some want it civil, and others want a mixture of the two. There are arguments for all three. I suggest you take the time to consider the personality of your jury and adjust your conduct accordingly. Give them what they want. Don't be rigid. They are, in effect, your bosses. All the world's a stage. And if you are unable to gauge what the majority of your jurors want to see, then revert to your natural style, whatever that may be.

Silence

Silence is more powerful than words. We don't use silence much in the United States. Silence focuses the listeners' attention, and it results in feeling and human emotion. The brain tunes in when there is silence to try and figure out why the talking stopped. Silence before an important question helps the listener focus on the question to come. Give it a shot.

The next time you are in trial and are about to ask an important question, wait five to ten seconds. Look knowingly at the witness and then the jurors. People will move forward in their seats. They will focus. Jurors will wonder, what is he going to say next? You won't be nervous, like you are when you can't think of what to say next. In fact, you'll probably feel powerful. A silence enhances the impact of any following question.

In another scenario, think of silence in the ballpark. A guy from the home team has a chance to win the game with a swing of the bat. The pitch, the crack of the bat, the ball sails out of the park. A winning home run. What happens in the stadium? After the crack of the bat, there is a collective hush. Everyone inhales and watches the ball's trajectory. Then all hell breaks loose as the ball clears the fence. Game over.

Why don't lawyers respect the collective hush? Time and again, I have seen a lawyer hit a home run in the courtroom, only to immediately move on to the next question. You know what I am talking about. You ask the perfect question and get the perfect answer.

Stop, and watch it sail out of the park. Savor it. Don't speak. Let the jurors watch it sail out too. Let them digest it. Write it down. Then wait for their cheers. OK, maybe not that. But by being quiet, and not moving immediately on, the impact on the jurors will be greater.

Repeat

Repeat important points twice and even three times. Lawyer Geoffrey Fieger says, "You can never say a good thing too many times." I agree. This forces the important point deeper into each juror's memory. The following simple example illustrates this.

> You're telling us the doctor did not take the cord blood gas for testing. He didn't take the cord blood gas test?

[Now make your I-can't-believe-it face and repeat.]

> He didn't take the cord blood gas test?

Use Your Notebook

Use your notebook as an "important point" technique. When a witness says something you consider to be very important, walk back to your table, open a notebook, and ask the witness to repeat it. When he does, write it down in your notebook. This signals to the jurors that they should do the same because you actually took the time to write it down, and you never write anything down. "Hey, check it out: the teacher is taking notes."

Look at the Jurors

During direct or cross, when you are about to ask an important question, turn away from your witness, and ask the question looking at the jurors. I've watched lawyers go through an entire examination of a witness without ever once looking at the jurors. On the other hand, I've seen Nick face the jurors and ask five or six questions in a row without ever looking at the witness. Here is what I think is going on. When Nick turns away from the witness, faces the jurors, and asks a question, he is communicating the following: "I know who is important here. The jurors are. That's why I'm focusing on you. I'm also telling you that you've got to get ready for this response. It's going to be a doozy. Let's enjoy it together." This is bonding and focusing.

No Podiums

Don't use podiums ever. You don't need protection in the courtroom.

No Typed Question Lists

Don't use typed question lists. The jurors can see the thickness of the paper pile and inwardly groan at their personal time guesstimate.

Look Confident after Sidebar Meetings

Always be confident and even smile when you come back from a sidebar. You won, didn't you? I mean, you always win sidebars, right? Let the jurors know it. You win every sidebar, like you're going to win this trial. But no fist pumping. People respond well to self-confidence, but not to arrogance. Jurors are fascinated by sidebars, as am I. What are they talking about up there? I've even heard jurors taking bets on how many sidebars there will be that day.

Move Around

When doing direct and cross, don't be static. Move around. Stand up. Sit down. When asking a question that is of particular interest to the jurors, move to the far side of the jury box and meld in with the jurors as much as possible. When referring to the defendant, move behind the defendant's chair, especially if he or she is not present. When talking about opposing counsel, move in front of their table and make eye contact with them while you ask the question. It's a chess game; you have to move.

Know Your Client's Birthday

Birthdays. Know your client's birthday. A major embarrassment for our legal team occurred in the *Sierra Charles* case. Sierra was our nine-year-old client. One day in court, the defense lawyer stood up and said, "On behalf of the entire defense team, I'd like to say happy birthday to Sierra." Ouch, we had no idea. Learn the major trial participants' birthdays if you can. No one is offended by having her birthday recognized. Now we're much better at birthdays. For example, we arranged the entire *Blunt* trial in such a way that the jurors began deliberation on Sofia's birthday. We didn't want to overdo the birthday angle, so we only mentioned it twelve times in the closing. All's fair.

Estimate Time Correctly

Try not to underestimate the time you need when the judge asks about it. Especially in front of the jurors.

"How much longer will you need with witness X?"

"About forty minutes, Your Honor."

Three hours later, the questioning drones on.

Jurors get annoyed with broken promises. As do judges and opposing counsel. It works against your credibility. Why do lawyers chronically underestimate? I can't believe an experienced trial lawyer really doesn't know how long he or she needs. My guess is they say these small amounts of time because they think that is what the judge wants to hear. Or they're afraid that if they say three hours, the judge will deny them the time. If it is the latter, I understand. If it is the former, just say three hours. Remember what mom always said? Honesty is the best policy.

Know When to Stop

Speaking of time, there is no rule of court that says you are required to fill up your allotted time. If you're done ahead of time and have nothing left to say, it's OK to sit down. In fact, it is impressive. Similarly, when questioning witnesses, develop your dramatic timing. Know when to stop. Often I have observed lawyers hit a high point in the questioning that wraps it up so well, where they could sit down in triumph. Yet they rattle off a few more questions and lose the advantage, because the questions were on their list. Then they sit down with a "Nothing further." Momentum lost. Go with your gut. If it feels right, sit down. If people congratulate you on your wrap-up, you'll know to trust your gut more often.

Stick to Your Story

Stick to your story line and keep pounding away at it. Call adverse witnesses in your case-in-chief and make them tell your story. It strengthens your veracity. Use cross-examination to continue to pound away at your story line. Everyone on both sides agrees the hospital and doctor screwed up. It's just a matter of the degree of the screw-up.

Balance the Courtroom

At the beginning of the *Blunt* case, there were three lawyers for the plaintiffs and three for the defense. This gave good balance at the tables. Then the hospital settled about two weeks into trial. The next day, during one of the breaks, the two lawyers for the hospital packed their bags and departed. Suddenly, there was one lawyer sitting at the defense table with his client. Soon thereafter, his client stopped attending the trial. The sole remaining defense lawyer looked abandoned. We had a perception problem with the jurors: three lawyers against one. The plaintiffs were ganging up on the defense. This was rich irony when you consider the resources of the two sides. However, would the jurors perceive the fight as unfair? I'm sure the defense lawyer was not opposed to the possibility. The gallery exacerbated the issue. A gallery is seated like an old-fashioned wedding. The plaintiff's guests sat behind the plaintiff's table, and the defense guests sat on their side. By the third week, it was looking too lopsided in favor of the plaintiffs—the boat was in danger of tipping. Simple rearranging solved this issue. We never had more than two lawyers at the plaintiff's table, and we had mandatory reseating in the peanut gallery. Balance and harmony was restored—feng shui in the courtroom.

Use Humor If It Is Natural

Use humor throughout the trial if your humor is quick and natural. Otherwise, don't. For example, Nick always forgets to ask permission to approach the witness. Judges will remind him in varying degrees of severity. One day in the *Blunt* trial, Nick was particularly remiss. Five or six times, he forgot to ask. It got to the point where the jurors and the judge looked forward to it. Even the witness anticipated it. As Nick moved toward the witness, caught up in the passion of the moment, smiles would start to appear. Everyone saw it coming, and they were looking forward to it. I wanted to wave a red flag. Nick charged forward for witness number seven, and the judge had "Mr. Rowley" on his lips. At the last second, Nick pulled up just short of the witness, turned to the judge, and said, "Gotcha." It brought the house down. Humans want to laugh. They look favorably on those who make them laugh. It's called human nature. Jurors are humans.

Lighting

Turn the lights down before showing something on the screen, then turn the lights back up when you are done. If the goal is to have whatever is on the screen have maximum impact with the jurors, this tactic makes sense. The jurors can see it better with the lights down. Ask the jurors if you don't believe me. Likewise, when your screen presentation is over and the lights go back up, it causes the jurors to turn their focus back to you and what you have to say. It also demonstrates your efficiency and mastery of the courtroom.

I know this might seem obvious as you read it. But in a courtroom, most lawyers seem to be prisoners of their own thoughts. What is my next question? How do I get around what they said? And so on. Courtroom logistics are not a priority. Thus, time and again, I have squinted at screen presentations through fluorescent brilliance, and watched an hour of testimony in the dimness. Put the jurors' needs first. Lights on, lights off. Lights on, lights off. Try a Post-it note if you need a reminder.

Email Trial Progress to the Defense

If there are multiple defendants in a civil trial, use emails to stir up dissension among them. This is one of Nick's specialties. Suffice it to say that his emails stir it up. They are full of phrases such as "Personal assets at risk," "You've lost on the following issue," "This email should be communicated to the following parties," "Defendant will have a bad-faith claim against the insurance company," "These lawyers can represent the defendant in the bad-faith claim," "First to settle is the first out the door," "The policy is blown," and "Friday the train will leave the station regarding settlement."

This is good stuff that at a minimum sows dissension among the enemy ranks. It often results in a settlement with one of the defendants, providing financial security to the clients and legal team. With that security, the legal team can then go for a home run against the remaining defendants. This is exactly what happened in the *Landeros* case and the *Blunt* case.

Keep Track of Witnesses

As a long trial drags on, some of the minor witnesses get lost in the shuffle. For that reason I will do a short write-up on the content of each witness's testimony, as well as try to capture some of their personality. That provides Nick easier recollection when the closing comes around.

Recalling minor witnesses and their testimony when creating the closing can be challenging, so if asked, I'll try to capture the moment and mood of their testimony on paper the same day of their testimony. The goal is for Nick, weeks or months later, to read the memo and say, "Oh yeah, I remember this person. OK, here's how we'll use his testimony." The insights contained in the memo are often my opinions and might not be 100 percent accurate, but that is not the point. The point is to create a snapshot of an impression that serves as a memory jab somewhere down the road. The following is an example of a memo I wrote, designed to capture a minor witness's time on the stand.

Example: Witness Memo for Smith

Smith was a witness who appeared on behalf of Sierra Vista hospital, where she is a respiratory therapist.

Appearances. Smith's style could only be described as eclectic. My guess would be that she is much older than she appears. She had very long blond hair pinned up. She wore stylish glasses and her makeup was directed at age minimization. Her clothes were hippielike: a long flowing dress with cowboy boots. But her manicure (French manicure) contradicted the hippie clothes. Smith basically had the confidence to dress in a way that pleased her and not her lawyers, who probably would have preferred something along the lines of a medical professional.

Testimony. Smith's testimony was overburdened with pressure from both within and without. In other words, Smith's view of herself in the world clashed repeatedly with the practical considerations of her testimony. Smith sees herself as a kind, soft-spoken individual who has chosen to do good in a harsh world. Part of that good is protecting those without a voice, thus her specialization in neonatal respiratory distress. My guess would be that she practices, or is at least interested in, Eastern religion. So her personal belief system basically holds that a good, honest person who does kind acts will be rewarded with good karma, and also be applauded by society. In this case, Smith brought a baby back from the dead and is now ready for the applause.

Cue Nick. His attack on her conduct is a slap in the face and is confusing to her. Where is the reward for her good acts? At this point, the inconvenience of reality sets in. Smith is forced to confront some unattractive thoughts.

- One, some of her colleagues screwed up and committed medical negligence. She knows this, both through hospital gossip and her own observations.

- Two, being on the staff of a hospital is akin to belonging to a private club. Us and them. When attacked, circle the wagons and protect your own. Smith has or had a duty to protect, or become a pariah among staff.

- Three, financial considerations. I believe Smith is a contract employee. Her continued employment, increased hours, and financial security were directly threatened by her testimony. Perhaps the threat was verbal, or only implied. But make no mistake, it was there. Smith knew that if she wanted to keep working, she had better say the right things.

With this background, her conflicted testimony is easier to grasp.

My guess at Smith's internal mental dialogue: "I *will* tell the truth! Why is this man attacking me? I like his boots. I saved this baby's life! I can't believe I just admitted that; they are going to kill me back at the hospital. Cry, cry. There were no mistakes made! Well except for that ice cube Haupt and the other respiratory therapist. Fuck it, I'm going to tell the truth. Truth, truth, and so on."

Break.

Hieatt (hospital lawyer): "What the hell are you saying? You want to work anywhere in this town again? Get outta my woodshed!"

Back in the chair for Smith: "'Yes, cream in the lungs can turn into syrup.' Lie, lie. Cry, cry for the unfairness of it all, but I need the job. Sorry, I didn't understand the question. Could you repeat it? And in the end my karma knows I saved Sofia's life. The rest of this is just bullshit compromise. Cry, cry. Yes, I am upset, but to be honest, Mr. Rowley, it is because of my loss of innocence."

Use the Gallery

If someone is sitting in the peanut gallery, they are fair game. If someone new suddenly shows up to court the same day that a defense witness shows up, chances are they are connected. Try to find out ahead of time, but if you can't, you can still ask the defense witness the question.

"Who is that person is the front row?" Ask it nicely.

"Oh, that's my mom."

"Well, that's nice she can come in." And leave it at that. No harm.

But if it is like the *Blunt* case, several gallery sitters turned out to be relevant. For example, one day, a nurse was testifying. Nick asked her who the two ladies were in the front row.

NURSE: They are my supervisors at work.

NICK: Could you identify them?

[The nurse named them.]

NICK: Why are they here?

NURSE: To support me.

NICK: Are they here to keep an eye on you?

From there, Nick went on to show how her testimony might affect her job security and reveal the pressure she felt to answer correctly with her bosses in the courtroom. Every juror who has been an employee understood that pressure. They also understood the competing demands of truthfulness and financial security. All because of the gallery.

Corporate Defendants

Keep digging. The extent of some corporate webs is amazing. Who owns whom? This small defendant company is owned by a regional corporation, which operates under this umbrella of corporations, which in turn is part of a multinational conglomeration. And they all have their own insurance policies. Dig for the connections. Invite them all to the party. Then start sending out emails advising on how to escape.

Send trial reports every few days to the defendants and tell them to copy their insurance company decision makers and the actual clients. Tell them your analysis of how trial is going, and why the defense decision makers are making a bad choice not to reasonably settle the case. Nick has settled many cases during trial by ensuring that we are reporting the truth to the insurance company rather than allowing the insurance company to only have access to the defense lawyer's daily reports.

Trip Wires

I believe in the use of trip wires. A trip wire is a word or phrase that triggers an area of inquiry or argument that we've boiled down from a set of written questions, story lines, themes, or subjects that we have agreed we must cover during a certain part of the case. This is how we do the trial without having notes. We want a trial to be a natural conversation with the jurors and the witnesses who testify. You cover all your major subjects without boring the jurors with a rigid question-and-answer format if you learn and develop the method of using trip wires. We showed this extensively at the beginning of this chapter.

Conclusion

At the beginning of this chapter, I made some observations about a man in Africa and a Japanese room. I wanted to convey the attraction and wisdom of age-old minimalist approaches. This applies specifically to the complexities of the courtroom. Applying a simplifying approach to the testimony of both lay and expert witnesses will most powerfully convey your message to the jury. A conversation is the smoothest form of that conveyance, and one the jurors are most familiar with.

Back to our man in Africa. Imagine if you placed that man in the living room of a New York apartment. Chances are he'd be overwhelmed. But what if you placed him in the equally alien Japanese tatami mat room? I believe he'd make himself right at home. Keeping your message and testimony complex might be impressive and score points with those immersed in the case, but it will overwhelm many jurors. If juror comprehension and sympathy are your goals, then keep it simple so that everyone feels at home.

Direct Examination

Nick Rowley

Direct examination is the most difficult part of the trial. You don't want it to look contrived or rehearsed, yet you need to prepare it and have each direct examination timed and planned. I believe that making direct examinations as short as possible is the way to go. Also important is preparing your witness to be super effective when the defense is cross-examining him. Then have a redirect planned that blows the defense's attempt at destroying your witness out of the water.

Plan your direct examinations before the trial begins, at the very least a few days before the witness goes on the stand. Each direct examination should advance the story you are trying to tell.

Direct examination should never be a stale, boring, question-and-answer session that drags on and on. Direct examination is the time to connect, feel, and relive the story in the courtroom. The most important goal is to bring the direct examination to life through what I call the "action method." Do whatever it takes to be on your feet, reenacting scenes, drawing on a board, and creating physical movement in the courtroom.

Direct Examination Begins before Trial

First, direct examination begins outside of the courtroom and long before trial. I am going to use another case as an example to tell you how I do this. As I write this chapter to you now, I am sitting in a hotel room with Kimberly, a victim of a mild traumatic brain injury. It is 5:30 a.m., and she is taking a shower. I got her a nice hotel suite with a separate living room close to where the defense exam is taking place. I came here myself to make sure she woke up so we could be prepared for this morning's defense medical exam and neuropsychological interview. I was here last night. Before she went to sleep, I made sure we went over important issues in preparation for today. I want them in her mind as the last things she thinks of before she falls asleep. I have a close relationship with Kimberly. She is not just a client. She is somebody I care about. We have become friends, and we trust and care for each other. We are a team. I will not leave this important job to somebody she does not know and trust. I am not too good or so important that I won't get up at 4:30 a.m., have breakfast, and drive Kimberly to the defense examinations. It is very important, and I do it myself as often as I can.

I spend time with my clients and their families so that when we stand in front of a jury, we are connected on a human level. If I am not able to do this, then Tiffany Chung, my young loyal partner and part of my trial team, does it. If you were to ask Tiffany what the most important part of being a trial lawyer is, she would tell you: "Caring and spending time with your client."

Another reason for me personally to be at Kimberly's examination is so that I can meet the defense examiner and tell him I am the lead trial lawyer on the case who will be cross-examining him. I bring him a file of paperwork that establishes Kimberly's case. I offer this expert the opportunity to talk to our experts and to collateral source witnesses (laypeople who can talk about the before and after of your client as a noninjured versus now injured and damaged person), and I offer to answer any questions he has. I bring photographs of the vehicles, and all the information that helps our case. This way, if the examiner leaves anything out of his report, I discredit him. I am going to make sure that he has every opportunity to treat Kimberly fairly and issue a report that upsets the defense's frivolous position on the case.

Most of our clients and witnesses smile when they see us in court because they are not used to seeing us dressed up in suits. I am wearing jeans and a regular shirt to the defense expert exam today. I don't dress up, not only because I don't like to wear suits and dress pants, but also because when I am not in court, I am a regular person. Uniforms add labels to humans that separate them from being ordinary. A uniform shows the world that the person wearing it is different, and it sets them apart. Taking the uniform off takes away a barrier that can disconnect people from each other.

You Are the Director of the Story

As the directors of the story, we need to have a relationship with the humans whom we will tell the story with. We must understand the story we want these humans to help us tell. We must know it in our core and be able to see and feel it alive within us. We accomplish this better if we do it as regular people. Developing trusting relationships allows us to truly feel and relive the chapters of the story. It is only after this, having lived and walked as much of each chapter as possible, that we are ready to share the story with our jury.

Bringing the story to life means we must show the story to the jury rather than just tell it to them. I am sure you are wondering how we do this in court. Here's how:

- Get witnesses off of the stand.

- Draw, set, and reenact scenes.

The Trial Lawyers College[1] can teach you how to do this. Attend a regional seminar. Find a local TLC group and attend. Learn how to reenact scenes and events. You cannot learn this

---

1. For more information, visit www.triallawyerscollege.com.

from reading a book; you have to do it and learn through the "action method" of learning. If you have not attended a Trial Lawyers College regional seminar, you cannot afford *not* to take the time to do so—that is, if you really want to become an effective Trial by Human lawyer.

Human feelings are the universal truth within the story, and showing the audience the scenes and expressing the human feelings and experiences associated with your case is the credible way to conduct an effective direct examination.

If you have a scene that is important to the story, you can ask the witness: "If you were to take us to that day that your sister was hurt, if we were standing there in the emergency room when your sister was being examined by the doctor, tell us what we would see through your eyes."

You can ask the witness, "Would it be helpful for you to explain what you saw and experienced if we were to have you come down off of the stand and show us where you were in the room, and what the room looked like in comparison to this courtroom?" Then ask the judge for permission to have the witness come down off of the stand. Often, the judge will allow you to do this.

In the case of a client with a brain injury, you could ask the witness questions like the following. Note that once you begin questioning using this strategy, present tense is important.

Q: I want you to tell us, where were you at in the room? If where I am standing is the door to the room, tell us where you are.

Q: What does it smell like in the room?

A: The room is dirty and I can smell urine.

Q: What do you see and who is there with you?

Q: What do you hear? What are the sounds?

A: The sounds are loud because the doctor and nurses attending to my sister were doing CPR in the room next door. We could hear everything.

Q: Do you hear what the doctor says to your sister?

A: My sister was out of it and she was in and out of consciousness. We were having to keep her awake.

Q: Do you hear your sister responding to the doctor?

A: The doctor was in a rush and did not spend much time with her . . . He was attending to a gunshot victim that came in.

Q: Describe for us how your sister is interacting with the doctor.

A: We waited five hours before any doctor really spent any time with my sister and she was on morphine. She was nauseated and kept vomiting and telling us her head was hurting.

This direct examination is what trumped the defense experts and defense lawyer who were trying to establish that the ER records showed my client was not badly injured, and that she did not have any of the initial signs and symptoms of a traumatic brain injury. We were able to show that the ER people were busy and didn't do a thorough job, therefore they overlooked obvious signs of traumatic brain injury.

Examining Expert Witnesses

Even with expert witnesses, you can bring a direct examination to life. You have a choice here. You can ask the expert witness to go over his curriculum vitae (résumé) and summarize his education, training, and experience, or you could ask the witness to go back to 1973 and tell us where he was in the world. What was he doing in life? You could show the jury a picture of an ordinary human being who is beginning an educational path as a medical doctor, or engineer, in a specific place in the world. You could then go through years of education, training, experience, maybe even the date and time of the expert's first surgery. Now the jury has a foundation from which to trust your expert. The jury has gone to medical school or engineering school and seen how long it took. You could then take the jury to the time when the expert first met your client. "What is going through your mind as you first hear about this case?" Set up the examination room or the room where your expert is reviewing the MRI films that show the brain injury or the neuropsychological testing.

You could direct the expert to the scene of the injury or alleged crime and ask, "If we are there together in the emergency room and we see the client going in and out of consciousness while the emergency room doctor and nurses are in the room next door doing CPR on another patient, what would that mean, the fact that your client is going in and out of consciousness, feeling nauseated, having head pain, and having problems staying awake?"

Have the expert explain what it is that you see when you are portraying the scene. For example, you could say, "Imagine we are all students here in this courtroom. Tell us what it is we are looking at."

A plaintiff's direct examination should take place at different scenes that the jury can see and feel. Set a scene whenever possible, and personally know in your core what the smells, sounds, and feelings are. "We" is an important word in direct examination and throughout the entire trial. Ask the witness, "If we are there with you, by your side, what would you tell us we are looking at?" You must bring the chapter to life, to the lives of each of your jurors.

Direct examination is simply directing a chapter of a drama. Think of the title of your story and the most important chapter that the witness needs to tell. Identify the protagonist and the auxiliary characters, and direct the scene.

Examining Lay Witnesses

With lay witnesses, do your best to meet with them in person in ordinary clothing. When preparing for trial, go to scenes of the story if you can, and ask them to meet you there. If you can't go there, ask them to imagine the scenes or the chapters that they witnessed, and ask them to tell you what you would see if you were standing there with them.

Go slow. Do not rush the process. Ask them to slow down and do their best to reexperience what it is that they witnessed. Be thankful to them for their time, and be sure to tell them how important they are to the case.

Some witnesses will not want to be involved. Be prepared for that. Tell them why you need them. Use the word "please." It is a magic word.

"Please, Mr. Johnson, I really need your help. The insurance company is refusing to pay Jim's medical bills, and they are blaming Jim for the accident. We really need your help."

In a liability dispute case, the police report might say something that is wrong and have wrong conclusions. Ask the witness on the stand:

Q: The police officer who showed up after the car crash says and testified that the crash happened this way: _____, and the expert witness for the defense testified that it happened this way: _____. Is that consistent with what you saw? You were there; tell us what you saw with your eyes.

[If there is an objection, say:]

Q: Tell us what you saw with your own eyes on June 5, 2005, at the intersection of Foothill and Haven Avenue.

Conclusion

The strength of your direct examination comes from your connection with people as human beings. The jury will see it and believe it if you have spent the time to connect with people on a human level. There is no substitute for spending time with your client and with your witnesses.

Cross-Examination

Nick Rowley

General Rules for Cross-Examination

First, never ever ask an open-ended question during cross-examination. Don't do it. Stop yourself. If you start to do it, then stop and reask your question over again. All competent trial lawyers will tell you to not ask open-ended questions. In a recent trial, the defense lawyers kept asking open-ended questions, and 90 percent of the time, they were killing their own case. It was hard not to smile as the witness kept retelling her story.

Do not start each question with the word "and." It is annoying. Also, don't acknowledge the answer and validate the witness you are cross-examining by saying "OK" or "Thank you" or by nodding your head every time you get an answer.

Try this out the wrong way by speaking aloud this quirky and incorrect way of doing a cross-examination. Speak this out loud to yourself, and say it while looking in the mirror so you can see what is going on, how it is goofy, and then go watch a few different trials. You'll see other lawyers doing exactly what I am talking about.

CROSS-EXAMINER: The car was red, correct?

WITNESS: Yes.

Q: OK. [Nods head] And the car was a Toyota, correct?

A: Yes.

Q: OK. [Nods head] The car was driving south on Pine Avenue, correct?

A: Yes.

Q: OK. [Nods head] What was the other car, which my client was driving, doing?

A: . . .

[You have no idea what this answer is going to be because you asked an open-ended question.]

Q: Thank you. [Nods head] And . . .

Now try this by speaking out the right way to do a cross-examination:

CROSS-EXAMINER: The car was a red car, the car you were traveling behind, correct?

WITNESS: Yes.

Q: It was a Toyota, isn't that true? You were driving behind the red Toyota on southbound Pine Street, isn't that true?

[Look at the jury when you say "red Toyota" and look back to the witness when you say "isn't that true?" Do it smoothly and politely, and make eye contact with one or more jurors with each statement of fact you want to establish.]

A: Yes.

Q: As you were driving behind it, on southbound Pine, you saw the Toyota approaching the intersection of Fifth Street, true?

WITNESS: Yes.

Q: There is a stop sign at Fifth Street, requiring all vehicles to stop, your vehicle and the red Toyota in front of you?

A: Yes.

Q: The red Toyota does not stop at the stop sign, does it?

[Pay attention to and communicate with the jurors during your cross-exams of witnesses. Make soft eye contact and deliver your statements of facts to the jurors. Then turn back to the witness and simply say, "Isn't that true?"]

Let's make it even simpler. In this example, the witness you are cross-examining is on the stand, and you want to establish that the color of the car was blue.

[You look at the witness.]

CROSS-EXAMINER: I want to talk to you about [pause] . . .

[Or you can say, "Can we please talk about" and then pause. Either way, you now partially turn your body, extend an open hand, and completely turn your face and focus your eyes on the jury. Scan the jury, find a juror, and *now* you can finish your question or statement of fact. Look the juror in the eye, softly but with truth and credibility. Finish your pause, and say:]

CROSS-EXAMINER: The color of the car. The color of the car was blue.

[You have delivered this to a juror. There is no doubt that the color of the car was blue. You now turn back to the witness.]

CROSS-EXAMINER: Isn't that true?

Here is another example, this time of a series of questions you can use to paint the scene of an expert and his bias:

Q: Sometimes you are sitting at a desk in your office when you first learn about a case like this, true?

Q: Sometimes you get a letter about a case like this and a $5,000 check from the defense, true?

Q: Getting $5,000 feels good?

Q: Sometimes you get five new cases per week, true?

Q: Five cases, five $5,000 checks, $25,000? Good money, true?

Q: Then you just need to see the five people and write five reports, true?

Q: When you write these reports, you don't have to reinvent the wheel, do you?

Q: You have a person in your office who types the reports?

Q: The money doing this work is much easier than seeing patients, isn't it?

Q: The people you see for the defense are not patients of yours, are they?

Q: People like my client cannot call you and set up another appointment and complain about the job you did or what you wrote, can they?

Q: There is no physician–patient relationship, is there?

Q: If you misdiagnose them, if your opinion is wrong, you cannot be sued, can you?

Q: So, sitting there at your desk, you get this envelope with another $5,000 check. It is easier money for you than dealing with a waiting room full of patients where you only get paid $150 per visit and have to deal with billing Medicare or Medicaid?

Q: You can also do this work from your home or a coffee shop, or on an airplane coming here, and you have done this work outside of your clinic, isn't that true?

You have told the story of bias and brought it to life. The point is that there is a way to bring the expert review to life, to get the jury imagining him sitting there getting that fat check that pays him thirty times better than having to deal with a patient whom he has to care about. And no matter how the expert answers the questions, your questions have told the story.

Cross-Examining on Standard of Care

This example is more complex, but it is just as simple. This example comes from the defense expert on Sofia's case.

[Look at the jury and repeat:]

Cross-examiner: Standard of care. I would like to ask you some questions about standard of care; is that OK?

[Look at the jury.]

Q: When we say "standard of care" [look at the jury], we are talking about the level of carefulness, the level of attention and competency that a patient in this community deserves [look at the jury], isn't that true? [Look back to the witness and keep going.] Complying with the standard of care involves giving the patient the reasonable attention with reasonable competency, isn't that true?

Q: When it comes to delivering a baby that is hooked up to a fetal heart monitor, if a physician and nurse fail to pay reasonable attention to the fetal heart monitor, a baby in severe distress can end up being ignored, isn't that true?

Q: Ignoring a baby in distress can result in a baby being born with brain damage, isn't that true?

Q: Doctors, nurses, and hospitals—the medical system—charge money to patients in exchange for the promise to deliver reasonable care and attention to mothers and babies during labor and delivery?

Q: Delivering a baby in a hospital with a board-certified obstetrician and surgeon is not free. The Blunt family was charged and the hospital and doctors got paid good money for the delivery of baby Sofia, true?

Q: Baby Sofia was born with brain damage. She looked dead when she came out of her mother, true?

Q: Baby Sofia's fetal heart monitor strips showed that her heartbeat was dropping during contractions for more than an hour, isn't that true?

Q: She came out looking dead and never cried or took her first breaths, did she?

Q: Baby Sofia had to be intubated and resuscitated after she was delivered, and now she has cerebral palsy, true?

Q: She will never walk because her legs do not work, true?

Q: She cannot hold her head up and cannot eat food. She eats through a feeding tube that is surgically implanted into her stomach?[1]

Cross-examination is where we establish our credibility and show the jury that what we say is the truth. We are polite and we are courteous. We show that we know this case better than anybody. We know the story, all of its chapters, all the witnesses, all the evidence. If the witness we are cross-examining is tricky and evasive, we don't let him get us off track: we stick to the basic facts. And if we have to, we politely repeat our very simple questions, and the expert's bias and evasiveness will become clear.

During cross, it is our goal to establish the facts for our closing argument. We do this continuously through the witnesses we cross-examine. We are making statements of fact that we know are true. We make them to the jury, and then we politely turn to the witness and say the magic words: "Isn't that true?" or "True?" or "Correct?"

Cross-examination is not a time to be rude. It is not a time to show off. It is so easy to kill a witness on cross-examination. Anybody can learn how to do that. The skill to develop is kindly making the witness your witness.

There is a book by Larry Pozner and Roger Dodd called *Cross-Examination: Science and Techniques*.[2] It is a good book to read to

---

1. *Blunt v. Sierra Vista Medical Center*, case number CV 100071, Superior Court of San Luis Obispo County, San Luis Obispo, CA.
2. Larry S. Pozner and Roger Dodd, *Cross-Examination: Science and Techniques* (New York: Lexis Nexis, 2004).

give you structure. The Trial Lawyers College also teaches you to tell the story through cross-examination, and it is much simpler than reading a long book. I teach cross-examination by making it as simple as possible.

The Storybook Cross

Maren Chaloupka taught me this method of cross-examination at the Trial Lawyers College. It is the "storybook cross." It makes things very simple. Each question is actually a statement describing a page in the story. Think of the nursery rhyme "Jack and Jill" as you read this.

Q: [Look over at the jury.] There was Jack [look back to the witness], isn't that true?

A: Yes, but there was also Jill, and Jill had a red sweater!

[Do not let the witness you are cross-examining get away with not answering your simple question.]

Q: [Look back at the jury and repeat.] There was Jack [look back to the witness], isn't that true?

A: Jill was a pretty girl. She had freckles. But she behaved badly.

[All of that may be true, but the witness is still not answering the question. Look back at the jury, and repeat, firmly:]

Q: There was Jack, isn't that true?

A: Yes, there was Jack!

[Finally, a response to the question. The witness is clearly annoyed to have to have answered the question, and the jury will see this annoyance.]

Q: Thank you for answering my question. There was Jill, isn't that true?

A: As I told you, Jill had freckles, was pretty, but behaved badly.

[Again, all of that may be true, but the witness has not answered the simple question that was asked.]

Q: [Look at the jury.] There was Jill [look back to the witness], true?

A: Yes, there was Jill.

Q: Thank you again.

[This is witness training. Eventually, the witness will learn that he or she looks biased and bad by not answering simple questions.]

Q: Jack and Jill were at the bottom of a hill, isn't that true?

A: Yes.

Q: Jack and Jill went up the hill, true?

A: Yes.

Q: When they were on the top of the hill, Jack fell down, true?

A: Yes.

Q: Jack fell down and broke his crown, yes?

A: Yes, that is what happened.

Q: After Jack fell down and broke his crown, Jill, that little girl Jill, she came tumbling down after, didn't she?

A: Yes.

Q: Jack was hurt pretty badly when his crown was broken, isn't that true?

A: Yes.

Q: Jack is still hurt pretty badly, isn't he?

A: Not in my opinion.

Q: You did not see Jack until three years after he broke his crown, true?

Q: Of the thousands of hours that have passed since Jack broke his crown, you have only spent thirty minutes with Jack, isn't that true?

A: . . .

Q: And those thirty minutes were minutes you were being paid by [point over to the defense] the defense in this case, isn't that true?

A: ...

Q: And before you spent those thirty minutes with Jack, or even knew what he looked like, you had already formed an opinion about him, isn't that true?

A: ...

Q: You had already written reports for the defense in this case and been paid thousands of dollars?

A: I was paid for reviewing records.

Q: And you knew that your thirty minutes with Jack were just to try and look for reasons to help the defense in this case, isn't that true?

A: No, of course not. I did a thorough, objective examination.

Q: And if you were in fact biased and motivated by money, you would look us in the eye and tell us?

A: Of course.

Q: Thank you for being so fair. I have no further questions.

The point of this simple example is that you can simplify every cross-examination to help you tell the story. Write it out. In every question you ask, involve the jurors, look at them, and make every question a statement of fact, part of your closing argument. Do this politely. Repeat your simple questions if the witness refuses to answer. Maintain control.

One way I quickly cross-examine biomechanical or kinesiology experts and get them off of the stand and make them look like fools is as follows:

Q: Dr. Adams, your job in this case has been to determine the movement of my client's body as a result of the forces that occurred during the collision, true?

A: Yes.

Q: In order to do that, you have formed opinions about the position of Kimberly's body at the moment of impact and how her body moved as a result of the forces, true?

A: Yes.

Q: I have this chair here [which I have placed in front of the jury box], and I am wondering if you would be able to show us how you believe she was sitting at the time of the collision. Would you be able to demonstrate that for us using your own body?

A: Yes.

Q: Now that you are sitting and holding your body and arms and hands in the position that you believe, in your opinion, was her body position at the time of the collision, I am wondering if you would be able to show us with your own body how Kimberly's body moved from the point of the impact to the point of both vehicles coming to rest. I am going to go to the end of the courtroom and come at you, and when I slap my hands together and say, *"Crash,"* please move your body the way that Kimberly's body moved for the first five seconds after impact.

A: OK.

[I go to the entrance to the courtroom and start walking fast toward the witness. Then I slap my hands together and loudly say, *"Crash!"*]

A: Well, the first thing that happened was . . .

Q: Doctor, wait. I am asking for you to just show us, move your body like Kimberly's body without saying a word. I am not asking for an explanation. I am just asking that you show us without saying a word. Are you able to do this?

A: Yes.

[I go back to the entrance of the courtroom, walk toward the witness, and say:]

Q: *Crash!*

[The witness moves like a fool and the jurors are trying not to laugh. Or the expert admits he does not know how her body moved.]

Making a point and establishing a fact through cross-examination is much more powerful and effective than doing it on direct examination. Show pictures and anatomical illustrations. Bring the defense expert down off the stand and reenact things if you feel comfortable. And take risks. Do things you have never done before. Plan them in advance. Have a plan B if it goes wrong, and don't get upset or stop trying if something doesn't work. The courtroom can be a fun place. Cross-examination is the time when most judges let you get creative. Have fun with it, entertain the jury, advance your case, and bring the courtroom to life.

Keeping Connected with the Jury during Trial

Steve Halteman

One way I try to help out during trial is to watch the jurors and monitor their reactions. Throughout the trial, I keep my focus on the jury box. Why? Well, because that's what I've been asked to do. But it's also where I think I can do the most good. And maybe part of the reason is just because no one else is doing it. Let's face it: who goes to the movies and watches the audience the entire time? The same thing happens in a courtroom. The action is center stage, where questioning and presentations are taking place. That is where everyone's focus naturally goes. I fight that urge, and instead, I watch people watching the show. I try to read their facial expressions and body language. Are the jurors reacting favorably or unfavorably to the day's conversations and themes? How do they react to each lawyer? Do they seem persuaded?

Observing Isn't an Exact Science

I wish I could say that this work of observing the jury is an exact science. "Juror number four touched her ear during your cross of expert X; therefore, she did not approve of the harshness of your tone." But it is not like that. Perhaps there are people who can pull that off, but I'm just not one of them. I must swim against the tides of my limitations. Still, if you watch with patience, over time, you will develop a sense of a given juror's inner emotions. Adding up these observations allows you to predict which way the juror is leaning and which approaches impact him or her.

Obviously, not all jurors are the same. Just like there is a range of comprehension on a jury, so there is a range of emotional display. Some jurors are open books, there to be read by anyone who takes the time. Others give away nothing, at least to me. It's the ones in the middle that make me work. Nothing for days, then a backhand to a neighbor's arm and a roll of the eyes when the defense lawyer is making excuses for his client. This is a good sign from both of the jurors—they've been talking. Add up the signs and go with your gut.

At the start of closing in the *Blunt* case, I told Nick I was pretty certain that seven jurors were with us, one was leaning away from us, and I had no idea about the other four. Does that help? I believe so. Based on the backgrounds of the four unknowns, we could tailor parts of the closing to appeal to them. If settlement negotiations are ongoing, believing seven out of twelve jurors are with you allows a position of strength. Or the opposite: if seven out of twelve are against you, start bluffing and begging. If seven out of twelve are with you, your need to take risks in the closing is lessened. If seven are against you, swing for the fences in closing.

Watch for Group Cohesion

Another observation I made during the *Blunt* trial was the remarkable cohesiveness of the jurors as a group. During short breaks, there was a lot of chatting going on in the box. During longer breaks, the jurors sat together in the hallway. At lunch, they ate together. I've seen trials where there was very little interaction among the jurors. I've even seen a trial where the jurors did not exchange one word between each other during the two-week duration. That, to me, introduces volatility into guessing how things will go in the deliberation room. But when jurors are cohesive as a group, it points to consensus in decision making. This increases the likelihood of a unanimous verdict, which can be good or bad, but never inconsequential.

LISTEN TO QUESTIONS

Questions from the jurors can be a way to keep a connection and stay in tune. If the court or law allows juror questions, tell the jurors in opening that they can ask questions and tell them how to do it.

In the *Blunt* trial, the jurors were permitted to submit written questions. The frequency of this increased as the trial wore on and the jurors' confidence increased. The juror would hand her question to the courtroom attendant, who would pass it to the clerk, who would pass it to the judge for approval, who would pass it back to the clerk for copying, who would hand the copies to the courtroom attendant, who would distribute them to the lawyers. The lawyers would then read the question and decide whether to ask them.

What I found interesting was the jurors' reactions when their letters were delivered. As I was focused on the jurors, I was usually aware of who had written and passed the question to the courtroom attendant. Almost without exception, the writers would pay very close attention to how the lawyers received their questions. Did the lawyers read them and consider them, or toss them aside? Everybody, including jurors, wants to feel they are pitching in. That they are part of the process. Not considering jurors' questions well is a form of rejection—do it at your peril.

So, based on this, I suggested to Nick that he read every question thoroughly and nod up and down as he did so. His face should suggest, "Wow, great question. Why didn't I think of that?" Then, if it was his turn, he should ask the question, whether it was a good or bad question for us.

I suggested this for two reasons:

1. It showed respect for the writing juror's efforts. That respect perhaps had more value than the actual answer.

2. Nick told the jurors in voir dire that there were no bad questions. Why should the trial change things?

And that is what Nick did. I don't know how much it helped, but as the trial continued, the jury questions trended toward favorable questions for the plaintiffs.

Keep Track of Reading Material

Whenever book and magazine covers are visible, I make note of what jurors are reading. If it is a book, I will track it down and read it. Why? Because I believe that libraries reflect personalities. If a book appeals to a juror, then maybe there is something in the content relevant to the trial. For example, if a juror is reading a book about a conspiracy, he should be receptive to our theme of a hospital cover-up by disposing of medical records. So we would emphasize that in closing. Every little move is aimed at an eventual checkmate.

The Foreperson

Early on in the *Blunt* trial, I picked the person whom I thought would be the foreperson. The lawyers on our legal team concurred. In the end, we were lucky, as our guess proved correct. Our effort to focus on that juror was not wasted. As to the jurors' verdict, seven with us, one leaning away, and four unknown going into closing was my guess. But what caused me to be optimistic as the jurors began deliberations was their cohesiveness. I believed this would lead to consensus. This was another lucky guess, as the jurors came back twelve to zero on negligence and causation in favor of the plaintiffs. As to the damage questions, the vote was ten to two and eleven to one back and forth. It would have been nice to guess twelve to zero going into the closing though. Maybe next time. The verdict was $74.2 million in favor of the Blunts.

Conclusion

To have a paid observer in trial every day giving you feedback is not a luxury everyone can afford. Still, most lawyers have access to volunteers they can draft. Anybody can watch and listen. Preferably, it should be someone unbiased and not afraid to say it like it is. Check in with your observer throughout the day for her observations. Her insights might surprise you, and they might even help your case. Buy lunch for her and try out some of your ideas for the afternoon session. You might end up writing a book together.

Closing Argument

Nick Rowley and Steve Halteman

Nick's View of Closing Argument

Empowerment, righteous indignation, passing the responsibility, and putting your client in the jurors' hands. In closing, we are giving our case—everything we have worked hard for—away. What we believe, what we have been able to control, everything that the case is to us and our client—we give it to the jurors.

Closing is the time to rally up your team and give them the ball. This is the time when someway, somehow, you must make it important and personal to the jurors. This is not a violation of the golden rule. We are not asking the jurors to pay the amount of money in a civil case that they would take if they suffered similar injuries. That is the golden rule. Instead, we need to talk about the importance of the verdict to the community, to safety, and making sure that the defense team knows they cannot act this way and get away cheap.

Closing is the time to teach the jury how to deliberate back in the jury room and go about their job. I do this sometimes by setting two chairs in front of the jury box, facing each other. I model what arguments jurors might make back in the jury room that I am afraid of, and I show the jurors how to respond. I point to the door to the jury room. I always go in the jury room before closing so I can set the scene and tell the jurors what it looks like. I say:

> Back there in that jury room, there is a table. There are chairs around the table. The table is made of wood. As you sit around that table, you will all be able to look at each other for the first time during the trial.
>
> What happens at this table is up to you. There might be a few people who work at that table to send this case out of court and help the defendants escape justice, avoid responsibility. I sure hope that isn't so, but just in case, I hope there are a few of you who fight hard for Sofia and who won't give up. It is easy to give up. It is hard to stay and fight for what you believe in.
>
> Nothing I say is evidence. Nothing you say to each other is evidence. But it is the only thing that matters, the only thing that makes a difference, and what jurors say in their verdict, I believe, is the most powerful thing we have in our system of justice.

I then go on:

> Back in the jury room, somebody might say medicine is not perfect. That person is 100 percent right. We are not asking for perfection and that is not the issue. The question here is what the standard of care is in your medical community. If you check "no" to the first question, the defense walks out of here not only having their experts to excuse them whenever they need to call on their experts, but now they have a stamp of approval from the patients in the community saying that this is acceptable medicine, we can practice medicine this

way, and if a person gets hurt, well, too bad. We get away with it. The jury has said this is the standard of reasonableness and safety in this community.

Folks, that scares me. It is scary to think that not only can medical providers who we trust our lives to—not only can the medical providers practice this way, hurt a person, shove it under the carpet and deny that they did anything wrong, and not only can they get their experts to back them up and make excuses for them, but they got the community to support anything they do. That is scary. Your verdict is so important. Your verdict is something the hospital can come back to month after month, year after year, patient after patient, case after case, and say: "We get to practice medicine this way, and the community says it is acceptable!" I hope that is not what they get to say. Giving a stamp of approval on medical care like this would be a scary thing for this community.

I will go through a number of issues, sit in the chair as a juror, and model what I fear jurors will say and what the defense lawyer will say in his closing. This way, when the defense lawyer gets up to talk, the jurors have heard it all. There is nothing new to hear.

Judges instruct jurors not to be passionate, not to have sympathy, and to "decide the case on the facts and only the facts." Human sensations are facts, aren't they? Love can be a fact. Happiness can be a fact, and so can sadness, embarrassment, and loss of comfort, companionship, independence, and identity. How can a person judge and value these vital facts without applying his or her "humanness"? Jurors often translate a judge's instructions into believing that it is wrong for them to be human.

We want jurors to know that they are in the courtroom as regular everyday human beings of the community, that they are there to use everything that makes them human to carry out justice. They need to make an important decision about justice, and it is OK for them to apply their humanness, to make a community decision with their combined hearts, guts, and minds.

Slides for Closing

I use metaphors and slide presentations during closing, but I make sure that the presentation is something that complements what I am saying, not something that substitutes, and not something that interferes with my connection with the jury.[1]

I have a number of slides I've used in closing, but I try to limit the number to the select few that I feel convey the most important points I want the jury to remember. Sometimes these are new slides the jurors haven't seen before, and sometimes they're repeats of slides they saw during trial.

This slide comes from the *Von Normann* case, when the defense's position was that they saw nothing, heard nothing, and knew nothing. They were playing dumb and behaving like the proverbial three monkeys.[2]

The defense's position in the **Von Normann** *case*

---

1. Available in the downloadable content are transcripts of closings I have done in *Blunt, Wall,* and *Von Normann.* I talk about equal trade value, and you will see how I pass the responsibility of making sure justice is served over to the jury.
2. *Von Normann v. Newport Channel Inn,* case number 30-2010-00423312, Superior Court of California, Orange County, CA.

In other cases, I've used an image like the following to show that the defense is ignoring what happened and refusing to see.

The defense behaving like an ostrich

Slides are images the jurors can carry with them into deliberation. Often a simple picture will stick with them after several days of testimony.

Steve's View of Closing Argument

Greater minds than my own have written mounds of articles about the art of closing argument. The authors have certainly had more experience with closing arguments than I do, because I have never actually done one.

Closing is your last chance to make a lasting impression. If the trial has not gone well for you, it's your last chance. If the trial has gone well for you, it's still your last chance. I suspect most people prefer a bad movie with a good ending to a good movie with bad ending. Good endings leave a better taste in your mouth. What I'd like to talk about is how Nick prepares for closing, and my observations of the process.

Preparation for closing normally has an informal and a formal stage. In the informal stage, the lawyers gather and start to organize information. In the formal stage, the attorneys organize this information into an actual closing argument, which they then practice and polish. Because Nick is opposed to anything formal, we never actually reach that stage. And if the informal stage has any structure to it, I'm still looking for it. Basically it goes like this. Early on, working with Nick, I noticed that great ideas for closing were always popping up during the trial. Nick or one of the other lawyers would say, "Why don't we try this or say that?" Problem was, in a long trial, these ideas were often lost to the passage of time and memory. So I started keeping a file and taking notes. Ideas shouldn't go to waste. Now, when Nick and I are batting around closing ideas and come up with something, he'll say, "Write that one down in your file." That's about the extent of the long-term preparation.

Short-term preparation starts with the arrival of our AV specialist, Pat Logan, and his cases of computer stuff, Diet Coke, and candy bars. About a week out, Pat starts to put together the audiovisual section of the closing. He reuses some of the slides from the opening and creates some new ones. This is really the only time during preparation for closing that the whole team gathers together. We run through the slides one by one and agree what works and what doesn't. Pat makes the needed changes. We hold another meeting and introduce more changes. Pat's torture is ongoing up to and including the morning of the trial.

The results are always worth Pat's suffering. Why? I believe a slide provides a reference point for the entire jury. There are relatively few slides in any closing. There are thousands upon thousands of words. A picture's impact on the brain is stronger than words. Thus the jurors can recall it more easily. "Remember the slide that showed the connection between the hospital, Stanford, and the doctor?"

Chances are that jurors' joint recall of that slide will be much greater than if Nick had just made the connection orally. The same is true with words shown on a screen, reinforced by Nick speaking them at the same time.

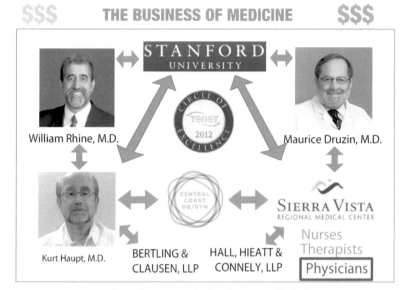

Relationships between defendants in the Blunt *case*

I can't imagine a closing that isn't made stronger by an AV presentation. For example, we spent a lot of effort in the *Blunt* trial educating the jurors about our version of the fetal monitoring strips. I was dubious about their value. To me, they looked like a seismograph showing various earthquakes. I didn't really understand them. The rest of the team, however, held them in high regard. We agreed to disagree.

That was before Nick and Pat created an ongoing series of relevant fetal monitoring strip slides with large red circles around the crisis points for Sofia's heart. "Danger" was spelled out next to many of these crisis points. Now I was onboard with the value of fetal monitoring strips. Because it was visual, I could now understand how much the defendant doctor had dropped the ball. How could he miss all those, I wondered? Judging by the jurors' comments after the verdict, the doctor's failure to monitor the monitoring strips also hit them hard. My bet is that all those red circles brought the danger home.

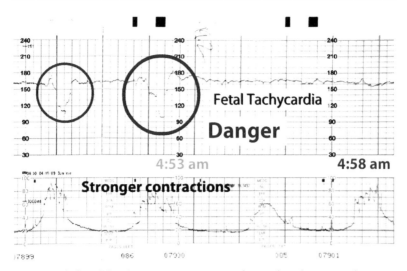

Slide of fetal monitoring strips from the Blunt *trial*

Meanwhile, as Nick and Pat are developing the slides, the rest of the team works independently on their parts of the closing. I tend to focus on the human angle of the case. My guideline is: *what do the jurors want to hear?* Not "What is the best legal argument?" but rather "What is the best emotional argument?"

For example, in the *Blunt* trial, there was a lot of discussion about Sofia's life expectancy. There were many parents sitting in the jury box. I am a parent. No parent wants to hear about his or her child dying young. Everyone can agree on that. So a strong emotional argument would be: *What gives the right to any person to say another's child will die young, especially when the premature death will benefit the speaker economically?* The trip wire for this argument would be "life expectancy."

Here are three actual trip wires with their respective arguments, followed by the trip wire in action during the *Blunt* closing. Hopefully this will give you a familiarity with the process.

Trip Wire: Alarms

A video was made during Jennifer Blunt's delivery. The video ended because the batteries in the video camera ran out. During the video, which ended not long before the actual delivery, several alarms could be heard going off in the background. The alarms did not seem to cause the doctor or nurses to react in any significant manner. Our position was that an alarm is a warning designed to prevent a larger disaster. People ignore alarms at their own peril. In the *Blunt* case, for the medical team to ignore the alarms implied negligence.

This excerpt shows the trip wire in action during the *Blunt* closing:

> At the beginning of the case, I told you that the monitor was beeping, the monitor was beeping. And folks, the point of that is, is whether it's—if it wasn't the fetal monitor, because they turned the volume down on that, but the family heard the sound, and they tell me, "Hey, there's beeping going on. We don't know what it is." That's a scary thing for a patient.
>
> So that may not have been the monitor beeping. You know where it would have been beeping is at that nurses' station. And when you're supposed to read it, and you're supposed to be looking at the strip, as a doctor. And if you're supposed to be reviewing that and paying attention to it, and you're supposed to be looking at it, whether it's beeping or not, it's their responsibility to look at those strips, because that's the lifeline of the baby. And that's telling us what's going on. That's telling us, is she being choked? Is that cord strangling her? Is her body, as her head pushes away, is that cord putting a noose around her neck? Let's see what's happening to the heartbeat. What's Sofia saying to us? And we're going to go over what she was saying to us.[3]

Trip Wire: Cord Blood Gas Test

Our argument was that when a baby is born distressed, it is standard procedure in the medical community to do a cord blood gas test. This test will show whether the baby was damaged during the delivery process. Basically, was Sofia's brain starved of oxygen while Dr. Haupt delivered her? Our position was that it was, and

---

3. *Blunt* closing, page 25 to page 26.

Dr. Haupt knew this because of her low Apgar score at birth. The doctor knew that the cord blood gas test would confirm the damage and expose him to liability. Thus, as a matter of self-preservation, he failed to order the test, despite having an hour to do so.

This is the trip wire in action during the *Blunt* closing:

NICK: So here we go. The criteria sufficient to define intrapartum injury. Evidence of acidosis in the fetal umbilical cord blood established that.

MR. BERTLING: Objection; arguing facts outside of the evidence, Your Honor.

THE COURT: Overruled.

Nick: Established that with something that—I'll get to that. We established that this is the criteria. He's right; Mr. Bertling is right. We didn't establish that the cord blood had acidosis, and there's a reason why. She's got all three of those, according to everybody. The only question is this—

[Nick shows a plastic model of the clamped umbilical cord.]

—this cord blood. This is the criteria that ACOG [American College of Obstetricians and Gynecologists] defines. That says this is how you make the slam-dunk, definitive diagnosis, not a more-likely-true-than-not diagnosis. Remember, the standard here is more likely true than not true. This is the standard from ACOG, saying that this is what gives us cerebral palsy, from hypoxic brain injury while the baby is in Mom. Well, folks, this is the instruction.

When the cord is clamped—the cord has three vessels in it, and it has something very precious in there. And when a baby comes out looking dead, when a baby comes out with Apgars in the one percentile, Dr. Haupt knows. Dr. Haupt knows. And the cord is always clamped, like this—

[Nick shows his plastic model of the clamped umbilical cord again.]

—so that the cord blood can be tested. So Dr. Haupt, he had sixty minutes, sixty minutes, while this cord blood was there. And during that sixty-minute period, Dr. Haupt was looking at the cord blood. He knows it's there. Dr. Haupt—it's just sitting there. It's probably in a little tray. And so during that sixty-minute period, I imagine Dr. Haupt is looking at the strips, looking at this baby. Dr. Ochoa comes in. This is bad news. This baby is badly damaged. The blood gas taken shows she's badly damaged.

But there is something in this room, there is something here that would show whether Dr. Haupt, the nurses, together, the team, let this baby go through three hours of something she should have never been put through. There is something that would prove it. There is something that is the smoking gun, the picture of the smoking gun. There is something, according to ACOG. And all of a sudden, after this, Mr. Bertling stopped talking about ACOG.

He stopped talking about ACOG.

And so, within that hour, this cord blood, which was in the control of Dr. Haupt and his team, he had a choice of what to do with it, of what to do with this cord blood. And it was Sofia's cord blood; it belonged to her. It was her. And it would tell us what happened while she was in her mama's tummy. And it would tell us about the acidosis. And it would give us that one final check to show that this hypoxia happened, that this brain injury happened while she was inside her mom. And it's there, and it belongs to her. And we all have the right to know what the test shows. And if a baby comes out looking that bad, you test the blood. But Dr. Haupt never—what went on? This is what happened to the cord blood.

[Nick throws the plastic cord model in the courtroom trash can, with a loud bang.]

That's what happened to it.

[Nick removes the cord model from the trash can.]

And the law tells you what you can do with that. Intentionally concealed or destroyed. Well, folks, this is intentional.

[Nick throws the cord model in the trash again.]

And so, the cord blood, that last factor to show you conclusively that Sofia's cerebral palsy happened in Mom's tummy—I don't get to put that check there. But I do, and you do, each and every one of you do get to put that check there with this instruction with 204.

[Nick removes the cord model from the trash can.]

Because this instruction from His Honor says, it says that if you take evidence that you know—and they all knew. These are smart people. These are the higher-ups, all the powers that be. They know. They choose to do that.

[Nick throws the cord model in the trash again.]

You may decide the evidence would be unfavorable to the party. You may decide that that other check mark exists, and that's the law of the case. You take something, you chuck it. You chuck a record, you chuck some blood, the baby's blood you should test. That means each and every one of you get to say, you know what, you shouldn't have chucked that. You should have known better. You did know better. And we're going to check that extra box, and we're going to say this is what did it. That gives you permission to check that box.

[Nick removes the cord model from the trash can.]

Anyone in here, who thinks it's reasonable to have chucked that cord blood, with everything we heard, and the truth that we found out?

He knew. Mr. Bertling said he was all up to date with ACOG. That means he knew those four factors. He should know them inside and out. He knew. And that's more likely true than not true, folks. You know in your gut. More likely true than not true, folks. You know in your gut. More likely true than not true. And have they proved otherwise? This is called destroying.

[Nick throws the model in the trash again.]

> That's what happened here, in your community. Because everyone cared about protecting themselves and their reputations, and Dr. Haupt chose that.

[Nick removes the cord model from the trash can.]

> And you know what? Does that make him a bad, evil person, or is that just self-preservation of a doctor who has standing in the club of the community, the club? Because, you know, to be in that club. And he wants to protect his reputation and his standing in the club. Maybe it's just self-preservation. You know.

[Nick throws the model in the trash.]

> So—whatever it is, it's sad.[4]

Trip Wire: Doctor Wouldn't Change Course

Our argument in this trip wire was that there are a number of ways for a doctor to deliver a baby. When one method isn't working, perhaps it is time to try another instead of just repeating the same thing over and over again. In this case, Dr. Haupt continued to simply massage Jennifer's vagina despite the obvious signs that Sofia was in distress. Nor did he discuss alternative methods of delivery with the Blunts. We believed this was negligence on Dr. Haupt's part. Earlier in the closing, Nick pointed out Dr. Haupt's failure to do anything other than continue to massage Jennifer's vagina.

During the *Blunt* closing, we could show this trip wire in action. During this part of the closing, fetal heart rate monitor strips were shown on the screen behind Nick, with circles around the times when Sofia's heart rate raced upward and plunged downward. The racing and plunging were caused by the oxygen to Sofia's brain being repeatedly cut off and restored. The circles were in red and labeled with red letters spelling out: "DANGER."

What follows is Nick explaining to the jurors the doctor's failure to change course.

---

4. *Blunt* closing, pages 53–57.

NICK: So we see what's happening here, and they take it off. We move forward in time. We look as these strips. This is danger [indicating on the slide]. Danger, danger. Mom's heart rate is being picked up. Sofia's heart rate. You see, it's dropping off, right here [indicating on the slide]. Just really quick, Your Honor, if I may [indicating on the slide]?

THE COURT: That's all right.

[Courtroom lights are dimmed.]

NICK: Right here. [Indicating on the slide] This is what's happening to her heart rate. It's coming down, and then it's shooting back up. And you're going to see a pattern. So this is Mom. This is Mom [indicating on the slide]. Dr. Schifrin [the plaintiff's OB-GYN expert] testified. He said, "I'm sure this is Mom." And he showed you how he linked it together. So Sofia's heart rate then is going down here [indicating on the slide], and then shooting up. So she's not getting oxygenated blood, and then when her heart rate is racing, it's just—it's racing but there's not oxygenated blood going to her brain. So this period starts, that's dangerous. Now at any point here, as we move on, at any point during this danger, Dr. Haupt could have rescued Sofia.

So starting at 6:00 a.m., Sofia could be rescued. Again, it's that. It's going down [indicating on the slide]. He can rescue Sofia by doing an episiotomy. No reason not to. He could have rescued her by just stop pushing. Let's put the monitor back on. He could have rescued her, you know, push with every other contraction. Let's wait. Mom, stop pushing, because that puts more pressure on the baby. He could have changed—they are pushing this medication through her. He could have given Mom more oxygen. He could have done an episiotomy. You look at the video. Come on. As reasonable people, would you say, just make the cut. She tore anyhow. She tore. She tore. What's easier to stitch up, a nice incision or a tear? He didn't even give her the option. You know, this baby is not coming out. Dystocia. Dystocia. Would you like an episiotomy? Yeah. She asked in the video, "Why is this taking so long?"

She's out of energy. She can't even feel herself because of the epidural. Give her the choice. Talk to her about it. Didn't at all. Vacuum, forceps. Dr. Haupt did nothing. This wasn't an alternative method. He did nothing, and let's continue. And what evidence do we have that anybody—I know that, Mr. Bertling, you know, had the nurses say, "Oh well, there was nothing wrong with the strip at any point." Really, what part of the strip did you look at? I don't know. When did you pay attention to it? I don't know. When did Dr. Haupt look at it? I don't know. All these "I don't knows" and "I don't remembers," unless it favors them, the team.

But we know, because we look at it ourselves. And we know by looking at it, by what we've learned in this trial, this ain't OK. This is danger. We need to rescue Sofia. That's what a reasonably careful doctor would do.[5]

Props

In addition to compiling a list of arguments and their respective trip wires, I come up with props. For example, the defendant doctor never testified in the *Blunt* trial. It is very unusual in a civil case with contested liability for a defendant not to testify. The opposition made a stipulation that the defendant wouldn't testify, and this failure to do so wouldn't be mentioned in front of the jurors. In fact, the defendant stopped attending the trial several weeks before closing.

My idea was to have Nick set up a folding chair in front of the defense table at the start of his closing. He would never refer to the empty chair. But it would remain there throughout Nick's closing, its symbolism obvious to the jury. Unfortunately, I forgot the chair on closing day, so it didn't happen. But you get the point.

Another prop example was when Nick decided to demonstrate how the defendant doctor had failed to take an umbilical cord blood gas test after Sofia's delivery. Doctors do this test by taking a section of the umbilical cord and having it tested for acid levels. The acid levels show whether brain damage took place

---

5. *Blunt,* page 71 to page 73.

while the newborn was still in the womb. When a baby is born in respiratory distress, it is a standard test to perform. Nick had a mock-up of a clamped-off section of umbilical cord made. He wanted to show what Dr. Haupt had in his hands right after the birth. I suggested one way to demonstrate Dr. Haupt's failure to do the test was to throw the model umbilical cord into a trash can, preferably one of those metal ones common in courtrooms. A nice big sound. Before Nick could answer, I said, "But you probably don't have the guts to do that." He smiled, and then threw the cord away in closing several times, retrieving it after each toss. (This occurred while Nick was discussing Dr. Haupt "chucking" the umbilical cord in the cord blood gas test trip wire above.) Point taken.

When we are working on a case together, a day or two before closing, I will meet with Nick and present my ideas. He'll listen and use what he wants. The same thing happens with other members of the team. Then, usually the day before closing, Nick will compile all the trip wires, put them in the order he wants, make sure all our themes are represented, and then drink wine. The morning of closing, we go for a run and then head to court. That is the end of the informal stage of closing. There are no dress rehearsals. There is no formal stage of presentation and polish. The first time we hear the closing is the first time the jurors hear it. It's fresh and interesting for all. At least it never sounds canned.

Other Observations about Closing

A few other observations about the actual closing. All of these are my opinions, nothing more.

1. Some lawyers use anger in their closing. I've never seen it work. It smacks of desperation and lack of control.

2. I like alternating emotional and logical arguments in closing, just like alternating expert and lay witnesses. There is a balance that is attractive. It's like the lawyer is saying to the jurors, "Here is something for your heart, and here is something for your head." If both are well fed, the juror is happy.

3. Silence still has a place in closing. Like right after the metal clamps hit the bottom of a metal trash can.

4. In closing, take all your time available, unlike the rest of trial. If you run out of allotted time during your initial phase of closing, ask the judge if you can use some of your rebuttal time to wrap things up.

5. Tearing up is OK, as long as there are no crocodiles. I have never seen a lawyer completely break down, so I don't have an opinion in that regard.

6. Have some good stock stories memorized. The kind of stories that send chills up the spine. Finish up your closing with one. Nick often uses the "fire in the museum" story and the "bird in the hand" story, which are both included as follows.

Stock Story: Fire in the Museum

I want to tell you a story. A story about the Louvre, in France. It's a museum where they have the most precious artwork. One time, there was a bad, bad fire, and the Louvre was in flames. Everyone rushed to get outside. The firemen came, and the firemen started rushing in to look for people. They'd bring people out. Just when everyone was out, and they thought it was safe, beams are coming down. It's burning. The manager of the museum told a fireman, "You have to go in and you have to save the Picasso. It's a $100 million painting. You've got to save it."

The fireman ran in. As he got there, he ran in, and he saw the Picasso when he got to the point, and there's all this fire. He looks at the Picasso, and underneath the painting is a little girl. Picasso and the little girl. Without hesitating, he throws the little girl over his shoulder. He runs out. The Louvre goes up in flames, and so does the Picasso.

The manager of the museum, the keeper of the museum, starts screaming at the fireman, "You imbecile, you fool. How could you have left the Picasso? That was made by a master! It was one of a kind!"

The fireman looked at the man and said, "Well, this girl. This girl, she's one of a kind. She was made by the greatest of all masters, and she is worth more."

 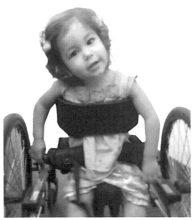

Picasso — Sofia

This is a slide we made for the Blunt *trial.*

Stock Story: *The Bird in the Hand*

Once upon a time, there was a wise old man, and there was a smart-aleck young boy. The young boy always wanted to outwit the wise old man. One day, he came up with a plan. He said, "I'm going to go into the forest, and I'm going to find myself a baby bird. I'm going to come up to the old man, and I'm going to say, 'Old man, what do I have in my hands?' The old man would say, 'A baby bird.' 'Well, is the baby bird alive, or is it dead?'"

If the old man said the bird was alive, the boy would squish it and say, "You're wrong." If the old man said the bird was dead, the boy would open his hands and let the bird fly away, thus outwitting the wise old man.

So the boy goes into the forest, and he searches and searches, and he comes up and finds a baby bird. He gets the nest, and brings the baby bird to the wise old man. He says, "Old man, what do I have in my hands?"

The old man says, "It's a baby bird."

"Well, is the bird alive or is it dead?"
And the old man says, "The bird is in your hands. You decide."

• • •

Sure, other lawyers use these stories. They're not Nick Rowley originals, but what are the chances the jurors aren't hearing the stories for the first time? In the *Blunt* trial, Nick used the latter as his summing up. The jurors were visibly delighted. Deep down, despite what television and the Internet have eradicated, we are still a people that loves live music and a good live story around the campfire. We appreciate gifted storytellers. Tell the jurors a good story and you will be rewarded.

Talking about Money

Nick Rowley

Money. It's such a dirty word when it comes to lawsuits. Too bad it's not four letters. It's the only way a civil plaintiff can get true justice, yet it's the sole reason our legal profession is often belittled in society. Headlines scream: "Money-hungry lawyers," "Plaintiffs' verdicts skyrocketing out of control," and "Caps on medical malpractice damages upheld."

We're taught from a young age that it's not polite to discuss issues of money. Don't ask how much something costs. Don't talk about how much your parents make or how much anyone else's parents make.

When we walk into a courtroom, we have no credibility, and we are asking for money. How do you feel when somebody asks you for money? Does it make you happy? Would you rather *not* have been asked for money? How do we get over the hurdles of lack of credibility and asking for something that makes people uncomfortable? Imagine asking an acquaintance how much her salary was last year. Or asking your boss for a raise. The mere thought of this probably gives you a queasy feeling. Money makes people uneasy.

In your case, you're going to need to talk about money. There's no way around it. So talk about it early, and talk about it often.

Example: Money in Voir Dire

Talk about it in voir dire.

For example, sometimes the issues of religious beliefs and people's relationships to money come up. In those cases, I've asked:

"Can there be forgiveness, and also compensation?" If my clients say, "We go to church. We have our beliefs, and we forgive," yet they're still bringing a lawsuit for compensation to take care of their daughter for the rest of her life, I'll ask the jury, "To make this all right, is that something that is OK with you, in terms of being a juror on this case?"

In another instance, I've tried to get the jurors to think about valuing their own losses or tragedies in terms of a dollar amount:

> Talking about the issue of money, and brutal honesty, is that something that is an uncomfortable thing to talk about? Right now, think of something tragic that you've gone through in your life. Can you pause for a minute and think of that? I won't ask you what your tragic situation is. I'm thinking of mine. Can you imagine being asked to equate that to a dollar amount of money? "Here's a dollar amount it's worth." For me, I couldn't fathom it either. Even though it's what I do for a living as a lawyer.

> Even though money doesn't wipe away any of the pain or the injuries, it is the *only* way to compensate for injuries at trial. The only way. I'm acknowledging with the jury that equating pain and suffering to money is extremely difficult, yet absolutely necessary.

Example: Money in Opening Statement

Talk about money in opening statement. In Jim Von Normann's brain injury case, this is part of what I said in opening statement about money damages, after apportionment was dealt with:

An important thing at this point is, now that the only thing we're talking about is damages, is to have no sympathy for the defense. When you're adding up what something is worth, what a dollar value is of a day of pain, or a day of harm, you figure, "What's the reasonable compensation? What's the equal trade dollar value for that day of harm of a life?" It's not to say, "Well, if we believe that is a lot of money, we felt sympathetic, so now we're going to drop that down." Or, "We're going to drop that number down because the man who was hurt was drunk." That's already done and dealt with. So now it's just a matter of figuring out what things are worth.

And I mentioned to you at the beginning that if we got to this point, it was going to be many millions of dollars. We're dealing with a lifetime of care for a person whose brain is shrinking. And I'm going to tell you what it is at the end I'm going to ask you for. I'm going to be brutally honest with you. I'm going to tell you what the evidence is going to show, and it's a bit of a sad story.

But we're going to have to project out for the next almost fifty years, because this is Jim Von Normann's one and only trial. He doesn't get to come back and get more money for damages that he suffers twenty years from now. This is it. So your job will be to forecast, to look ahead in time, and project. And look at him when he's a fifty-year-old man, and what's going on with his brain, and what's going on with his life, and figuring out the equal trade dollar value for reasonable compensation when he's fifty, and when he's sixty. I want to show you what the evidence will prove in that regard.

* * *

Now, I want to tell you and be brutally honest with you about what I'm going to ask you for at the end of the day, and tell you why the evidence will justify that. Your job will be to evaluate damages for the fifty-one years of a human being's life. Fifty-one years. The total verdict we're going to ask you for is many millions of dollars. I'll tell you how that will add up as fair

> justice and equal trade dollar value for fifty-one years of a severe traumatic brain injury, and how that is going to be a number that will persevere. I'll show you how that is. That's a shocking big number, but I'll show you the reasons why that's a just number to take care of a person with a brain injury, so it doesn't fall back on the taxpayers to take care of him.
>
> Your job will be just to determine what the numbers are, and it will be the court's job to determine how that gets paid. Your job is just, "What is something really worth? What is the equal dollar value of the damages?"

• • •

> He's been diagnosed with dementia by the doctors that have seen him. And dementia is something we hope we're never going to get. If we are going to get it, then maybe medicine or some pills will help. When you have dementia from a brain injury, there's no medicine to really help. You can slow it down, but you can't stop it. So it's not something that he's going to get when he's in his sixties. It's something he has now as a man in his twenties, and it's progressively getting worse.

[I then go on to describe all of his injuries and the care he will need. After that description, I continue:]

> So, future damages. What I have is "equal trade dollar value." Your job will be to determine reasonable compensation. If you went out, and there was a building or car that was ruined, you'd look at the Kelley Blue Book or Edmunds.com and ask, "What's the equal trade dollar value of that vehicle?" That's the reasonable compensation. It shall be 100 percent of the equal trade dollar value of the item that's been lost.
>
> Your job will be to figure out what the equal trade dollar value is of human happiness, of human life, for 47.8 years, to the year 2060 in the future. You'll have to figure out what 47.8 years of that equal trade dollar value is, what the fair trade is, for what's been done to him. That's 570 months.
>
> Physical pain.

[I then describe the physical pain.]

Loss of independence. Living a brain-injured life. Being inconvenienced. Not being able to just go to the store when he wants to go, or go out and work a job. He's not employable anymore. He's not going to be able to go to college, to do the things that a normal young man would do. And the enjoyment of his life? A lot of that has been lost.

Each of those, you'll be instructed, are separate issues of harm. And each separate item must have a dollar amount assigned to it. So, you'll go back in the jury room and say, "What's the reasonable compensation, the equal trade dollar value, for a life of seizures?" Is it cheap? "What's the 100 percent value of a trade for a life of seizures? A life of everything he has?"

To balance that out for the future, with all the medical bills, the medical care is going to be just about $20 million. I'll explain to you how I believe that all adds up to be an equal trade, a fair trade, for the life he has now. An equal trade for a human being's damages.

The past damages, past medical bills, just up to now are about $1 million. That has to be paid. It's owed to the community, and the hospital in this community. They're waiting to be paid for their bill.

And you'll figure out the past value of 3.4 years of a shrinking brain, 3.4 years of pain, 3.4 years of humiliation, 3.4 years of his life in his twenties. I'm going to ask you for the past, just what he's gone through up until today, through this point in trial, to give $3.4 million as the trade for what he's been through up to this point. His justice for everything that's been done to him and his brain.

Now, this is a decision, listening to the medical witnesses, and what this patient is going to need for the rest of his life, and what he's going to go through. It's a decision that I'm going to ask you not to make with any sympathy. Sympathy? You leave that outside of the courtroom. No sympathy. If we figure this is what it's worth, there's no sympathy for the defendant. We're not asking you for a verdict based on sympathy. We're asking you for a verdict based upon the evidence and your humanity. You look at this as human beings, apply your collective humanity and common sense, look at the evidence, and ask, "What is it worth to have a brain and a life that's injured for fifty years?"

The question will be, "Is it worth a lot in Orange County, or is it something that's cheap?"[1]

Example: Money in Closing Argument

Talk about money in closing argument.

In Matthew Wall's case (the young man whose pelvis was injured and his penis smashed in a motorcycle accident), this is how I addressed the money issue in closing:

> Think about what he has gone through as a human being to take away a chunk of his twenties, and say "Here is a trade for that." Can you imagine that? When you say reasonable compensation, and it is equal trade, I take reasonable compensation for a vehicle, an expensive painting, or an airplane. Something that is destroyed. Or some expensive Bugatti car. Reasonable compensation, if it is ruined, is the equal trade dollar value of what was taken. It is the equal trade dollar value. Anything less is unreasonable compensation. To take his life, twenty-three to twenty-seven, put him through all of this, that is reasonable. If you go for the rest of his life, the next fifty years, that is not unreasonable. It is not unreasonable.
>
> You are all told in the instructions that if public opinion says, "You know what? Giving people big jury verdicts is bad." That is public opinion, and push that aside.

---

1. *Von Normann v. Newport Channel Inn,* case number 30-2010-00423312, Superior Court of California, Orange County, CA.

Prejudice and prejudice, push that aside. What is the equal trade dollar value, the reasonable compensation, of taking this kid and sentencing him to this?

Let's just look at what the number is. If it was some expensive horse that was going to run the Kentucky Derby, and he broke his ankle and couldn't run anymore, I could ask for $50 million, and nobody would blink an eye. Well, it's an expensive horse. One of a kind. Well, Matthew's body, and himself, he's one of a kind too. And society tells us, "Well, we can put big dollar amounts on things like a racehorse, a baseball player, or a painting, that goes for hundreds of millions of dollars, but when it comes to a human being, let's go cheap."

Well, what I say to corporations is, "You get no discount. You pay 100 percent of the true value of the human being. You pay 100 percent. You get no discount." And folks, with what has gone on, I'm asking you to give them no discount at all. No discount at all. The law says 100 percent of the damages.

If for some reason, you find that Matthew is at fault, and he shares a percentage, you still add up the total number of his loss. You add up the percentage of whatever the apportionment of responsibility is afterwards. That number doesn't change. If you believe this is the number, the fair trade of what he has lost, the judge makes the adjustment, but you don't reduce the number yourselves.

When it comes to economic loss, noneconomic loss, all those damages, every one is a separate item. Every one is a separate item. What you do is, you take pain and a fractured pelvis. He has pain that he lives with every day. He lives with that every day. If he starts to jog or he stands for a long period of time, or he wants to go out and do something active, it starts to throb. It starts to throb.

That is one item of damage. That is one time. If you take that, and if he had it for the past 4.2 years, it is likely that he's going to have it for the rest of his life. And, as he gets old, and his bones are more brittle, as that happens, if the pain is throbbing now after four years from that bone break, that broken pelvis, that will continue. This is his only shot at getting compensated for the equal dollar value of having to walk around with that for the rest of his life.

The evidence is undisputed on that. You take that, and you ask, "What is that worth? How much per day is it worth it to have that? Here is $100, Matthew Wall, to have pelvic pain when you walk around, if you stand for too long, or if it starts to throb. You get $100. Every day." It is every day. That is a separate item of harm. The law tells us every separate item of harm must be compensated for.

You take that, and you take the next separate item, which is anxiety. The next separate item is disfigurement. It changed him down there. That does something to a man. That is disfigurement.

What is that for every day of the rest of his life? "Fifty dollars, Matthew, for each day you have a penis that is an inch shorter, or an inch and a half shorter. You get $50 to have that and live with that every day. For every day of your life: $50." That is not enough. It is not enough. Some of us need every inch we have got. That is not something you take, and then say it's not worth anything. That is a separate item.

• • •

Then, it comes down to the total damages.

If someone says, "Well, you know, if we gave Matthew Wall this much money, he could invest that, and that is going to give him money in the future." Sometimes, anyone with any background in math or accounting or anything might say, "Well, he can make a good investment with that, and make money over time." The law actually tells you, you can't do that. That is improper.

The law says: Here are all of the separate items. There is physical pain and suffering, loss of enjoyment of life. These are each separate items that deserve a dollar amount: disfigurement, physical impairment, inconvenience, grief, anxiety. Each one of these. It says that the amount of noneconomic damages should not be further reduced to present cash value.

That means you don't say, "Well, we want to give Matthew Wall the $17 million for what he has gone through, and what he is going to go through over the years, but we're going to give him this much, because he can invest that, and get that amount." The law says you don't do that.

・・・

So, for Matthew Wall's past damages. If we were to add these up, each separate item, and say to Matthew, "We have got a deal for you." It's that morning, and a stoplight comes up. Right at that intersection is where Matthew Wall is going to pass the base. He stops. There is someone in a black limousine who waves at him, and tells him to pull over to the parking lot. So he pulls over and takes off his helmet.

The man in a dark suit gets out with a briefcase, and he says, "Here, I've got something for you. Mr. Wall, look in here. I've got $1 million, and you are going to get $1 million each year for the next four years.

"You're twenty-three years old. You are going to get this. You are serving our country, and you are doing all these things. You're going to get this. This is yours, but here is the trade.

"This is reasonable compensation, Mr. Wall, because this is going to be the equal trade dollar value for something very personal to you. Something very special to you. And something very special to people who you are in love with and who you are intimate with.

"I am going to take both your testicles, and I am going to crush them, put a lot of question marks as to your whole future, your whole life. I am going to damage the arteries to your penis. I am going to damage the nerve. You are going to go through more pain than you could ever imagine.

"I am going to fracture your pelvis. It's going to break; something you can't put a cast on. I am going to break your foot. I am going to hurt you. But here is the deal: you get this. Will you take it? Will you take it, Mr. Wall?"

Mr. Wall says, "No."

"But, this is what you get. You don't have any say in the matter. You don't get to choose. It is going to happen. But this is reasonable compensation. This is reasonable compensation. It is the equal trade dollar value for your intimacy, for your humanity. Take it. It is all you get."

If you ask Matthew Wall, "Is that an equal trade? Is that fair?" It is not. If you ask me, it is not. It should be more. Take someone in the ages of twenty-three to twenty-seven, and you mess them up like this. And then when he needs a surgery, he has to wait. He can't afford to get the surgery. The surgery is only temporary. He is still damaged. Goes through needles, all these different things he has to go through, and what he will have to go through for the rest of his life. A lot of question marks. He will be going through it, to some degree or another. "But here is what you get for 4.25 years."

Future? Going to give you fifty years of pain in your pelvis. When your bones change, and they become brittle? We can apply our common sense. Fifty years of being humiliated yourself. "You'll learn to live with it." It doesn't change the damage.

Fifty years of inconvenience. "Well, OK, I am going to take a pill and do this." The spontaneity is gone. Have to deal with the risk of blood clots in that small little artery. Fifty years of mental anguish, fifty years of disfigurement. These are all of the separate items you have been instructed on. To say, "Well, here is what you get for fifty years. Fifty years, Matthew Wall. There you go."

"No, corporations. No. No. I don't want that. I will take all of that and trade it to get back what I had, and to just be a twenty-three-year-old, a twenty-seven-year-old, and a thirty-five-year-old. To have every chance in the world when it comes to this part of me." If he could pay for a magic wand, that took all of that money and trades it, that is an equal trade dollar value.

If you say it is more, you can say it is more. You have that power to say it is more. I sure hope you don't say it is a lot less, because that is an insult to injury with what he has gone through.

So when you are back in that jury room, if someone says, "You know what? That Nick Rowley and Courtney Yoder? They are just crazy. That is way too much." Ask yourselves. If you go forward in time fifty years, your job here as a jury is to compensate him for the year 2061, for the year 2050. When you look at what money is now versus then, your job is to project, because he only gets this one trial. One shot.

You ask, "Well, how do we know what is right to compensate him for his pain and suffering from all those different separate items, for all of the years, for each of those years?"

One way to look at it is to go back in time and think about it. The first man was put into space in 1961, and it was a Russian. Russia put the first man into space. Big differences.

If you were to take a jury back in 1961, and a man suffered an injury like this, and you projected forward to give him damages for fifty years, and decided to give him $1.5 million to compensate him for everything he is going to go through from the year 1960 to the year 2010, back in 1961, you would say, "That is crazy." But if you look at it using your common sense and your intelligence now, you would say that for fifty years, that's not crazy. Equal trade dollar value. That is not outrageous. It is something that makes sense when we look forward, and we know that our job is to give him these damages for the rest of his life.

So imagine yourselves as that jury back in 1961 with the same injury. The lawyer says, "Hey, $1.5 million for fifty years?" Then, put yourselves forward in time as the jury, looking back at what you gave. I don't think it is unreasonable.

You all get to tell these defendants what Matthew Wall was worth, and what he went through. You all get to have a verdict form, which will be here in this courthouse for many, many years. For fifty-four years, it will be in this courthouse, your verdict form. Look forward in time. Fifty years from now would be 2061.

In 2061, you look back and say, "Well, this is what a jury gave back in 2011 for something that happened to a young man and changed his life. That is justice." Or, in 2061, you may look and say, "Actually, that is really not enough justice, looking at what things cost now."

You get to say in the community something that everybody in this courtroom can go back, and look at, and say: "This is what no discount is. This is what full justice is."[2]

The law tells the jury not to have any sympathy for the defense, even if the damages were a billion dollars. We want the jury to know this when they are figuring out what the equal dollar value (E$V) is for each of the separate items of damage.

I use slides to convey this idea of time, that this is the one shot that the plaintiff gets to cover him for fifty years. Some of these slides are included as follows. What did bread cost in 1961, and what does it cost now? The same with gas and milk. A picture is worth more than words.

---

2. *Wall v. Miramontes,* case number 37-2009-00068436-CU-PA-EC, Superior Court of the State of California, County of San Diego, East County Division.

Talking about Money   269

25 cents

$3.50

1961 - 49 cents

2011 - $3.67

1961 - 21 cents

2011 - $2.49

The Deliberation: Closing and Rehearsals

Teach your jurors how to deliberate when they go back in the jury room. Tell them that sometimes there are a couple of jurors back in the deliberation room (point to where the deliberation room is) who will fight for the defense and for the defense experts. These people will try everything they can to keep the verdict low and to not give justice. That it is OK if a person has made up his or her mind to help the defense, because we only need nine out of twelve.

Conclusion

Own the dollar value you're asking for. Bring it into every part of the trial. Get used to the number, explain it, have it be a part of who you are. If you believe in it, the jury will believe it with you. If you're afraid of the number, the jury will sense that too.

18

LIFE LESSONS

Nick Rowley

IF YOU CANNOT TALK ABOUT IT, IT IS OUT OF CONTROL

Anxiety is the anticipation of pain and injury. Whatever is going on that is stressful or that bothers you, talk about it. Put it out in the open. Be prepared to listen and care about what others have to say. Client, family, judge—whomever you need to talk to: talk.

YOUR JURY NEEDS TO SEE YOU

Don't leave during deliberations. Be there waiting and showing you care. I sometimes show up the day after the verdict in regular everyday clothes. I am more comfortable that way. I have somebody else wear the suit and deal with the court issues.

Protect Your Verdict

If you and your client have won the case, don't go celebrate. Get a good night's sleep. Your opponents are not sleeping; they are working. Investigators who specialize in getting juror declarations and overturning verdicts are knocking at the doors of your jurors' homes. Do you think the defense is going to shake your hand, apologize, give you a check, and pay for your experts and pre-judgment interest? You need to protect your verdict. Depending on the jurisdiction, and being careful about what you write down on paper, you need to make sure to educate your jury, even the jurors who may have been against you, that the defense is bought and paid for by an insurance company. The insurance company will be sending investigators out to interview them with the goal of getting declarations from the jurors that they will use to overturn the verdict on appeal or get a new trial. You need to be armed when those jurors come out with their verdict. Connect with them, talk to them, and if they won't talk to you, have a letter delivered to them by hand, email, fax, mail, or any method you can think of.

Losing and Losing Faith

I know what it is to lose a case and to lose faith. I have felt like giving up, throwing in the towel, and never trying another case. I have tried cases where everything went right and we lost, with the only explanation being the existence of pure injustice, bias, and prejudice. I have lost cases I should have won, and those are something I can handle because I know I can do better next time, or otherwise pinpoint what went wrong. It is the cases that go perfectly, the cases we know we should win, but nonetheless lose, that cause us to lose faith and want to give up. The pain of failure, rejection, and self-doubt is unbearable. I have experienced these feelings of loss and seen how others have given up faith. My message to you is that you must not give up. Do not lose faith. The best thing you can do is pick yourself up and try another case, and if you lose again and again, then try another.

There is also more to winning than the end result. I represented a prisoner whose case was a long shot. My ego and need for self-preservation almost had me walk away and leave the trial to the lawyers who had asked for my help. Walking into the case, I expected we would lose. I tried the case and fought hard. In the end, the verdict we got was not what we had hoped for by any stretch, and the case ended up being exactly what I knew it would be walking into the trial. The win was when I sat down after closing argument and my client, a man who had spent twenty-seven of his twenty-nine adult years in prison, passed me a note with the words "Excellent!" and "Thank you." I left the courtroom that day while the jury deliberated and said to myself, "This is what matters more than anything." I have framed that note, and the man who was the prisoner remains my friend.

You must give yourself permission to lose some battles, understanding that this is inevitable if we are to be warriors and fight more than a few times. Losing battles is part of winning the war. George Washington lost almost every battle before winning the Revolutionary War. General Patton lost many of his battles. Public defenders generally lose the majority of their cases, trial after trial, yet they pick themselves up and try the next case. We rarely hear about losses from the leaders in our trial lawyer communities, and that is sad. The losses are what teach us how to win. Losing can be a gift, as painful as it is. (One of my favorite movies is *Fight Club,* with Brad Pitt and Edward Norton. They start a fight club, and one of the things they make their club members do is go out and lose a fight.)

The best trial lawyers that I know try and lose cases. If you aren't getting knocked down, you aren't trying tough enough cases. Anybody can try the easy cases. Anybody can try a multimillion-dollar case and get a million-dollar verdict. Prosecutors with a 95 percent win rate don't impress me. The public defender with a 10 percent win rate does. If you are a loser, then so am I; stop feeling sorry for yourself and get back up again and fight.

Be Very Careful about Calling People Liars

Someone may be lying, but there is no reason for you as the lawyer to slice them and use that word in front of the jury. Jurors do not like to see people mistreated or beaten down, even when it's obvious that they deserve it. Instead of using the word *liar*, expose the lack of brutal honesty and the lies. If you do that, the jurors will draw their own conclusions and restore the truth.

Rather than calling somebody a liar, I might demonstrate his or her lies by saying this:

> When someone gives us their word, we expect them to keep it. When someone tells us that if we do something, they will do something for us in return, when we do what they have asked, we expect them to do what they have promised they would do.
>
> The defendant doctor and the nurses broke their promise. They took money in exchange for a promise to deliver a certain level of professionalism and care to a patient. They broke that promise and patients were hurt; a family tree has been changed forever.
>
> Courtrooms are places where we see so much dishonesty, so much dishonesty even though everybody takes the oath to tell the truth. You don't need to call the defendant and the nurses liars in order to find them negligent. There is something called "self-preservation" that might be the reason for them not being brutally honest with us. Self-preservation is why the doctors and nurses came in and backed up everything the defendant said and everything that the defense lawyers wanted them to say. Your jury verdict does not take away a medical license or their ability to continue treating patients.

When You Are In and Out of Court, Don't Get Angry

I have a bad temper with a short fuse. There is a book a friend gave me called *Anger: Wisdom for Cooling the Flames* by Thich Nhat Hanh. If you need therapy for your anger, get it. I have.

Look to the root of your anger. If you are angry, it might be because you are wounded and hurt. It might be because you are afraid. Talk to the jury about what is going on within you. It is OK to show your vulnerability and ask for help. What human who cares can deny a fellow human who is hurt and needs help?

Many humans will turn their heads away from and avoid listening to the rage and anger of an attorney-at-law who points and shouts. Remember, it is not just the voice that shows anger and rage. Don't ever point at jurors or raise your voice to a yell or shout in court, and certainly never do it while facing the jury or any other human in the courtroom.

A friend, mentor, and fellow trial lawyer Jim McCallion once opened his arms, looked up to the ceiling during his closing argument, and started crying out loudly for justice. He asked the defendant doctor how in the world he thought he could get away with treating and caring for Jim's client the way he did. It was effective because Jim didn't yell or show anger; instead, he cried out with frustration. He did not send that loudness to any human in the courtroom; rather, he sent it up above. I loved it.

Embrace and Talk about the Ugly Part of Your Case

Tell the jurors what is ugly about the case. Be brutally honest. There are ugly parts of all of us. There are ugly parts of who I am, but without my ugliness, I would not be me. Maybe I would be much better. But I am what I am. This case is what it is, and like most things in the world, it is not perfect.

Be a Happy Person

My friend Aldwin Ali, a man from the island of Trinidad, has taught me a bit about humans over the years. Aldwin is a professional driver who has worked hard picking people up at airports, transporting lawyers and witnesses to and from court. Aldwin impresses me most because he is a single father who has raised his son Josh, who is now twenty-three years old. Aldwin brought Josh here to the United States because he was an infant with cerebral palsy. Josh's mother decided life would be better off without having to raise a child with cerebral palsy. Aldwin has done it all on his own. As I write this, Aldwin is driving me to Victorville, California, so that I can discuss a disagreement I have with a recent order from a judge who has shown some bias.

I love Aldwin because he is always positive, and no matter how bad the day is, he shows happiness. Aldwin says: "A happy person is a good person." We have a tendency to trust happy people. What we can take from this is this: if we are in a courtroom, even though we are dealing with tragedy, we can be happy, we can be upbeat, and we can be positive. We can motivate jurors to be proud of their job because they get to make a difference in the world that will start a wave of change. They will cause a change in a human life. Maybe in turn, that will create a wave of change in the lives of other humans.

You Cannot Say a Good Thing Too Many Times

Geoffrey Fieger taught me this. One thing that Geoff does is repeat things in sequences. For example, he would say, "Dr. Jones[1] is not telling us the truth. He is not telling us the truth. We know he isn't telling us the truth, and we know it because . . ." When Geoff looks the jurors in the eye and repeats what he says, they believe it. Humans only retain a third of what you tell them, so if you say it three times, and you do it in a way that is entertaining and that communicates, it will sink in and sear into the neurons in their brains.

Don't Fight with the Judge, Especially in Front of the Jury

I tried this recently when the judge was a tyrant dictator who was actually an insurance defense lawyer in a black robe. The fight was

---

1. This name has been fictionalized.

inevitable and I engaged in the battle, but I regret it. The judge and my fight with him significantly affected the money verdict. The insurance defense lawyer sucked, as they often do. I could have avoided my fight with the judge. As we walked out of court, I told the young lawyer who I came in to teach and try the case with, "Don't ever do what I did in court today, that fighting with the judge. I probably lost this jury today."

By what I just said doesn't mean that you should just submit to a biased advocate in a robe. You must stand up for yourself—and, more importantly, your client. If it is inevitable that the judge is going to screw your case every chance he gets, then find the courage to make a challenge to the judge before you get to trial. Gather declarations together from other lawyers and call the judge out. If there are bad judges, work to get them removed or to help them change. Make challenges to the judge for cause. Be respectful, make a record, and give specific examples of how the judge is biased. We all have dealt with tyrannical, biased judges. As officers of the court, we have the duty to find the courage to either change bad judges or get them removed.

Many lawyers have succeeded in getting judges and justices removed from the bench, which in turn helps thousands of humans. File a challenge in writing with declarations from other lawyers. If you get stuck with that judge, file declarations each day about the facial expressions, the rulings, and the bullying. In the end, even the worst judges want to see themselves as fair and just. They are the way they are because of their emotions and feelings. Just make sure you are very careful, 100 percent accurate, and respectful when you do this.

• • •

As I write this section, I am sitting in front of a judge in Victorville, California. I am upset with his ruling and am here on my motion for reconsideration. He compelled my client to submit to an MRI. I am looking at him right now as he is doing a minor's comp hearing, and he seems ever so nice. But when it came to my client and my young associate a couple weeks ago, he made an order that is unheard of, and compelled my client to put her body into the MRI scanner of defense counsel's choice.

The law does not allow defense lawyers to get MRIs on plaintiffs in injury cases. The law even says X-rays are not allowed because they are invasive. An MRI is much more complex. An MRI requires informed consent and a medical provider–patient relationship. This judge just gave the defense what they asked for.

It just so happens that the defendant is the County of San Bernardino, and the judge is a San Bernardino County judge. I am going to tell the judge that even if he does not change his ruling, I will not follow it, and that I want to know the sanction now so I can take an appeal. My job is to protect my client, not just roll over and accept any ruling, even if it is an unlawful order.

So here I am. We will see what happens. I will tell you, with brutal honesty, what happens in a few minutes. I think he is reading my papers right now. I was very strong-worded in my reconsideration motion. I told the judge that his ruling was wrong, against the law, without foundation, and that he made a mistake. I spoke very plainly. Well, here we go. My heart rate is increasing; my case is being called next.

* * *

Whew! The judge ruled in my favor. He read my papers and declaration, and said that his prior ruling was wrong. No MRI for my client by the defendant and its scumbag insurance company. When I got up in front of the judge, I was soft and respectful. He agreed with everything I wrote. He saw that he was wrong.

Closing Thoughts

Steve Halteman

Most readers of this book chose to enter a profession with a negative public perception. The hostility rating toward lawyers is high. The list of complaints is long. But that is public opinion in the big world. There's nothing we can really do to change that perception. Just like when we watch the national news, 99 percent of the time, we are powerless to impact events. However, if we narrow the focus to our community—and by that, I mean wherever you are in trial at a given moment—you are no longer powerless. I'm not talking about general public opinion in the local community. There will always be hostility toward big verdicts, lawsuits, and the aspects of human nature that cause lawsuits to be brought in the first place. Trying to change local public opinion about lawyers through conversation, publication, or deed is like trying to talk someone into switching his or her favorite baseball team. It won't happen, though Nick repeatedly bangs his head against that particular wall, trying. What I am talking about is the community of the courtroom. Looking at the big picture through a narrow lens. How to influence that narrow band of public opinion and turn it in your favor, like I have seen Nick do time and time again.

I humbly suggest that the answer to that question boils down to quite a simple concept—caring. I'd like to talk more about caring, but first this: If you already are a truly caring trial lawyer, then the rest of this chapter isn't for you. I congratulate you and hope you have enjoyed the book. But if you've had doubts, by all means, read on.

I am talking about permeating your efforts in a case with caring. Caring about your client, his or her family, and your jury. Being aware of the needs of these people not so you can manipulate them, but so you can help them. Sometimes even making sacrifices personally to do so. Caring about the judge when he or she is at his or her worst, the courtroom staff, the audience, and yes, even your opponent. Caring is an attitude. It is perceptible. It is genuine. It is not kissing ass with various courtroom participants for future benefit. It is transparent to those who receive it. It is recognizing that we are all cogs in a process, without which justice would grind to a halt and no one would reach verdicts. Caring is realizing that most of these cogs will never see the big payday you are shooting for, and yet they still soldier on. Care about them, even when they are being petty, even when it is of no benefit to you.

Caring does not mean being a pushover or always being the nice, soft-spoken lawyer. In fact, it has very little to do with courtroom strategy. You will still have to play hardball, make financially based decisions, and compromise against your better judgment, among other things. Caring will not stop you from being so harsh in a courtroom that observers wince. Caring will not stop you from making mistakes. Caring will not make you a more skilled lawyer. What caring will do is make you a better, more focused lawyer as well as a more sympathetic figure in the courtroom. It will make you aware of the big picture and not just the battle you are fighting.

Caring lawyers seem more self-confident. My hunch is that this leads to better verdicts. Jurors will perceive that you care about them, your client, the judge, and the process. In return, jurors will care about you and your efforts. They might say, "A genuine trial lawyer who actually gave a shit. Who would have thought?" And if you're just going through the motions and don't really care for your client and the process? Well, how can you ask jurors to do what you can't? Are you afraid to change your ways midstream? Just look to Ebenezer Scrooge as a role model.

But you are busy. So many trials, clients, and demands. And that's just your job. Technology keeps inventing ways to interrupt your life. Family, friends, obligations, and so on. So little time. You're thinking about getting a tattoo that says *Burnt out*. I hear you. Unfortunately, there are no easy answers, other than the best one, which is to simplify yourself. Nor are there any shortcuts to a caring attitude. You have to go through the steps outlined in this book. Spend time with your clients and break bread. Develop ways to care and ways to demonstrate it.

Don't try to fake it. You can't fake it effectively, although some actors pull it off. And, truth be told, most good lawyers would also make it as actors. They can turn a performance on and off at will. Still, faking caring is risky. Even great actors need a couple of takes to get it right. This is not something available in the courtroom, although it would be handy. "Take three on plaintiff's cross, and this time more passion, caring, and angst!"

No, you can't fake caring. There are just too many components to it—conscious and unconscious, subtle acts, and overt demonstrations, to fake it over the long course of a trial. The jury notices all of your actions. They hear your words. Let's face it: the lawyers in action are the only channel on the TV. And people are perceptive in many ways—consciously, subconsciously, and unconsciously. By people, I mean everybody sitting in the courtroom. Your words and actions will span that range of consciousness. By the end of the trial, everyone involved will have a definitive and concrete opinion as to whether the lawyers cared about their clients and jurors. The cool thing is, once you really care, you don't have to stress about faking.

Why is it important to be perceived as caring? Back to that range of consciousness we discussed earlier. It's human nature, across the spectrum of consciousness, to reward people who care. For example, see the Nobel Prize. The opposite is also true: we want to punish those who don't care. Lawyers are people—humans, according to this book. If a lawyer cares, the jury will know it, period. If a lawyer doesn't care, the jury will know it, period. All the courtroom strategies and maneuvering in the legal universe will not change this.

Now, the reward and punishment I mentioned above is not always possible out in the real world, with its complexity and size. But in the microcosm of the courtroom and its simple, straightforward structure, it damn well is possible for judges and jurors to punish and reward. They do this in a thousand different ways, big and small, throughout a trial, culminating in the biggest decision of all. Rewards and punishments accumulate and create a momentum toward the verdict. Caring won't dictate the outcome, nor will it overcome bad facts, but it will influence the process. You want the jury to think, "We can't just award them nothing. It would break their hearts." My guess is that the caring lawyer wins the toss-ups in the jury room. Think of caring as your secret weapon. Who knows, it may even create a glacial shift in the negative perception of lawyers, one trial and one micro community at a time.

Everything in this book is an attempt to bring you to a place where you can stand up at the end of trial and say, "I care about my client" with complete sincerity. The jurors need to then receive that comment with unquestioning acceptance. Caring is the foundation upon which you should build your trial practice and trial voice. Demonstrate it throughout your case. Don't cynically ridicule the concept, although that is easy to do. Caring is hard, often annoying work. We create it through effort. Spend the time with your clients, become friends, and help the jurors to understand by putting their needs first. Take the time to pity the poor defense lawyer who must summon up love for a corporation, who must take the time to break bread with a bottom-line client that is actually an insurance company, and who can never risk it all because hours are billable and subject to oversight. Sniff out the passion in that if you can.

A true plaintiff's trial lawyer knows it is not just a job, it is a calling. A caring attitude is mandatory when we are called. Without it, the steps in this book are hollow and will be of little assistance. We've all seen trial lawyers just going through the motions.

Why not go the extra step? Why not care? Why not throw yourself into the fight with passion—for your newfound friends and community? Everything flows from that first step—caring. Trial lawyering is a big part of your life, so why not care about all aspects of it? That way, when the jury files past you while you are playing with your nine-year-old client in the hallway, during a break, you won't have to wonder, how is this playing to the jurors? Do they think I am pandering to their sympathies? Am I? Are the jurors reacting negatively? Positively? Did the jurors like my suit today? Is it demeaning for me to get down on my knees to play?

No, if you care, and the jurors know it, then you're just playing with your bud. Everything else will fall into place.

Now go kick some ass with a caring attitude.

Appendix

THE *BLUNT* TRIAL IN SIX ACTS

Steve Halteman

Act One: Just the Facts

At the time of Sofia's birth, Jennifer Blunt managed the Head Start program for San Luis Obispo County, California. She had a master's degree. Andrew Blunt was a marine veteran. He served in Iraq and managed Kennedy Fitness Center in San Luis Obispo. Jennifer and Andrew were married. They lived in San Luis Obispo.

Upon learning of her pregnancy, Jennifer decided to use her gynecologist for the delivery. The baby was to be delivered at Sierra Vista Medical Center. It was Jennifer's first pregnancy. On April 18, 2009, Jennifer's water broke, and she went to the hospital. She was admitted at 7:19 a.m. Jennifer was hooked up to a fetal heart rate monitor at 7:30 a.m. She began labor at around 9:15 a.m., when she was put on Pitocin (a labor-inducing drug). At around 4:00 a.m. on April 19, one of the nurses repositioned Jennifer. Two labor and delivery nurses were in attendance. The defendant doctor was called at 5:28 a.m. to come down to the hospital. He arrived at 5:45 a.m.

At some point before delivery, the birth was videotaped. The video showed the defendant doctor massaging the vaginal opening. The tape ends before Sofia is delivered. At 6:30 a.m., the defendant doctor described the fetal monitoring strips as nonreassuring. At 6:38 a.m., Sofia was delivered. Her Apgar score (the Apgar score is a simple numerical assessment, from zero to ten, of how a baby is doing at birth) at one minute was 3. One of the nurses assigned the Apgar score.

Three grandmothers (two biological grandmothers plus a step-grandma), as well as Andrew Blunt, were present when Sofia was born. The defendant doctor asked Andrew if he would like to cut the cord. Andrew did so. The defendant handed Sofia to a nurse, who took her to the warming table. The defendant sewed up Jennifer, who tore during delivery. The defendant did not take a cord blood gas test.

The NICU (neonatal intensive care unit) team was called at 6:39 a.m. They arrived at 6:42 a.m. Sofia's Apgar at five minutes was 1. A respiratory therapist made multiple attempts to suction Sofia's airway and get an air tube into her. Then, a second respiratory therapist tried to do so. At some point, Sofia's heart stopped. After twenty minutes, Sofia began to breathe again. At 10:50 a.m., Sofia was flown to Stanford Medical Center because it was suspected she had brain damage. Sofia was at Stanford for about three weeks before being released to her parents.

Sofia has cerebral palsy. Sofia is now three years old. She is unable to walk, talk, or eat. She is fed through a tube attached to her stomach.

Act Two: The Blunt Family's Human Story

Jennifer and Andrew were your typical all-American couple: in their twenties, active, happy, and in love. When Jennifer got pregnant, she decided to use her gynecologist. But after a few visits, his poor bedside manner convinced her to find another doctor to deliver her baby. His nurse talked her out of it, saying, "He's the best. All the nurses use him to deliver their babies." So she stayed.

When Jennifer entered the hospital, she was forty-one weeks pregnant. Sofia was estimated to be 8.5 pounds. Jennifer is very petite. It was her first baby. Upon arrival at the hospital, Jennifer was placed on the fetal heart rate monitor and put on Pitocin.

There were warning signs from the beginning. The first and second stages of labor predicted the difficult childbirth to come. Jennifer's labor continued through the night. At around 4:00 a.m., the charge nurse repositioned Jennifer twice due to cord compression. For over three hours before Sofia's birth, the fetal heart rate strips showed Sofia's heart rate dropping and disappearing for a period of time, then spiking dramatically upward. No one was paying attention.

Eventually, at 5:45 a.m., the defendant sauntered in eating a sugar doughnut. He did not review the fetal heart rate strips from the time before he arrived, so he was not aware of Sofia's distress up until that point.

At some point before Sofia's birth, Andrew began videotaping. Andrew's mother was there, as well as Jennifer's mother and stepmother. The tape showed Dr. Haupt massaging around Sofia's head as Jennifer tries to push Sofia out. In the tape, Dr. Haupt rarely interacts with Jennifer, only telling her when to push. The tape captured the mood change in the room from joy to fear. Despite Jennifer's inability to push Sofia out, the defendant never changes his tactics. Then the tape stopped.

Despite the increasingly alarming fetal heart rate strips, the defendant did not change his approach. In the thirty minutes before Sofia's birth at 6:38 a.m., the signs from the fetal heart rate strips were dire. Her cord was being blocked. She was in trouble. Even the defendant admitted that the strips were nonreassuring at 6:30 a.m. Still, the defendant did not change his approach of basically waiting for Sofia to be born. He did not speed up the delivery by cutting the vaginal opening (episiotomy) and thus allowing for an easier exit. He did not use a vacuum (a cup applied to the baby's head that helps guide the baby out of the birth canal) or forceps (an instrument used to pull the baby's head out of the vagina) to help him deliver Sofia. He did not reduce the Pitocin and have Jennifer throttle back on the pushing, thus allowing both Jennifer and Sofia to rest and recover. He did not perform a C-section. He did not discuss these alternatives with Jennifer and Andrew. He did not call the NICU team when he found the strips nonreassuring at 6:30 a.m., something hospital policy required him to do. He just went on massaging. The defendant kept Jennifer in stage-three labor for three hours, which is unacceptable. Because Sofia's cord was blocked so often and for so long, she was brain damaged in the womb.

At 6:38 a.m., Sofia was finally delivered, tearing Jennifer in the process. Sofia looked pale, limp, and lifeless as she came out with the cord around her neck. The grandmothers were horrified to see their granddaughter born dead. The defendant calmly cleared some mucus and lifted the baby up to Andrew so that he could cut the cord. Andrew was shocked that he was being asked to cut the cord of a dead baby.

Sofia's Apgar score was 3 at one minute, primarily because she still had a heart rate. In newborns, this is the last body function lost before death. A nurse who assigned the Apgar score called the NICU team after seeing Sofia born due to her appearance. The defendant did not ask to have the NICU team called when Sofia was delivered. The defendant simply handed Sofia over to the nurse and was done with her care. He stitched up Jennifer and either "forgot" (deposition) or "decided not" (opening statement) to take the cord blood gas test. Obviously, because it is a guideline of the American College of Obstetricians and Gynecologists (of which the defendant is a member) and hospital policy to take cord blood gas when a baby is born in respiratory distress, Dr. Haupt knew to take the cord blood gas. Because the defendant had been a practicing OB-GYN for thirty-five years, delivered four thousand babies, and had up to an hour to take the cord blood gas, obviously he did not forget. The defendant knew that if Sofia was brain damaged, her cord blood gas would show it occurred while she was still inside her mother. The defendant did not take the cord blood gas as a way of protecting himself against liability. Instead of participating as the only doctor in the room with Sofia's ongoing medical emergency, he stayed with Jennifer and told her everything was going to be OK.

The NICU team arrived in three minutes and began to try to get Sofia to breathe. The first respiratory therapist was called. He tried repeatedly to put the breathing tube into Sofia's airway. He failed. His excuse was that he encountered thick, copious secretions of a substance unlike any he had ever seen before. Throughout trial, the secretions were called "pizza dough," "taffy," and "syrup," among other things. No one took a sample of these mysterious secretions to be tested. When the respiratory therapist was finally able to get the breathing tube in, he put it in the wrong place (esophagus). This cut the oxygen to her brain and Sofia's heart stopped. Sofia's Apgar at five minutes was 1. After a period of time, a second respiratory therapist arrived. The second respiratory therapist was able to get Sofia breathing again by putting the breathing tube in the right place. Sofia was not breathing for twenty minutes.

Andrew watched this entire process and never saw any secretions, nor did he see the defendant doctor participate in trying to get Sofia to breathe. No one else in the room, other than the defendant doctor, was qualified to administer drugs through Sofia's umbilical cord. As Sofia's airway was blocked for some time, there was a delay in getting her needed drugs, because the defendant doctor did not participate. Eventually, a neonatologist (a specialist doctor who works with newborn infants born prematurely or facing serious illnesses) arrived and was able to get the situation stabilized. Sofia was transported to Stanford Medical Center by helicopter to be placed on a cooling blanket. Such blankets are meant to reduce brain damage in newborns.

As Sofia was taken to Stanford, Andrew and Jennifer lay in the hospital bed together crying. The defendant doctor had left the room. The grandmothers were in the hallway, where they saw the delivery nurses in the hallway crying hysterically. No one from the hospital took the time to explain what had happened to the Blunts. Sofia was at Stanford for about three weeks.

Soon after Sofia's birth, a cover-up began. Records were rewritten and falsified. Reports were lost. The defendant doctor wrote in his report that Sofia came out fine with a strong heartbeat, but started deteriorating quite quickly. Another nurse wrote that Sofia was crying when born. Nurses' notes were rewritten by someone else long after the event. A long report that one healthcare provider wrote was lost. A neonatologist wrote a report that did not mention "copious secretions."

The standard of care for the community of San Luis Obispo was not met. Sofia Blunt was put through the wringer twice: first by the defendant doctor's negligence in the manner in which he delivered her, and second by the defendant hospital's negligence in the care they provided after she was born—especially considering that the defendant hospital is a level three NICU, which is supposed to be able to handle the worst of newborn trauma.

Act Three: The Defendant's Response and Point of View

Jennifer and Andrew chose the defendant doctor to deliver their firstborn child. He was a well-respected OB-GYN doctor who practiced in San Luis Obispo for thirty-five years and had delivered four thousand babies.

He had a reputation for excellence.

The defendant doctor was a man of few words, but a very caring man.

As Jennifer's pregnancy progressed, they developed a bond. Jennifer trusted the defendant doctor. The Blunts also chose to have their baby delivered at the defendant hospital, the only hospital in the area with a level three NICU team.

Jennifer came to the defendant hospital looking for excellence on April 18, 2009. Her first and second stages of labor were uneventful. At around 4:00 a.m., as her labor progressed, the charge nurse repositioned Jennifer. From her admission, Jennifer had been hooked up to a fetal heart rate monitor. The nurses continually monitored the fetal heart rate strips. The readings were within normal ranges.

At 5:28 a.m. on April 19, Jennifer's labor had progressed to the point that the defendant doctor needed to be called. He arrived at the hospital at 5:45 a.m. and promptly made his way to the delivery room. The defendant doctor immediately took control of the delivery. The defendant doctor and the caring, loving nurses carefully studied the fetal monitoring strips, and nothing they saw told them that the delivery needed to be sped up or that there was anything to worry about. Sometimes deliveries just take time.

At around this time, Andrew was videotaping Sofia's birth. The videotape shows the defendant doctor actively assisting Sofia's birth by massaging around her head. There is audio of the defendant doctor calmly giving Jennifer instructions, as well as the nurses encouraging her efforts. The defendant doctor is calm and professional. The tape shows Sofia's head getting closer and closer to coming out. Then the tape ends.

At 6:03 a.m., the defendant doctor removed the IUPC monitor (a device that monitors contractions) in preparation of delivery. But Sofia was stubborn and wasn't yet ready to come out, so the defendant doctor put a tocotransducer (also known as a tocodynamometer, a device that measures the duration and frequency of contractions) back on at 6:34 a.m. At 6:30 a.m., the defendant doctor noted in the records that the fetal heart rate strips were "nonreassuring" but his professional opinion was that it was OK to continue to wait longer to deliver Sofia by having Jennifer continue to push. There was still no rush.

At 6:38 a.m., Sofia was born. As she came out, she let out a cry. Her heart rate was strong. The defendant doctor cleared out some mucus from her airway. With all his years of experience, the defendant could tell the baby was fine, though he can understand lay witnesses might be shocked the first time they see the trauma of birth. The defendant offered to let Dad cut the cord, which Dad did. The defendant doctor handed the newborn Sofia to a nurse to take her to the warming table, where nurses could take measures to help Sofia.

Then, suddenly, for some unknown reason, Sofia began to fail. The defendant was torn between helping Sofia and helping Jennifer. For a while, the defendant participated in Sofia's care, but after some time, he returned to Jennifer. Jennifer's vaginal opening tore during delivery, so the defendant sewed it up. Then he soothed her concerns about Sofia. The defendant did not take a cord blood gas test at his discretion. Sofia's Apgar score at one minute was 3, which is a reflection of Sofia's rapid decline following her birth. Immediately, when Sofia's decline began, the NICU team was called. They arrived quickly and set about doing what they do best.

The cause of Sofia's distress became apparent right away. Extremely unusual amounts of thick, copious secretions were blocking Sofia's airway. Neither Dr. Haupt nor the nursing staff had ever witnessed such extreme secretions. Clearing out the secretions proved difficult and time-consuming. The decision was made to put a breathing tube down Sofia's airway, but unfortunately, because of the thick secretions, intubation (getting the tube into the airway) was nearly impossible.

First, a respiratory therapist attempted to get a breathing tube into Sofia, but the blockage proved insurmountable. Finally, with the help of a second respiratory therapist, they were able to get Sofia breathing again. Sofia's Apgar score of 1 at five minutes demonstrates her continued rapid decline that took place after birth. A neonatologist at Sierra Vista arrived on the scene soon thereafter to augment the NICU team.

When Sofia was born, she was a normal, healthy baby. Due to the unforeseeable blockage in her airway, her condition worsened rapidly after her cord was cut. This blockage prevented the NICU team from promptly getting an air tube down Sofia's airway, despite superhuman efforts. Unfortunately, during this time period that Sofia wasn't breathing, her heart stopped, and brain damage occurred. Because of this brain damage, Sofia developed cerebral palsy. At no time was the defendant doctor or any of the staff at Sierra Vista negligent in the performance of their duties. In fact, all performed admirably well. Sometimes bad things happen in childbirth, through no one's fault. The blockage in Sofia's lung was one of those bad things that "just happens." And everybody involved was devastated. It was a terrible day for the Blunt family and the hospital.

After Sofia was stabilized, she was transported to Stanford Medical Center by helicopter so that she might be placed on a cooling blanket. Stanford is at the forefront of hospitals that are using cooling blankets to reduce brain damage in newborns. Sofia was cared for at Stanford for about three weeks before being released to her parents.

The hospital kept thorough and comprehensive notes and reports during Sofia's stay at Sierra Vista. Sofia's birth was traumatic for all of the staff involved at Sierra Vista. They felt the impact deeply. Thus, there are some "inconsistencies" in the medical records and reports, but that is to be expected when staff is writing them up so soon after the trauma occurred. But that is no big deal. We are all "human," and we all see common events in slightly different ways. Then we write them up in our own styles. Some variations in observation are bound to happen. Certainly, there was no cover-up. The possibility of a lawsuit did not even exist at the time the reports were written.

The standard of care for the community of San Luis Obispo was absolutely met. Neither Sierra Vista nor Dr. Haupt were negligent in their care of Sofia Blunt. Sofia's brain damage was caused by an unforeseeable blockage in her airway. The defendant doctor delivered Sofia and the staff at Sierra Vista saved her life. Unfortunately, they could not prevent her brain damage.

Act Four: The Experts' Opinions

For the Plaintiffs: Barry Schifrin, MD, OB-GYN

Barry Schifrin, MD, OB-GYN, testified about the defendant doctor and the hospital's failures and the brain damage that Sofia sustained while still inside her mother. He explained how the brain damage was caused by intermittent and prolonged cord compression. Dr. Schifrin was critical of the defendant's failure to recognize Sofia's fetal distress based on the fetal monitor strips. He also took issue with the defendant's failure to explore other options, such as an episiotomy, vacuum, forceps, C-section, or to have Jennifer labor down (take a break from pushing and putting squeezing pressure on Sofia).

The defense focused on attacking Dr. Schifrin's knowledge of the defendant's credentials and whether Dr. Schifrin was aware that the defendant doctor had read and followed various bulletins from ACOG (American College of Obstetricians and Gynecologists).

For the Defendants: Maurice Druzin, MD, OB-GYN

Dr. Druzin testified that the defendant doctor complied with the standard of care in terms of his interpretation of the fetal monitor strips. Dr. Druzin could find no indication of fetal distress, and therefore, there was no reason to speed up Sofia's delivery. Dr. Druzin did not believe that Sofia suffered any brain injury while still inside her mother.

Dr. Druzin worked at Stanford. Stanford had a long-standing relationship with the defendants. Sierra Vista was a feeder hospital for Stanford Medical Center. Dr. Druzin knew the defendant doctor. Dr. Druzin was there to protect the defendants. Dr. Druzin was an advocate of tort reform who sought to take power away from jurors. Dr. Druzin had testified in three hundred to five hundred medical malpractice cases. Only once had he testified on behalf of a patient. This was perhaps a bias.

Interestingly, both Dr. Druzin and one of the jurors were originally from South Africa. The odds against having two South Africans in a courtroom in San Luis Obispo, California—one as a witness, the other a juror—must be astronomical.

For the Defendants: Dr. Rhine

Dr. Rhine was a member of the Stanford/Sierra Vista family. He was a good physician but was victimized by the defense. The defense did this by not allowing Dr. Rhine to see Sofia's fetal monitoring strips. Nor was he provided Jennifer's labor and delivery records. On top of that, he only saw select portions of Sofia's records from the defendant hospital, some of which were not accurate. Dr. Rhine's opinion of when Sofia's brain damage took place would have changed had he had access to all the records. We showed that Dr. Rhine was misled, just as the plaintiffs were.

For the Plaintiffs: Dr. Kawai, Life Care Planner

The life care plans of the plaintiff and defense were mostly similar with one significant difference: the plaintiffs wanted twenty-four hours of care per day by an LNP (licensed nurse practitioner) to protect Sofia and make sure she lived as long of a healthy life as possible. The defense, on the other hand, felt that four hours of care a day by a helper would be sufficient. The amount of hours and skill level of the helper would vary throughout Sofia's life, depending on her needs. The defense said that twenty-four-hour care was certainly unwarranted and was really just a money grab, adding $12 million to the value of Dr. Kawai's plan for a total of $15 million.

For the Defendants: Kimberly BeDell, MD, Physical Medical Rehabilitation

Dr. BeDell testified as to Sofia's future medical needs. She believed that Sofia's life expectancy was fifteen to twenty years.

For the Defendants: Linda Olzack, RN, Life Care Planner

Nurse Olzack testified about her life care plan, which included her own recommendations as well as Dr. BeDell's. The cost of nurse Olzack's life care plan was $3.5 million.

ACT FIVE: STANDING UP FOR THE BLUNT FAMILY OUTSIDE THE COURTROOM AS THE LOCAL NEWS ATTACKS

"Family Seeks Millions in Malpractice Lawsuit"

The defendants in the Blunt trial had a lot of influence in the small community of San Luis Obispo, California. Coincidentally, the local news and news blogs reported the trial and made the case very unpopular. It started with a news article that stated:

> Dr. Kurt Haupt has denied any wrongdoing, saying that his care was standard and that he handled the prenatal and labor treatment appropriately.
>
> According to the expert opinion of Dr. Connie L. Agnew, who testified on behalf of Haupt, his care was standard, court documents show.
>
> Sofia Blunt had to be resuscitated after she was born, and Haupt handled those procedures appropriately as well, according to his attorneys.[1]

Internet blogs from countless members of the community, including some of Dr. Haupt's patients, called the case frivolous and made the Blunt family look bad day after day during the trial. This was very upsetting to Jennifer and Andrew, who did not want a jury trial but had no choice because the defendant refused to offer anything other than a nuisance value settlement.

"Parents Awarded $74 Million in Malpractice Suit against Doctor"

Even after the last story, blogs continued to attack the family. The last story had a number of statements that we thought would validate the case and show that members of the community made the right decision. The following was reported in the posttrial news report:

> After two days of deliberation, a jury of eight women and four men found that Dr. Kurt Haupt was responsible for a botched delivery on April 19, 2009, at Sierra Vista Regional Medical Center.
>
> Several jurors hugged the family, who watched over the three-year-old girl in a stroller with a harness, after the verdict.
>
> "Damage to this little girl happened, and the evidence showed us that, more likely than not, the

---

1. Nick Wilson, "Family seeks millions in malpractice lawsuit," *The Tribune*, April 3, 2012, http://www.sanluisobispo.com/2012/04/03/2016596/family-seeks-millions-in-malpractice.html.

doctor was negligent," said Melody Eltrich, the jury foreperson. "Nobody wants to make someone pay for no reason. This was a life-changing event."

Juror Daniel Harris said that the case, to him, was about an American family overcoming an injustice to "come out on top."

"The doctor was complacent," Harris said.[2]

Despite the validation from the jury of the merits of the reports showing that Sofia was a legitimate victim of malpractice, there was a lot of public outrage. We responded to the blogs to make sure that the community knew the truth of the case, because if we didn't, the branding effect could taint jurors in future trials.

Act Six: The Jurors Speak

The jurors deliberated for two days. Then they came back with this to say: They found in favor of the plaintiffs on liability, twelve to zero. They believed Sofia would reach sixty-three years of age before dying. Their verdict was for $74.2 million.

The foreperson had this to say about the verdict: "Damage to this little girl happened, and the evidence showed us that, more likely than not, the doctor was negligent. We are setting the bar for our community. We don't care what the public has to say."

---

2. Nick Wilson, "Parents awarded $74 million in malpractice suit against doctor," *The Tribune,* April 20, 2012. http://www.sanluisobispo.com/2012/04/20/2037565/blunt-malpractice-lawsuit-haupt.html.

Index

A

ACOG (American College of Obstetricians and Gynecologists) 246–248, 294
action method 211, 214
Ali, Aldwin 275–276
American College of Obstetricians and Gynecologists (ACOG) 246–248, 294
Anger: Wisdom for Cooling the Flames (Thich Nhat Hanh) 274
attorney–client privilege, thirteenth juror and 77
audiovisuals. *See* props and audiovisuals

B

Ball, David 48, 85, 146
barbecue test 140
BeDell, Kimberly 295
betrayal (theme) 147
biases of expert witnesses 59, 115–116, 221–222, 224
Bird in the Hand story 254–255
Blunt v. Sierra Vista Medical Center
    about 61, 285–286
    cross-examination in 223–225
    defense response and point of view in 290–295
    establishing themes 44
    expert witnesses in 293–295
    gathering facts 42–46, 62–67
    human story in 41–46, 49–51, 67–70, 286–290
    juror cohesion in 232–233
    jurors asking questions 233–234
    jury verdict in 297
    local news attacks 295–297
    mini–opening statement 90–92
    props and audiovisuals in 243–252
    telling story with medical records 168–172
    thirteenth juror in 66–67, 82–83
    trial strategies in 201, 203, 205, 207–208
    trip wires in 140, 160–161, 182–197, 244–251
    voir dire in 100–103, 108–119, 129–130, 137–139
    witness testimony 182–197
Boag, Finlay 86, 148
body language
    of jurors 231
    during voir dire 97–98, 108
brutal honesty
    mini–opening statement on 91–92
    in opening statement 145
    about ugly part of case 275
    in voir dire 100–101, 105–106, 109–110, 118, 125, 136–138
brutal honesty exercise
    about 7–11
    Halteman's story 19–28
    Rowley's story 11–19
burden of proof 113–114

C

Carpenter, John 20, 59
Chaloupka, Maren 225
children in court 197
Chung, Tiffany 212
civil cases
    burden of proof 113–114
    stirring up dissension in 204–205
civil rights cases
    on money 122
    voir dire in 120–126
clients
    connecting with 30–31, 36–38, 42–47, 49–51, 62–67, 152–153, 212–213
    day-in-the-life experiences 45, 49

discovering their human stories 61–74
establishing trust with 45, 62, 72
knowing birthdays of 201
listening to 35, 45
promises made to 67
thirteenth juror and 82, 84
closing arguments
about 237–239, 241–244
focus groups writing 86
mentioning client's birthday in 201
on money 262–269
props and audiovisuals 240–244, 268–269
slides for 240–241, 242–244
on standard of care 238–239
stealing defense's case in 239
suggestions about 252–253
conflict of truth
depositions and 46
medical records and 46, 48
testing with focus groups 48–49
courage in battle 4
criminal cases, burden of proof in 113–114
cross-examination
establishing facts during 229
general rules 219–222
preparing witnesses for 211
on standard of care 223–225
storybook cross 225–229
Cross-Examination: Science and Techniques (Pozner and Dodd) 224

D
day-in-the-life experiences 45, 49
defense and defendants
balancing courtroom 203
in *Blunt v. Sierra Vista Medical Center* 290–295
corporate defendants 208
jurors distrusting 152, 163
lying during testimony 167
steaing case in closing arguments 239
stealing case in opening statement 145–147, 151–152, 162
stirring up dissension among 204–205
defense experts
biases of 59
discrediting 50
lay witnesses versus 51
questions for 56–60
reversing roles with 53–56
vanities of 178–179
deliberation
focus group 86
jury 238, 270, 297
depositions
conflict of truth and 46
gathering facts from 66
informal meetings versus 40
videotaped expert witnesses 52–53, 56
developing human story. *See* human story
direct examination
action method 211, 214
connecting with clients before 212–213
difficulty of 211
directing the story 213–215
of expert witnesses 215–216
of lay witnesses 214–215, 216–217
settings scenes in 216
discovery focus groups 85–86
Dodd, Roger 224
Dordick, Gary 120–121
Druzin, Maurice 294

E
economist expert testimony 80–82
Eltrich, Melody 297
emotional intelligence 158
equal dollar value 260, 268–269
evidence, opening statement on 147–148
exercise, brutal honesty 7–11
exercise, importance of 77–78
expert witnesses

biases of 59, 115–116, 221–222, 224
in *Blunt v. Sierra Vista Medical Center* 293–295
credibility of 114–116, 181
defense experts. *See* defense experts
economists 80–82
examining 215–216
first-person opening on 154–155
not understanding testimony of 177–181
ordering appearance of 151–152
simplifying testimony of 179–181, 209
vanities of 177–178
videotaped depositions 52–53, 56
eye contact
during cross-examination 220–221
as trial strategy 200
during voir dire 93, 98, 106, 108, 134

F
fact gathering 62–67
fear of trial lawyers 40, 98
feeling, reflective 97, 105–108
feng shui in the courtroom 203
Fieger, Geoffrey 200, 276
Fight Club (movie) 273
Fire in the Museum story 253–254
first dates, voir dire like 142–144
first-person opening statement 153–155
focus groups
attending 86
deliberation 86
discovery 85–86
importance of 85–86
in *Landeros v. Torres* 86–87
on noneconomic damages 87
purpose of 85
testing discovery of truth with 48–49
thirteenth jurors as 77, 83
writing closing arguments 86
writing down themes 86

writing opening statements 86
foreperson of juries 141–142, 234–235
fridge test 62, 66
Friedman, Rick 146

G
gallery seats in courtroom 203, 207
gathering facts for human story 42–47, 62–67
Girardi, Tom 119

H
Halteman, Steve 19–28, 148
Harris, Daniel 297
Haupt, Kurt. *See Blunt v. Sierra Vista Medical Center*
Henry, Patrick 123
Hidalgo, Rolando 46
honoring jurors 106–108
human story
applying to cases 37–38
in *Blunt v. Sierra Vista Medical Center* 41–46, 49–51, 67–70, 286–290
caring about 280–283
continuing involvement with 25, 49–51
depositions and 40, 46
developing 39–42, 49–51, 67–70
direct examination and 211
establishing themes from 44, 48
exercise questions 29–31
expert witnesses and 50, 52–60
gathering facts for 42–47, 62–67
insights gained from 37
lawyers as directors of 213–215
lay witnesses and 49–52
medical records and 41, 46, 48
in opening statements 36
optimism in 68
humor in courtroom 203–204

I
ignorance
intelligence and 156–158

thirteenth juror and 76–77, 83, 155–156
intelligence, measuring 156–158

J
judges, fighting with 276–278
jurors
    asking questions 136–139, 233–234
    barbecue test 140
    body language of 231
    brutal honesty and 100–101, 105–106, 109–110, 118, 125, 136–138
    connecting with 93–99, 106–108, 125, 131–139, 231–235
    deliberation 238, 270, 297
    distrusting defense 152, 163
    educating 178–181, 238, 270
    emotionally invested in case 145–146
    foreperson of 141–142, 234–235
    gender-specific injuries and 130
    group cohesion of 232–233
    hierachy of abilities in 158–159
    honoring 106–108, 125
    implanting witness themes with 182–197
    letting scenes tell the story 165–174
    on money 110–111, 125
    perceptions of 140
    promises to 202
    role reversal with 66–67, 98–99, 135–136
    selecting. *See* voir dire
    tracking reading material of 234
    validating 97, 107–108, 125
    what they need in opening statement 155–163
justice system, disease affecting 4–5

K
Karton, Josh 93

L
labels (client) 38

Landeros v. Torres
    about 75
    focus groups in 86–87
    psychological strategies in 77–79
    stirring up dissension among defendants 205
    thirteenth juror in 76–77, 80–84
lay witnesses
    credibility of 116
    examining 214–215, 216–217
    implanting themes with 181–197
    importance of 49–52
    ordering appearance of 151–152
    simplifying testimony 176, 209
    thirteenth juror and 82
legal team sizes 156
liars and lies 274
life lessons 271–278
listening
    to clients 35, 45
    reflective 97
    during voir dire 93–94, 96–99, 103
Logan, Pat 162, 242, 244
losing cases 272–273
Low, Joey 96, 98, 120–122

M
Malone, Pat 146
Mardirossian, Garo 120–121
McCallion, Jim 275
medical malpractice cases
    simplifying words in 179–181
    voir dire in 118–119
medical records
    conflict of truth and 46, 48
    discrediting 50
    mistrust of 41, 46
    storytelling with 168–174
mini–opening statements
    about 89–90
    in *Blunt v. Sierra Vista Medical Center* 90–92
Miramontes, Wall v. See Wall v. Miramontes
money
    civil rights cases and 122

closing arguments on 262–269
jurors' opinions about 110–111, 125
opening statement on 151, 258–262
owning the dollar amount 162
uneasiness about 257–258
voir dire on 258

N
neutrality of thirteenth juror 76, 83
Newport Channel Inn, Von Normann v. 52, 240, 258–262
Nhat Hanh, Thich 274
Norton, Edward 273
note-taking 200, 242
Nugent, Jim 98

O
objections to first-person opening 154–155
Olzack, Linda 295
open-ended questions 219
opening statement
  adjusting complexity of 159
  arguing case in 162
  avoid speeding up at end 163
  be ready 159–160
  brutal honesty in 145
  connecting with clients 152–153
  demeanor during 152
  drawing in audience with 161–162
  on evidence 147–148
  first-person 153–155
  focus groups writing 86
  human story in 36
  mini– 89–92
  on money 151, 258–262
  objections to 154–155
  owning dollar amount in 162
  passion in 147
  props and audiovisuals in 162
  Pulp Fiction 148–151, 161
  role reversal to improve 152–153
  stealing defense's case in 145–147, 151–152, 162
  storytelling in 161
  strong witnesses following 151–152
  suggestions for 159–163
  themes in 145–147
  using breaks advantageously 161
  what jury needs in 155–163
optimism in human story 68
Ounjian, Robert 42

P
paradigm planting 103–126
photo albums 30, 36, 45
physical exercise, importance of 77–78
Pitt, Brad 273
planting paradigms 103–126
podiums 200
Polarizing the Case (Friedman) 146
Porter, Grover 96
Posner, Larry 224
preparing for trial
  about 71
  being ready 159–160
  for closing arguments 242
  lay witnesses 181–197
  trip wires in 71
private faces 24, 62, 141
promises
  to clients 67
  to jurors 202
props and audiovisuals
  in *Blunt v. Sierra Vista Medical Center* 243–252
  in closing arguments 240–244, 268–269
  lighting considerations 204
  in opening statement 162
  of themes 162
public faces 24, 62, 141
public opinion about trial lawyers 257–258, 279–280
Pulp Fiction opening statement 148–151, 161

Q
question lists 201

questions
    jurors asking 136–139, 233–234
    open-ended 219

R
reading material, tracking 234
reasonable doubt standard 113–114
reflective feeling 97, 105–108
reflective listening 97
repeating
    important points 200
    questions during cross-
        examination 225–227
    things in sequences 276
Reservoir Dogs (movie) 148
reverse fluster 78–79
Ritner, Rod 71, 140
Rowley, Nick 11–20, 25
Rules of the Road (Friedman and Malone) 146

S
scenes
    setting in direct examination 216
    telling the story 165–174
Schifrin, Barry 293–294
sidebar meetings 201
Sierra Charles case 201
Sierra Vista Medical Center, Blunt v. See *Blunt v. Sierra Vista Medical Center*
silence
    in closing arguments 253
    as trial strategy 199
    validating jurors 97, 106
simplifying testimony 175–176, 179–180, 209
Spence, Gerry 8, 17, 19, 98
standard of care
    closing arguments on 238–239
    cross-examination on 223–225
stereotypes
    abandoning in voir dire 127–130, 141
    defined 129
    of trial lawyers 136–138
storybook cross 225–229

storytelling
    Bird in the Hand story 254–255
    from blood tests 172–174
    in cross-examination 225–229
    about expert witness biases 221–222
    from fetal heart monitor 169–172
    Fire in the Museum story 253–254
    from MRI machine 168–169
    in opening statement 161
success, true measure of 73

T
themes
    asking focus groups for 86
    betrayal 147
    establishing from human story 44, 48
    framing impressions 196
    opening statement and 145–147
    promoting with jurors 196
    props and audiovisuals of 162
    as trip wires 139–140, 182–197
Thich Nhat Hanh 274
thirteenth juror
    about 66–67
    attorney–client privilege and 77
    in *Blunt v. Sierra Vista Medical Center* 66–67, 82–83
    as focus group 77, 83
    in *Landeros v. Torres* 76–77, 80–84
    neutrality of 76, 83
    role of 135–136
    wall of ignorance 76–77, 83, 155–156
Torres, Landeros v. See *Landeros v. Torres*
trial lawyers
    adjusting conduct 198–199
    attending focus groups 86
    bag of tricks and 31
    becoming human again 30
    brainwashed view of 4–5
    caring about human story 280–283

defending clients against media
   attacks 295–297
  fear of 40, 98
  importance of physical exercise
   77–78
  public opinion about 257–258,
   279–280
  real 2–4
  reverse fluster 78–79
  stereotypes of 136–138
  tough cases and 119
  vanities of 178–179
Trial Lawyers College 213–214, 225
trial preparation
  about 71
  being ready 159–160
  for closing arguments 242
  lay witnesses 181–197
  trip wires in 71
trial strategies
  balancing courtroom 203
  confidence after sidebar meetings
   201
  corporate defendants 208
  estimating time correctly 202
  eye contact 200
  gallery seats 203, 207–208
  knowing client's birthday 201
  knowing when to stop 202
  lawyers' conduct 198–199
  lighting considerations 204
  moving around 201
  natural humor 203–204
  note-taking 200
  podium usage 200
  repeating important points 200
  silence 199
  sticking to story line 202
  tracking witnesses 205–207
  trip wires 208
  typed question lists 201
trip wires
  about 208
  in *Blunt v. Sierra Vista Medical
   Center* 140, 160–161, 182–
   197, 244–251
  conversation topics 138, 140

 themes as 139–140, 182–197
 in trial preparation 71
 trial strategies 208
trust
  establishing with clients 45, 62, 72
  trusting instincts 140–141, 202

V
Valens, Tom 31–36, 172
validating
  jurors 97, 107–108, 125
  opening statement 152
  witnesses 219
verdicts, protecting 272
videotaped expert depositions
 52–53, 56
voir dire
  answering hard questions during
   136–139
  barbecue test 140
  in *Blunt v. Sierra Vista Medical
   Center* 100–103, 108–119,
   129–130, 137–139
  body language during 97–98, 108
  brutal honesty in 100–101,
   105–106, 109–110, 118, 125,
   136–138
  in civil rights cases 120–126
  conversations in 133–135
  creating connections during
   93–99, 106–108, 125,
   131–139
  eye contact during 93, 98, 106,
   108, 134
  finding a leader 141–142
  getting started 99–103
  goal of 94, 96
  honoring jurors 106–108, 125
  importance of 94, 127
  inclusion and acceptance in
   95–96, 131
  jury box as classroom 139
  jury selection philosophy
   131–132
  like first dates 142–144
  listening during 93–94, 96–99,
   103

in medical malpractice cases 118–119
mini–opening statements and 89
on money 258
planting paradigms 103–126
reflective feeling in 97–99, 105–108
rejection in 94–95, 131
selling case throughout 139–140
stereotypes and 127–131, 141
suggestions for 133–134, 140–141
thirteenth juror and 82
validating jurors 107–108, 125
Von Normann v. Newport Channel Inn 52, 240, 258–262

W

Wall v. Miramontes
discovering human stories 63
juries and gender-specific injuries 130
money in closing argument 262–269
re-creating scene of tragedy 166–167
White, Steven 148
witnesses
brutal honesty with 40
expert. *See* expert witnesses
following opening statement 151–152
implanting themes 182–197
lay. *See* lay witnesses
permission to approach 203–204
preparing for cross-examination 211
simplifying testimony of 175–176, 209
spending time with 50
tracking 205–207
validating 219
witness training 226

Y

Yoder, Courtney 63, 148

About the Authors

Nick Rowley was born in Stormlake, Iowa, in 1977 and lived the first years of his life on a small farm. His parents split up when he was in the fourth grade, and after living back and forth between Iowa and Arizona, Nick moved out on his own at age fifteen. He signed up for active duty in the United States Air Force on his seventeenth birthday, trained as a pararescueman, and thereafter served as a combat medic and member of a special operations unit whose purpose was securing and extracting wounded soldiers and civilians. Nick received honors and recognition for his dedicated service during the United States' presence in Bosnia in 1995–1996.

Many consider Nick Rowley to be the most accomplished trial lawyer of his generation. He attributes his success to his knowledge of emergency medicine and traumatic brain injury, which he learned firsthand as a medic. He has also been personally trained and mentored over many years by Gerry Spence, Jude Basile, and Gary Dordick. Nick has received influence from and is thankful to Paul Luvera, Rick Friedman, and David Ball for their teachings. As a partner in the law firm of Carpenter, Zuckerman & Rowley, Nick focuses on jury trials and is a relentless courtroom warrior who has prevailed in the courtroom time and time again. He prides himself on his caring and empathic approach to working with his clients and their families, and his ability to help juries find the truth and deliver justice.

Steve Halteman lives in Costa Rica with his wife and daughter. He is also Nick Rowley's trial consultant. In his career, Mr. Halteman has consulted on cases resulting in verdicts of more than $120 million total. His trial philosophy demands that lawyers relentlessly narrow their case to its heart, eliminating ancillary issues that distract jurors from the truth. Mr. Halteman often analogizes his trial strategy to furniture building, his hobby. The strongest and most elegant chair or table has no unnecessary parts or flourishes. Likewise, he believes that every component of a trial must have an important purpose, or it must be shed.

Mr. Halteman credits his unclouded perspective of what jurors and judges really want with having lived overseas for all but four years of his adult life, his travels through over seventy countries, and having himself served as a court commissioner in Maryland. In his spare time, he has completed six marathons and a couple of ultramarathons, and soon plans to hike the 2,650-mile Pacific Crest Trail. He also credits himself with an archeological find, having discovered a perhaps unknown tomb in Jordan, or so he'd like to think.